THE SLAVE ECONOMIES:

Volume I
Historical and Theoretical Perspectives

PROBLEMS IN AMERICAN HISTORY

EDITOR

LOREN BARITZ

State University of New York, Albany

Ray B. Browne POPULAR CULTURE AND THE EXPANDING CONSCIOUSNESS

William N. Chambers THE FIRST PARTY SYSTEM:
Federalists and Republicans

Don E. Fehrenbacher THE LEADERSHIP OF ABRAHAM LINCOLN

Eugene D. Genovese THE SLAVE ECONOMICS
Volume I: Historical and Theoretical Perspectives
Volume II: Slavery in the International Economy

Paul Goodman THE AMERICAN CONSTITUTION

Richard J. Hooker THE AMERICAN REVOLUTION

Richard Kirkendall THE NEW DEAL AND AMERICAN CAPITALISM

Stephen G. Kurtz THE FEDERALISTS—
Creators and Critics of the Union 1780–1801

Walter LaFeber AMERICA IN THE COLD WAR

Walter LaFeber THE ORIGINS OF THE COLD WAR, 1941–1947

Donald G. Mathews AGITATION FOR FREEDOM:
The Abolitionist Movement

Douglas T. Miller THE NATURE OF JACKSONIAN AMERICA

Richard H. Miller AMERICAN IMPERIALISM IN 1898

Thomas J. Pressly RECONSTRUCTION

Richard Reinitz TENSIONS IN AMERICAN PURITANISM

Darrett B. Rutman THE GREAT AWAKENING

David F. Trask WORLD WAR I AT HOME

Patrick C. T. White THE CRITICAL YEARS, AMERICAN FOREIGN POLICY, 1793–1825

Harold D. Woodman THE LEGACY OF THE AMERICAN CIVIL WAR

THE SLAVE ECONOMIES:

Volume I
Historical and Theoretical Perspectives

EDITED BY

Eugene D. Genovese
University of Rochester

John Wiley & Sons, Inc.

New York • London • Sydney • Toronto

Library of Congress Cataloging in Publication Data:

Genovese, Eugene D   1930–
        The slave economies.

        (Problems in American history)
        CONTENTS: v. 1. Historical and theoretical perspectives.—v. 2. Slavery in the international economy.
        1. Slavery in America—Addresses, essays, lectures.
        2. Slave–trade—America—Addresses, essays, lectures.
        I. Title.

HT1048.G44   380.1'44   73-5519
ISBN 0-471-29615-5
ISBN 0-471-29616-3 (pbk.)

Printed in the United States of America

10 9 8 7 6 5 4 3 2 1

FOR IRV & GINNY FEDER

SERIES PREFACE

This series is an introduction to the most important problems in the writing and study of American history. Some of these problems have been the subject of debate and argument for a long time, although others only recently have been recognized as controversial. However, in every case, the student will find a vital topic, an understanding of which will deepen his knowledge of social change in America.

The scholars who introduce and edit the books in this series are teaching historians who have written history in the same general area as their individual books. Many of them are leading scholars in their fields, and all have done important work in the collective search for better historical understanding.

Because of the talent and the specialized knowledge of the individual editors, a rigid editorial format has not been imposed on them. For example, some of the editors believe that primary source material is necessary to their subjects. Some believe that their material should be arranged to show conflicting interpretations. Others have decided to use the selected materials as evidence for their own interpretations. The individual editors have been given the freedom to handle their books in the way that their own experience and knowledge indicate is best. The overall result is a series built up from the individual decisions of working scholars in the various fields, rather than one that conforms to a uniform editorial decision.

A common goal (rather than a shared technique) is the bridge of this series. There is always the desire to bring the reader as close to these problems as possible. One result of this objective is an emphasis on the nature and consequences of problems and events, with a de-emphasis of the more purely historiographical issues. The goal is to involve the student in the reality of crisis, the inevitability of ambiguity, and the excitement of finding a way through the historical maze.

Above all, this series is designed to show students how experienced historians read and reason. Although health is not contagious, intellectual engagement may be. If we show students something significant in a phrase or a passage that they otherwise may have missed, we will have accomplished part of our objective. When students see something that passed us by, then the process will have been made whole. This active and mutual involvement of editor and reader with a significant human problem will rescue the study of history from the smell and feel of dust.

Loren Baritz

CONTENTS

INTRODUCTION   1

PART ONE
Reference Points from the Ancient World   5

1. Harry W. Pearson, *The Secular Debate on Economic Primitivism*   9
2. M. I. Finley, *Was Greek Civilization Based on Slave Labour?*   19
3. Max Weber, *The Social Causes of the Decay of Ancient Civilization* 45

PART TWO
African Ramifications of the Slave Trade   69

4. Philip D. Curtin, *Major Trends*   73
5. Karl Polanyi, *The Challenge of the Slave Trade*   81
6. Rosemary Arnold, *A Port of Trade: Whydah on the Guinea Coast*   94
7. Rosemary Arnold, *Separation of Trade and Market: Great Market of Waydah* 120
8. Basil Davidson, *The Vital Contrast*   132

PART THREE
New World Slavery in the History of Capitalism   141

9. Eric J. Hobsbawm, *The Seventeenth Century in the Development of Capitalism* 145
10. Lewis Cecil Gray, *Genesis of the Plantation System as an Agency for the Colonial Expansion of Capitalism* 160
11. Stuart Bruchey, *The Planters: Sources of Operating Capital*   177
12. Eric Williams, *British Industry and the Triangular Trade*   183
13. C. L. R. James, *The West Indies in the History of European Capitalism* 195
14. Jay R. Mandle, *The Plantation Economy: An Essay in Definition*   214

THE SLAVE ECONOMIES:

Volume I
Historical and Theoretical Perspectives

Introduction

These two volumes treat modern slavery in its economic aspects, and the reader must therefore proceed at his own risk. The isolation of the economic aspects of a social system is dangerous and, in the end, false, for any such system is itself the general form of particular relationships among whole human beings, living and dead. The purest economic analysis rests on the assumption that strictly economic motives apply to strictly economic behavior. This procedure is useful, and in fact indispensable, for we cannot hope to grasp the complexities of a social system all at once, except on a level of abstraction that becomes a crude tool when applied to most problems. We are therefore forced to risk distortion and to isolate, so far as possible, certain variables. The only way to keep that risk to a minimum is to remind ourselves constantly that distortion is unavoidable. Even in the "purest" capitalist societies such nonrational factors as political decisions, military requirements, and the exigencies of family and community life impinge on market rationality. The slaveholding societies ranged much further from the capitalist model than have societies based on free labor, although some slave societies came much closer to the norm than did others. Each such society must be studied in its particularity—as a specific system of class relationships, political affiliations, and social mores—in order to evaluate the extent to which the economy moved according to its own inherent tendencies and therefore the extent to which economic models derived from marketplace capitalist economies may be deemed applicable. These volumes include selections that appreciate the wider social setting and should help to keep us on our guard.

If we read the economic story in too narrow a context—if we miss the social context within which economic activity takes place—we are certain to misinterpret the economic activity itself. It makes all the difference both to the economy and to the society whether or not they rest on slave labor or merely use slaves within a fundamentally different system of labor organization. The debates over ancient slavery bring this question into sharp focus. Finley's title, "Was Greek Civilization Based on Slave Labour?" speaks for itself, and we need not accept Weber's thesis to realize that its validity turns, in the first place, on the extent to which slave labor dominated the productive system as a whole.

Similarly, as the selections in Volume Two, especially, make clear, slavery played a different role in much of Spanish South America than it did in Brazil or the Caribbean. Accordingly, no single economic analysis could be expected to encompass the whole slavery experience. For a satisfactory general theory of New World slave societies we must go well beyond economics. But as the criticism of Frank Tannenbaum's institutional thesis shows, it is one thing to go beyond economics and another to try to do without economics as a major component of our theory.[1]

Volume One, in offering "Historical and Theoretical Perspectives," tries to draw attention to the similarity and difference between the problems that face the historian of the ancient world and those that face the historian of the modern world. And it also presents some of the important work on the economic impact of the slave trade on African society. The good work now

[1] See Frank Tannenbaum, *Slave & Citizen: The Negro in the Americas* (New York, 1944). For the debate see Laura Foner and Eugene D. Genovese, eds., *Slavery in the New World: A Reader in Comparative History* (Engle-Wood Cliffs, 1969). My own view is presented in Part One of *The World the Slaveholders Made* (New York, 1969). See also the recent important contributions in Chapters I–III of C. Vann Woodward, *American Counterpoint: Slavery and Racism in the North-South Dialogue* (Boston, 1971).

going forward on this subject ought to correct the distortions arising from the Euro-American view that has for so long dominated the history of Afro-American slavery. It ought, too, to demonstrate the limits of economic analysis, for it provides illuminating illustrations of how local systems of trade can feed into a world market without themselves being transformed internally into market economies. In these ways economic history and economic theory contribute to the restoration of the African historical experience to its rightful place and help bury the notion that Africa "had no history" until its contact with Europe. We find, rather, that Africa's slow but irreversible absorption into the world market signified the end of a long historical epoch and the beginning of the dissolution of traditional societies, as well as the advent of a revolutionizing new order.

Perhaps the greatest difference between the ancient and modern slave systems in both economy and society was the relationship of the modern slave systems, but not ancient ones, to a steadily expanding world market that came to form the center of both world economy and a developing capitalist society. Europe, Africa, and the Americas—and indeed Asia, which does not figure in these volumes—were drawn into a single economic orbit from the sixteenth century onward, and colonial slavery played an important role in the process. In Volume One we set the stage for an understanding of that process as a whole. In Volume Two we shall take a closer look at the slaveholding countries the exploitation of which contributed to the rise and expansion of European capitalism.

PART ONE

Reference Points from the Ancient World

Part One is designed to introduce the reader to a few of the many fascinating problems attendant on any consideration of slavery in the ancient world and to pose forcefully the problem of slavery as a peripheral or central labor system within a larger society. The selections, therefore, are meant to be suggestive, not "definitive," even in the restricted sense in which historians sometimes use that term. Indeed, the great historian of the ancient world, M. I. Finley, whose penetrating essay is included here, himself edited an invaluable volume, from which his selection is taken, that presents various viewpoints on the question to which he addresses himself. The essay by Max Weber is old and highly controversial, but it presents a challenging thesis that opens up the big questions. It is, then, the questions rather than the answers that chiefly concern us in a book devoted to modern, not ancient, slavery. Harry W. Pearson's essay may serve as an introduction to some of those questions.

Yet neither Pearson, nor Karl Polanyi, whose brilliant *tour de force*, "Aristotle Discovers the Economy" (in the same book in which Pearson's essay originally appeared), also called for a new departure, considered the epoch-making work of Marx to the discussion. Indeed, Weber's contribution, for all its brilliance and discrete importance, represented a backward step from the point at which Marx implicitly left the matter. By focusing on the socioeconomic system of the Roman Empire as a mode of production based on slave labor, Marx avoided the pitfall into which those whom Pearson and Polanyi criticized almost invariably

7

fell. That is, Marx insisted, in his general interpretation of history, as well as in his scattered remarks on primitive, ancient, and medieval economies, that the decisive forces of historical change had to be sought in the relations of production, not those of exchange. Hence, Marx outlined a theory of historical process that took full account of the possibilities for a high level of commerce and exchange in noncapitalist and precapitalist societies. The great advantage of this line of thought, as demonstrated in Maurice Dobb's pioneering *Studies in the Development of Capitalism*, is that it begins to explain the high levels of commercialization and of civilization, broadly considered, that were achieved by societies that were unable to generate anything like the capitalism that arose in early modern Europe.

But it should be clear at the outset that Marx's theory of the role of class forces in history cannot be made to rest on economics alone. Ironically, it was Weber, not Marx, who based his interpretation of the decline of ancient civilization on a narrowly economic argument, although Weber's great work on the sociology of religion, which includes much more than his well-known and little-understood *Protestant Ethic and the Spirit of Capitalism*, posed those great problems of cultural transformation to which Marx's work only implicitly addressed itself. Until recently, however, Marxists continued to cling too closely to an economic interpretation of class and so were unable to realize the full potentialities of their own theory. The Marxist contributions to these volumes reveal both the strengths and weaknesses of the school. The possibilities for reestablishing the claims of the Marxist interpretation with specific reference to slave societies are herein presented against sharply differing points of view. Specifically, the contributions of Eric J. Hobshawm, C. L. R. James, Octavio Ianni, Harold D. Woodman—to mention only a few of the Marxist authors—may be taken as a challenge both to Marxists and non-Marxists to produce what they preach and to study economics as one dimension of a multileveled development of social classes and historical process.

1

Harry W. Pearson
The Secular Debate on Economic Primitivism

For more than sixty years a debate has been raging in the field of economic history. Many features have faded out, some were irrelevant from the start. Yet it contained—and still contains—the elements of one of the most significant divergencies in the human sciences. It would not be easy to find a more suitable introduction than this controversy to the interpretive problems involved in the study of archaic economic institutions.

The theorem about which the storm of discussion ultimately centered was first propounded by Rodbertus in the middle 1860's. The actual controversy started some thirty years later between Karl Bücher and Eduard Meyer; it was at its height about the turn of the century. Subsequently Max Weber and Michael Rostovtzeff took their stand. Several others made important contributions.[1]

SOURCE. "The Secular Debate on Economic Primitivism," by Harry W. Pearson. Reprinted with permission of the Macmillan Company from *Trade and Market in the Early Empires: Economics in History and Theory*. Edited by Karl Polanyi, Conrad M. Arensberg and Harry W. Pearson. © by the Free Press, A Corporation, 1957.

[1] No attempt has been made in this chapter to summarize all of the contributions to this debate; the intent here is to present only the essential outlines. The best bibliographies are to be found in M. I. Rostovtzeff, *Social*

No more illuminating introduction to this conflict of views could be found than Friedrich Oertel's oft-quoted statement of the issues as he summed them up in 1925:

"Are we to conceive of the economy of antiquity as having reached a high level of development, or, on the contrary, as essentially primitive? Should the 5th and 4th centuries B.C. be regarded as an age of national and international business, a receding agriculture, an advancing industry, large scale manufacturing managed on capitalistic lines and growing in scope, with factories working for export and competing with one another for sales in the world market?

Or should we assume, on the contrary, that the stage of the closed "household economy" had not yet passed; that economic activity had not attained a national, even less an international scale; that no organized commerce involving long-distance trading was carried on and that, consequently, no large-scale industry producing for foreign markets existed? In brief, was the character of economic life still agrarian rather than industrial? Was commerce still restricted to a peddling of particular wares, the work of craftsmen producing without the aid of machinery and using the raw materials that were locally available to them?"[2]

Oertel termed the first the positive, the latter the negative theory. Johannes Hasebroek, more appropriately, called the first the modernizing, the latter the primitivist view. But careful examination of the terms employed by Oertel to describe the issues involved in the dispute as well as the various attempts to characterize the opposing positions serves well to indicate the lack of conceptual clarity which has dogged the controversy from the beginning. Debates such as this are resolved either by the appearance of new evidence or by the conceptual clarification of the problem so that the previously existing evidence falls into new perspective. In this case, the facts, on what we will call the

and Economic History of the Hellenistic World, III (Oxford, 1941), 1327–28, fn. 25; and, more recently in Eduard Will, "Trois quarts de siècle de recherches sur l'économie grècque antique," Annales, IX (January–March, 1954) .

[2] Friedrich Oertel, Supplement and comments appended to Robert Pöhlmann, Geschichte de sozialen Frage und des Sozialismus in der antiken Welt, 3d ed., III Munich, 1925) , 516–17.

operational level, can no longer be in dispute. It is, rather, the interpretation of these facts at the institutional level which remains unsettled.

THE OIKOS THEOREM: KARL RODBERTUS

The origins of this controversy go back to Rodbertus' essay on *Economic Life in Classical Antiquity,* which appeared over the years 1864–1867. The second part of this essay dealt with the "History of Roman Tributes from the Time of Augustus."[3] Here Rodbertus contrasted sharply modern and ancient taxation systems. His approach was highly suggestive. Modern taxation, he wrote, differentiates between personal and property taxes; these latter are either taxes on landed property or taxes on capital; capital, again, is either industrial or commercial, and the latter is invested either in goods or in money (i.e., either in industry or in finance). All these types of property appear as distinct from one another; indeed they appertain to different social classes. Distinctions analogous to those regarding property are also made in regard to incomes. We distinguish purely personal incomes, such as wages or salaries, which are due to the use of labor power, from income that derives from impersonal property, or title to ownership, such as rent; this latter may be either rent from land or profit; profit, again, is split up into interest and entrepreneurial profit.

"This state of affairs," Rodbertus concluded, "resulted in a modern expanding economy."[4] The various stages of production are here linked with one another through the process of buying and selling. In this fashion varying claims to a share in the national dividend are created which take the form of money incomes.

This remarkably modern view of the social function of money has not been sufficiently appreciated. Rodbertus realized that the transition from a "natural economy" to a "money economy" was not simply a technical matter, which resulted from a substitution of money purchase for barter. He insisted instead that a mone-

---

[3] Karl Rodbertus, "Zur Geschichte der römischen Tributsteuren," *Jahrbücher für Nationalökonomie und Statistik,* IV (1865), 339 and *passim.*

[4] *Ibid.,* p. 342.

tarized economy involved a social structure entirely different from that which went with an economy in kind. It was this change in the social structure accompanying the use of money rather than the technical fact of its use which ought to be emphasized, he thought. Had this point been expanded to include the varying social structures accompanying trading activity in the ancient world the controversy might have been resolved before it began.

Instead the "household" or "oikos" held the center of the stage. With Rodbertus the oikos was no more than a logical construct, a kind of anticipation of a Weberian "Ideal type." He invented the term, "lord of the oikos"[5] to designate the owner of all the various titles to property and the corresponding incomes listed above. All this was designed to illustrate how, instead of a multitude of differentiated taxes, the ancient Romans knew only one tax, the tributum paid by the lord of the oikos whose revenue was a compound of all those various kinds of incomes which had been fragmented by the modern "money economy."

For Rodbertus the oikos was typified by the vast Roman slave-worked domain, but historical confusion is apparent in a tendency to speak of the oikos without reference to any definite period. The term oikos thus became merely a peg upon which to hang the concept of economy in kind under which money, markets, and exchange were at a discount, in spite of the existence of an elaborate organization of production.

The essential element in this speculative theory upon which controversy later hinged was Rodbertus' statement that in this oikos economy.

"Nowhere does buying and selling intervene, nowhere do goods change hands. Since the national dividend never changes hands, it nowhere splits up into various income categories as in modern times. . . . All this necessitated economy-in-kind. No money was needed to make the national dividend pass from one phase of production to the other, since no change of ownership was involved."[6]

[5] Ibid., p. 344.
[6] Ibid., pp. 345–46.

KARL BÜCHER AND EDUARD MEYER

Here the matter might have rested had it not been for Karl Bücher's path-breaking work, *Die Entstehung der Volkswirtschaft,* first published in 1893. The great achievement of Bücher was to link the study of economic life in the ancient world with primitive economics. His aim was to establish a general theory of economic development from primitive to modern times. He did not equate classical antiquity with primitive society, but by emphasizing the relatively recent tribal origins of ancient Greek and Roman society, he suggested that ancient economic life might better be understood if viewed from the perspective of primitive rather than modern society.

Regarding our specific interest his thesis was that not before the emergence of the modern state do we find a *Volkswirtschaft,* i.e., a complex economic life on larger than a city scale. Up to the year 1000 A.D. the economy never passed beyond the stage of closed domestic economy *(geschlossene Hauswirtschaft)* where production was solely for one's own needs, involving no exchange between the household units. The economic life of the Greeks, Carthaginians and Romans, he said, was typified by this *oikos* economy. (Here he referred to Rodbertus.) [7]

Bücher later conceded that before the development of a large scale slave economy, there was a much larger amount of free wage labor, professional services, and exchange in general. However he still maintained his thesis in the following form: Complex economic life of a territorial character on a large scale *(Volkswirtschaft)* is the result of a development covering a period of thousands of years, and is no older than the modern state. Prior to this, mankind existed over long stretches of time without any system of exchange of goods and services that deserves the name of a complex economic life on a national scale.[8]

By settling on the self-sufficient *oikos* as the central unit of ancient society and placing this construct in a speculative theory of

[7] Karl Bücher, *Industrial Evolution,* English translation (New York, 1912), pp. 96–97.

[8] *Ibid.,* p. 88.

economic development, Bücher forced himself into the position of having to deny the significance of trade and money in ancient society. Thus the unfortunate *oikos* theorem cast the die of the controversy which was to ensue, and provided an easy target for Eduard Meyer who vigorously challenged Bücher's position in 1895.[9]

Meyer summed up his opposing thesis in the dictum that, ". . . the later period of antiquity was in essence entirely modern."[10] In support of this he adduced evidence on a number of points which seemed decisive: "The ancient world possessed an articulated economic life with a highly developed system of transportation and an intensive exchange of commodities."[11] "In the ancient Orient we meet from the earliest recorded time with a highly developed manufacturing industry, a general system of commerce, and the use of precious metals as the means of exchange."[12] Here he went on to say that since 2500 B.C. Babylonia produced numerous documents referring to private business transactions in regard to slaves, land and buildings, dividing of property at death, etc. There we find a developed system of accountancy in terms of gold and silver, which spread all over the civilized world and served as a basis for coinage. The central point which seemed to prove the economic modernity of the ancient world was that, "Trade and money were of fundamental importance in the economic life of the ancients."[13]

Meyer's position is what Hasebroek has called the "modernizing" attitude, what Oertel described as the "positive" approach, while Salvioli termed it the historians' view. A more precise designation for this position might be "the market-oriented" view. Our modern world is indeed characterized by an unprecedented

---

[9] This challenge was delivered in Meyer's address to the third meeting of the German historians at Frankfort in 1895. The address, "Die wirtschaftliche Entwicklung des Altertums," is published in Eduard Meyer, *Kleine Schriften* (Halle, 1924), pp. 79 ff.

[10] *Ibid.*, p. 89.

[11] *Ibid.*, p. 88.

[12] *Ibid.*, p. 90.

[13] *Ibid.*, p. 88.

development of productive power, an international trade network, and the use of money as a universal means of exchange. By suggesting that the ancient world had begun on the same line Meyer was, of course, adopting a "modernizing" attitude. It was also "positive" in the sense that it attributed these elements to ancient civilization; and it did represent the nineteenth-century historians' traditional view. But these terms do not convey the central feature of Meyer's position. The pivotal institution of the modern economy is the market. It is under its aegis that production, trade and money are integrated into a self-contained economic system. And the crucial point in regard to the position of Meyer and the "modernists" is that in asserting the *existence* of large scale manufacturing, trade and money, they also assumed their *organization* to follow the market pattern. But whether or not these elements of any specific economy are so organized is a point for investigation at least equally as important as the fact of their existence. The fact that the debate turned so much upon the exclusive importance of the *oikos* obscured this point and thereby weakened the position of the "primitivists." The "evidence" clearly turned against them.

The long-distance carrying and exchange of goods and the use of money objects were indeed widely spread features of ancient economic life, and in 1932 Michael Rostovtzeff was able to state that the *oikos* position was then held by almost no one.[14] But this was a pyrrhic victory for the market-oriented position. The *oikos* had been a spurious issue from the start. Once that thesis was thoroughly discredited the argument could move to the level on which it should have begun. On this level there is no disputing the "facts" regarding the physical movements of slaves, grain, wine, oil, pottery; their changing hands between distant peoples, nor can one deny some local exchanges between city and countryside. There is likewise no question of the use of money objects. The question is, how were these elements of economic life institutionalized to produce the continuous goods and person movements essential to a stable economy?

---

[14] Cf. his review of J. Hasebroek, *Zeitschrift für die Gesammte Staatswissenschaft,* 92 (1932), 334.

MAX WEBER AND MICHAEL ROSTOVTZEFF

It was the genius of Max Weber which eventually permitted the debate to reach this level. Accepting neither the "primitive" nor the "modern" approach to the problem, Weber admitted that there were some similarities between the economy of the European ancient world at the height of its development and that of the later medieval period, but he emphasized the unique characteristics of ancient culture which for him made all the difference.[15]

The force which moved the Greek and Roman economies in their special direction, according to Weber, was the general military-political orientation of ancient culture. War in ancient times was the hunt for men and economic advantages were won through the ceaseless wars and, in peace, by political means. Even the cities, although superficially like those of the Middle Ages in economic outline, were essentially different in total outlook and organization.

"Taken in its entirety . . . the city democracy of antiquity is a political guild. Tribute, booty, the payments of confederate cities, were merely distributed among the citizens. . . . The monopoly of the political guild included cleruchy, the distribution of conquered land among the citizens, and the distribution of the spoils of war; and at the last the city paid out of the proceeds of its political activity theater admissions, allotments of grain, and payments for jury service and for participation in religious rites."[16]

Weber thus opened the way to a new interpretation of the "facts," over which there was now little dispute. No victim of a preconceived stage theory of economic development, his approach showed the possibility of a relatively high level of economic organization existing in a societal framework basically different from that of the modern market system.

It can hardly be said, however, that Weber resolved the issues in this secular debate, for while he sketched in the outlines of a

---

[15] "Die sozialen Gründe des Untergangs der antiken Kultur," *Gesammelte Aufsätze zur Sozial-und Wirtschaftsgeschichte* (Tübingen, 1924), pp. 289–311. See also *Wirtschaft und Gesellschaft*, ch. 8 (Tübingen, 1922).

[16] Max Weber, *General Economic History* (Glencoe, Illinois, 1950), p. 331.

new approach, he did not provide the conceptual tools with
which to answer specific questions regarding trade organization,
money uses, and methods of exchange. And although Johannes
Hasebroek's detailed and masterful elaboration of Weber's thesis
in 1931[17] secured an important victory for the so-called "primitivist" side, Michael Rostovtzeff's questioning opposition proved
that all the issues had not thereby been resolved.

Rostovtzeff conceded that the class warfare and revolutions
which created the democracy of the Greek city states were of a
different character than those which established capitalism in the
modern western world, and that the ideals of the new society retained the color of the chieftain's society which had preceded
it.[18] But in effect this merely moved forward the time setting of
the controversy. Rostovtzeff argued that the debate should focus
on the high point of ancient economic development, that is, the
Hellenistic and early Roman period. And regarding this period,
Rostovtzeff stood firm: "As far as I am concerned, the difference between the economic life of this period and that of the
modern world is only quantitative, not qualitative."[19] To deny
this, Rostovtzeff declared, would be to deny that the ancient
world had achieved any economic development over four thousand years.

Like Oertel, Rostovtzeff maintained that the controversy was
made up of this dilemma: did the ancient world in its long existence go through a development similar to that of the modern
world or was the whole ancient world based upon a primitive
stage of economic life? He labeled the closed household theorem
an ideal construction which never existed, above all not in
Greece where there was an active trade with the highly developed Oriental empires. And did the Ionian Greeks gain nothing
from the cities of the Near East where they settled? "Surely
something must have happened!"[20]

This statement of Rostovtzeff's view of the issues in the *oikos*
controversy appeared in 1932, and thus represented the culmina-

[17] *Griechische Wirtschafts-und Gesellschaftsgeschichte* (Tübingen, 1931).
[18] *Op. cit.*, p. 337.
[19] *Ibid.*, p. 335, n. 1.
[20] *Ibid.*, p. 338.

tion of nearly forty years of debate since the publication of Bücher's book in 1893. Yet it is remarkable how little clarification of the issues had been achieved; opposing sides still clashed in a conceptual twilight.

The source of the confusion now appears obvious. *Both* sides, with the partial exception of Weber, were unable to conceive of an elaborate economy with trade, money, and market places being organized in any manner other than that of the market system. The "primitivists," who insisted that the ancient world was different from the modern, sought their support in the *oikos,* which to them represented an earlier *stage* in the development of the self-same market system. The "modernists" saw Greece and Rome resting on a foundation four thousand years in the building, which included the high economic and cultural life of the ancient Near East. Meyer emphasized the high economic development of this area and Rostovtzeff the contact between it and Greek and Roman culture. To them it was inconceivable that such a long period, full of cultural achievement, would not produce an economy at least up to the level of the later medieval period. As Rostovtzeff declared, "Something must have happened!"

But what if those four thousand years of development had moved along different lines than those of the modern world? Then the perspective from which Greece and Rome should be viewed would have to be shifted. Not capitalism, then, but a different organization of economic life would be the model from which to judge the high period of ancient economy. Bücher's primitivist perspective and Weber's military-political approach had suggested this view of the question. But neither Bücher nor Weber had provided adequate conceptual tools for recognizing what had happened, i.e., the institutional foundations of this different sort of economic development.

The following chapters of this work are devoted to this task. Exploring anew the position of trade, money, and market in the Mediterranean empires, a radically new perspective is gained from which to view the economic life of the people of the Old World. This perspective gives a much broader range to the issues of the *oikos* debate. For now the elements of markets and commercial trade which appear in the Greek classical and Hellenistic periods are seen not as the heritage of over four thousand years of Mesopotamian development, but as portentous new inventions seeking a place in Greek culture.

2   *M. I. Finley*

Was Greek Civilization Based on Slave Labour?[1]

I

Two generalizations may be made at the outset. First: at all times and in all places the Greek world relied on some form (or forms) of dependent labour to meet its needs, both public and private. By this I mean that dependent labour was essential, in a significant measure, if the requirements of agriculture, trade, manufacture, public works, and war production were to be fulfilled. And by dependent labour I mean work performed under compulsions other than those of kinship or communal obligations.[2] Second: with the rarest of exceptions, there were always substantial numbers of free men engaged in productive labour. By this I mean primarily not free hired labour but free men working on their own (or leased) land or in their shops or homes as craftsmen and shopkeepers. It is within the framework created by these two generalizations that the questions must be asked which seek to locate slavery in the society. And by slavery,

SOURCE. First published in HISTORIA vol. VIII, 1959. Franz Steiner Verlag GmbH, Wiesbaden.

[1] This is a slightly enlarged and revised version of a paper read at the triennial meeting of the Joint Committee of Greek and Roman Societies in Cambridge on 11 August 1958. No effort has been made to annotate fully or to provide more than a handful of modern references. I am grateful to Professors A. H. M. Johens and M. Postan in Cambridge, and Mr G. E. M. de Ste. Croix of New College and Mr P. A. Brunt of Oriel College, Oxford, for much helpful criticism.

[2] I also exclude the "economic compulsion" of the wage-labour system.

finally, I mean roughly the status in which a man is, in the eyes
of the law and of public opinion and with respect to all other
parties, a possession, a chattel, of another man.[3]

How completely the Greeks always took slavery for granted as
one of the facts of human existence is abundantly evident to anyone who has read their literature. In the Homeric poems it is assumed (correctly) that captive women will be taken home as
slaves, and that occasional male slaves—the victims of Phoeni-
cian merchant-pirates—will also be on hand. In the seventh century B.C., when Hesiod, the Boeotian "peasant" poet, gets down
to practical advice in his *Works and Days,* he tells his brother
how to use slaves properly; that they will be available is simply
assumed.[4] The same is true of Xenophon's manual for the gentleman farmer, the *Oeconomicus,* written about 375 B.C. A few
years earlier, an Athenian cripple who was appealing a decision
dropping him from the dole, said to the Council: "I have a trade
which brings me in a little, but I can barely work at it myself and
I cannot afford to buy someone to replace myself in it."[5] In the
first book of the Pseudo-Aristotelian *Oeconomica,* a Peripatetic
work probably of the late fourth or early third century B.C., we
find the following proposition about the organization of the
household, stated as baldly and flatly as it could possibly be
done: "Of property, the first and most necessary kind, the best
and most manageable, is man. Therefore the first step is to procure good slaves. Of slaves there are two kinds, the overseer and
the worker."[6] Polybius, discussing the strategic situation of By-

---

[3] It is obviously not a valid objection to this working definition to point
out either that a slave is biologically a man none the less, or that there were
usually some pressures to give him a little recognition of his humanity, such
as the privilege of asylum or the de facto privilege of marriage.

[4] I believe that the ερι θοσ, and perhaps the θησ of ll. 602–03 were slaves,
from the context, peculiar as that use of the two words may be. But even if
one rejects my interpretation of these two lines, slaves are so repeatedly taken
for granted in the poem that it is incorrect to imply a balanced alternative, as
does W. L. Westermann, The Slave Systems of Greek and Roman Antiquity
(Philadelphia 1955), 4, when he writes: "The peasant of modest means of the
type of Hesiod might well have slaves but he also used hired labour."

[5] Lysias 24.6.

[6] Ps.-Aristotle, Oec. 1.5.1,1344a22.

zantium, speaks quite casually of "the necessities of life—cattle and slaves" which come from the Black Sea region.[7] And so on.

The Greek language had an astonishing range of vocabulary for slaves, unparalleled in my knowledge.[8] In the earliest texts, Homer and Hesiod, there were two basic words for slave, *dmos* and *doulos,* used without any discoverable distinction between them, and both with uncertain etymologies. *Dmos* died out quickly, surviving only in poetry, whereas *doulos* remained the basic word, so to speak, all through Greek history, and the root on which were built such words as *douleia,* "slavery." But Homer already has, in one probably interpolated passage, the word (in the plural form) *andrapoda,* which became very common, and seems to have been constructed on the model of *tetrapoda.*[9] Still another general word came into use in the Hellenistic period, when *soma* ("body") came to mean "slave" if not otherwise qualified by an adjective.

These words were strictly servile, except in such metaphors as "the Athenians enslaved the allies." But there was still another group which could be used for both slaves and freemen, depending on the context. Three of them are built on the household root, *oikos—oikeus, oiketes,* and *oikiatas—*and the pattern of usage is variegated, complicated, and still largely unexamined. In Crete, for example, *oikeus* seems to have been a technical status term more like "serf" than any other instance known to me in Greek history. It was archaic even in Crete, however, and it dropped out of sight there in post-fifth-century documents. Elsewhere these *oikos*-words sometimes meant merely "servant" or "slave" generically, and sometimes, though less often, they indicated narrower distinctions, such as house-born slave (as against purchased) or privately owned (as against royal in the Hellenistic context) .[10]

[7] Polyb. 4.38.4.

[8] I am not considering the local helotage words here, although the Greeks themselves customarily called such people "slaves."

[9] Homer, Il. 7.475.

[10] The terminology needs systematic investigation in terms of a range of unfree and semi-free statuses. I have given only some examples. On the regional and dialectal variations, see Erika Kretschmer, "Beiträge zur Wort-

If we think of ancient society as made up of a spectrum of statuses, with the free citizen at one end and the slave at the other, and with a considerable number of shades of dependence in between, then we have already discovered two lines of the spectrum, the slave and the serf-like *oikeus* of Crete. At least four more can easily be added: the helot (with such parallels as the *penestes* of Thessaly) ; the debt-bondsman, who was not a slave although under some conditions he could eventually be sold into slavery abroad; the conditionally manumitted slave; and, finally, the freedman. All six categories rarely, if ever, appeared concurrently within the same community, nor were they equal in importance or equally significant in all periods of Greek history. By and large, the slave proper was the decisive figure (to the virtual exclusion of the others) in the economically and politically advanced communities; whereas helotage and debt-bondage were to be found in the more archaic communities, whether in Crete or Sparta or Thessaly at an even late date, or in Athens in its pre-Solonian period. There is also some correlation, though by no means a perfect one, between the various categories of dependent labour and their function. Slavery was the most flexible of the forms, adaptable to all kinds and levels of activity, whereas helotage and the rest were best suited to agriculture, pasturage, and household service, much less so to manufacture and trade.

II

With little exception, there was no activity, productive or unproductive, public or private, pleasant or unpleasant, which was not performed by slaves at some times and in some places in the Greek world. The major exception was, of course, political: no slave held public office or sat on the deliberative and judicial

geographie der altgr. Dialek'te. 1. Diener, Sklave", Glotta XVIII (1930), 71–81. On the interchangeability of the terms in classical Athenian usage, see Siegfried Lauffer, Die Bergwerkssklaven von Laureion (2 vols., Akad. Wiss. Mainz, Abh. Geistes- u. Sozialwiss. Kl. 1955, no. 12; 1956, no. 11), I 1104–8; cf. E. L. Kazakevich, "The Term δουλοσ and the Concept 'Slave' in Athens in the Fourth Century B.C." (in Russian), VDI (1956), no. 3, pp. 119–36, summarized in Bibl. Class. Or. II (1957), 203–205. (A former student, Mr. Jonathan Frankel, kindly abstracted the latter article for me.)

bodies (though slaves were commonly employed in the "civil service," as secretaries and clerks, and as policemen and prison attendants). Slaves did not fight as a rule, either, unless freed (although helots apparently did), and they were very rare in the liberal professions, including medicine. On the other side, there was no activity which was not performed by free men at some times and in some places. That is sometimes denied, but the denial rests on a gross error, namely, the failure to differentiate between a free man working for himself and one working for another, for hire. In the Greek scale of values, the crucial test was not so much the nature of the work (within limits, of course) as the condition or status under which it was carried on.[11] "The condition of the free man," said Aristotle, "is that he does not live under the restraint of another."[12] On this point, Aristotle was expressing a nearly universal Greek notion. Although we find free Greeks doing every kind of work, the free wage-earner, the free man who regularly works *for* another and therefore "lives under the restraint of another" is a rare figure in the sources, and he surely was a minor factor in the picture.[13]

[11] See A. Aymard, "L'idée de travail dans la Grèce archaique," J. de Psych. XLI (1948), 29–45.

[12] Rhet. 1.9, 1367a32.

[13] This statement is not invalidated by the occasional sally which a small-holder or petty craftsman might make into the labour market to do three days' harvesting or a week's work on temple construction; or by the presence in cities like Athens of a substantial number of men, almost all of them unskilled, who lived on odd jobs (when they were not rowing in the fleet or otherwise occupied by the state), those, for example, who congregated daily at Κολωγοσμιοθιοσ (on which see A. Fuks, in Eranos XLIX, 1951, 171–73). Nowhere in the sources do we hear of private establishments employing a staff of hired workers as their normal operation. Public works are frequently adduced as evidence to the contrary, but I believe without sufficient cogency. In the first place, the more common practice seems to have been a contract with an entrepreneur (even if he worked alone), not hire for wages; see P. H. Davis, "The Delian Building Accounts," Bull. Corr. Hell. LXI (1937), at pp. 110–20. Second, such evidence as we have—most fully from Delos—argues that such work was spasmodic and infrequent, and quite inconceivable as a source of livelihood for any but a handful of men. All this is consistent with the view that most of the craftsmen appearing in the accounts were independent masons and carpenters who occasionally accepted a job from the state just as they accepted orders from private clients. The key to the whole question is the absence of entrepreneurs whose regular labour force consisted of hired free men.

The basic economic activity was, of course, agriculture. Throughout Greek history, the overwhelming majority of the population had its main wealth in the land. And the majority were smallholders, depending on their own labour, the labour of other members of the family, and the occasional assistance (as in time of harvest) of neighbours and casual hired hands. Some proportion of these smallholders owned a slave, or even two, but we cannot possibly determine what the proportion was, and in this sector the whole issue is clearly not of the greatest importance. But the large landholders, a minority though they were, constituted the political (and often the intellectual) elite of the Greek world; our evidence reveals remarkably few names of any consequence whose economic base was outside the land. This landholding elite tended to become more and more of an an absentee group in the course of Greek history; but early or late, whether they sat on their estates or in the cities, dependent labour worked their land as a basic rule (even when allowance is made for tenancy). In some areas it took the form of helotage, and in the archaic period, of debt-bondage, but generally the form was outright slavery.

I am aware, of course, that this view of slavery in Greek agriculture is now strongly contested. Nevertheless, I accept the evidence of the line of authors whom I have already cited, from Hesiod to the pseudo-Aristotelian *Oeconomica*. These are all matter-of-fact writings, not utopias or speculative statements of what ought to be. If slavery was not the customary labour form on the larger holdings, then I cannot imagine what Hesiod or Xenophon or the Peripatetic were doing, or why any Greek bothered to read their works.[14] One similar piece of evidence is worth adding. There was a Greek harvest festival called the Kronia, which was celebrated in Athens and other places (especially

[14] Scholars who argue that slavery was unimportant in agriculture systematically ignore the *Hausvaterliteratur* and similar evidence, while trying to prove their case partly by weak arguments from silence (on which see G. E. M. de Ste. Croix in Class. Rev., n. s. VII, 1957, p. 56), and partly by reference to the papyri. One cannot protest strongly enough against the latter procedure, since the agricultural regime in Ptolemaic and Roman Egypt was not Greek; see M. Rostovtzeff, The Social & Economic History of the Hellenistic World (3 vols., Oxford, repr. 1953), I 272–77.

among the Ionians). One feature, says the Atthidographer Philochorus, was that "the heads of families ate the crops and fruits at the same table with their slaves, with whom they had shared the labours of cultivation. For the god is pleased with this honour from the slaves in contemplation of their labours."[15] Neither the practice nor Philochorus' explanation of it makes any sense whatever if slavery was as unimportant in agriculture as some modern writers pretend.

I had better be perfectly clear here: I am not saying that slaves outnumbered free men in agriculture, or that the bulk of farming was done by slaves, but that slavery dominated agriculture insofar as it was on a scale that transcended the labour of the householder and his sons. Nor am I suggesting that there was no hired free labour; rather that there was little of any significance. Among the slaves, furthermore, were the overseers, invariably so if the property was large enough or if the owner was an absentee. "Of slaves," said the author of the *Oeconomica*, "there are two kinds, the overseer and the worker."

In mining and quarrying the situation was decisively one-sided. There were free men, in Athens for example, who leased such small mining concessions that they were able to work them alone. The moment, however, additional labour was introduced (and that was the more common case), it seems normally to have been slave. The largest individual holdings of slaves in Athens were workers in the mines, topped by the one thousand reported to have been leased out for this purpose by the fifth-century general Nicias.[16] It has been suggested, indeed, that at one point there may have been as many as thirty thousand slaves at work in the Athenian silver mines and processing mills.[17]

Manufacture was like agriculture in that the choice was (even more exclusively) between the independent craftsman working alone or with members of his family and the owner of slaves. The link with slavery was so close (and the absence of free hired labour so complete) that Demosthenes, for example, could say "they caused the *ergasterion* to disappear" and then he could fol-

---

[15] Philochorus 328 F 97, ap. Macrob. Sat. 1.10.22.

[16] Xenophon, Poroi 4.14.

[17] See Lauffer, op. cit., II 904–16.

low, as an exact synonym and with no possible misunderstanding, by saying that "they caused the slaves to disappear."[18] On the other hand, the proportion of operations employing slaves, as against the independent self-employed craftsmen, was probably greater than in agriculture, and in this respect more like mining. In commerce and banking, subordinates were invariably slaves, even in such posts as "bank manager." However, the numbers were small.

In the domestic field, finally, we can take it as a rule that any free man who possibly could afford one, owned a slave attendant who accompanied him when he walked abroad in the town or when he travelled (including his military service), and also a slave woman for the household chores. There is no conceivable way of estimating how many such free men there were, or how many owned numbers of domestics, but the fact is taken for granted so completely and so often in the literature that I strongly believe that many owned slaves even when they could not afford them. (Modern parallels will come to mind readily.) I stress this for two reasons. First, the need for domestic slaves, often an unproductive element, should serve as a cautionary sign when one examines such questions as the efficiency and cost of slave labour. Second, domestic slavery was by no means entirely unproductive. In the countryside in particular, but also in the towns, two important industries would often be in their hands in the larger households, on a straight production for household consumption basis. I refer to baking and textile making, and every medievalist, at least, will at once grasp the significance of the withdrawal of the latter from market production, even if the withdrawal was far from complete.[19]

It would be very helpful if we had some idea how many slaves there were in any given Greek community to carry on all this work, and how they were divided among the branches of the

[18] Dem. 27.19,26; 28.12; see Finley, Studies in Land and Credit in Ancient Athens (New Brunswick 1952), 67. For another decisive text, see Xen. Memorab. 2.7.6.

[19] On the importance of the domestic slave as nursemaid and pedagogue, see Joseph Vogt's rectoral address, "Wege zur Menschlichkeit in der antiken Sklaverei," Univ. Tübingen Reden XLVII (1958), 19–38. (Dr. V. Ehrenberg kindly called my attention to this publication.)

economy. Unfortunately we have no reliable figures, and none at all for most of the *poleis*. What I consider to be the best computations for Athens suggest that the total of slaves reached 80–100,000 in peak periods in the fifth and fourth centuries B.C.[20] Athens had the largest population in the classical Greek world and the largest number of slaves. Thucydides said that there were more slaves in his day on the island of Chios than in any other Greek community except Sparata,[21] but I suggest that he was thinking of the density of the slave population measured against the free, not of absolute totals (and in Sparta he meant the helots, not chattel slaves). Other places, such as Aegina or Corinth, may at one time or another also have had a higher ratio of slaves than Athens. And there were surely communities in which the slaves were less dense.

More than that we can scarcely say about the numbers, but I think that is really enough. There is too much tendentious discussion of numbers in the literature already, as if a mere count of heads is the answer to all the complicated questions which flow from the existence of slavery. The Athenian figures I mentioned amount to an average of no less than three or four slaves to each free household (including all free men in the calculation, whether citizen or not). But even the smallest figure anyone has suggested, 20,000 slaves in Demosthenes' time[22]—altogether too low in my opinion—would be roughly equivalent to one slave for each adult citizen, no negligible ratio. Within very broad limits, the numbers are irrelevant to the question of significance. When Starr, for example, objects to "exaggerated guesses" and replies that "the most careful estimates . . . reduce the proportion of slaves to far less than half the population, probably one third or one quarter at most,"[23] he is proving far less than he thinks. No one seriously believes that slaves did all the work in Athens (or anywhere else in Greece except for Sparta with

[20] Lauffer, op. cit., II 904–16.

[21] Thuc. 8.40.2.

[22] A. H. M. Jones, *Athenian Democracy* (Oxford 1957), 76–79; cf. his "Slavery in the Ancient World," Econ. Hist. Rev., 2nd ser., IX (1956), at p. 187.

[23] C. G. Starr, "An Overdose of Slavery", J. Econ. Hist. XVIII (1958), at pp. 21–22.

its helots), and one merely confuses the issues when one pretends that somehow a reduction of the estimates to only a third or a quarter of the population is crucial.[24] In 1860, according to official census figures, slightly less than one third of the total population of the American slave states were slaves. Furthermore, "nearly three-fourths of all free Southerners had no connection with slavery through either family ties or direct ownership. The 'typical' Southerner was not only a small farmer but also a nonslaveholder."[25] Yet no one would think of denying that slavery was a decisive element in southern society. The analogy seems obvious for ancient Greece, where, it can be shown, ownership of slaves was even more widely spread among the free men and the use of slaves much more diversified, and where the estimates do not give a ratio significantly below the American one. Simply stated, there can be no denial that there were enough slaves about for them to be, of necessity, an integral factor in the society.

There were two main sources of supply. One was captives, the victims of war and sometimes piracy. One of the few generalizations about the ancient world to which there is no exception is this, that the victorious power had absolute right over the persons and the property of the vanquished.[26] This right was not exercised to its full extent every time, but it was exercised often enough, and on a large enough scale, to throw a continuous and numerous supply of men, women, and children on to the slave market. Alongside the captives we must place the so-called barbarians who came into the Greek world in a steady stream— Thracians, Scythians, Cappadocians, etc.—through the activity of full-time traders, much like the process by which African slaves reached the new world in more modern times. Many were the victims of wars among the barbarians themselves. Others

---

[24] It is remarkable how completely Starr misses this point in his very belligerent article. Although he says over and over again that slavery was not "dominant" or "basic" in antiquity, I can find no serious argument in his article other than his disproof of the view that slaves did all the work.

[25] Kenneth M. Stampp, The Peculiar Institution: Slavery in the Ante-Bellum South (New York 1956), 29–30.

[26] See A. Aymard, "Le partage des profits de la guerre dans les traités d'alliance antiques," Rev. hist. CCXVII (1957), 233–49.

came peacefully, so to speak: Herodotus says that the Thracians sold their children for export.[27] The first steps all took place outside the Greek orbit, and our sources tell us virtually nothing about them, but there can be no doubt that large numbers and a steady supply were involved, for there is no other way to explain such facts as the high proportion of Paphlagonians and Thracians among the slaves in the Attic silver mines, many of them specialists, or the corps of 300 Scythian archers (slaves owned by the state) who constituted the Athenian police force.

Merely to complete the picture, we must list penal servitude and the exposure of unwanted children. Beyond mere mention, however, they can be ignored because they were altogether negligible in their importance. There then remains one more source, breeding, and that is a puzzle. One reads in the modern literature that there was very little breeding of slaves (as distinct from helots and the like) among the Greeks because, under their conditions, it was cheaper to buy slaves than to raise them. I am not altogether satisfied with the evidence for this view, and I am altogether dissatisfied with the economics which is supposed to justify it. There were conditions under which breeding was certainly rare, but for reasons which have nothing to do with economics. In the mines, for example, nearly all the slaves were men, and that is the explanation, simply enough. But what about domestics, among whom the proportion of women was surely high? I must leave the question unanswered, except to remove one fallacy. It is sometimes said that there is a demographic law that no slave population ever reproduces itself, that they must always be replenished from outside. Such a law is a myth: that can be said categorically on the evidence of the southern states, evidence which is statistical and reliable.

III

The impression one gets is clearly that the majority of the slaves were foreigners. In a sense, they were all foreigners. That is to say, it was the rule (apart from debt bondage) that Atheni-

[27] Herod. 5.6.

ans were never kept as slaves in Athens, or Corinthians in Corinth. However, I am referring to the more basic sense, that the majority were not Greeks at all, but men and women from the races living outside the Greek world. It is idle to speculate about proportions here, but there cannot be any reasonable doubt about the majority. In some places, such as the Laurium silver mines in Attica, this meant relatively large concentrations in a small area. The number of Thracian slaves in Laurium in Xenophon's time, for example, was greater than the total population of some of the smaller Greek city-states.

No wonder some Greeks came to identify slaves and barbarians (a synonym for all non-Greeks). The most serious effort, so far as we know, to justify this view as part of the natural arrangement of things, will be found in the first book of Aristotle's *Politics*. It was not a successful effort for several reasons, of which the most obvious is the fact, as Aristotle himself conceded, that too many were slaves "by accident," by the chance of warfare or shipwreck or kidnapping. In the end, natural slavery was abandoned as a concept, defeated by the pragmatic view that slavery was a fact of life, a conventional institution universally practised. As the Roman jurist Florentinus phrased it, "Slavery is an institution of the *ius gentium* whereby someone is subject to the *dominium* of another, contrary to nature."[28] That view (and even sharper formulations) can be traced back to the sophistic literature of the fifth century B.C., and, in a less formal way, to Greek tragedy. I chose Florentinus to quote instead because his definition appears in the *Digest,* in which slavery is so prominent that the Roman law of slavery has been called "the most characteristic part of the most characteristic intellectual product of Rome."[29] Nothing illustrates more perfectly the inability of the ancient world to imagine that there could be a civilized society without slaves.

The Greek world was one of endless debate and challenge. Among the intellectuals, no belief or idea was self-evident: every conception and every institution sooner or later came under attack—religious beliefs, ethical values, political systems, aspects

[28] Dig. 1.5.4.1.
[29] W. W. Buckland, The Roman Law of Slavery (Cambridge 1908), v.

of the economy, even such bedrock institutions as the family and private property. Slavery, too, up to a point, but that point was invariably a good distance short of abolitionist proposals. Plato, who criticized society more radically than any other thinker, did not concern himself much with the question in the *Republic,* but even there he assumed the continuance of slavery. And in the *Laws,* "the number of passages . . . that deal with slavery is surprisingly large" and the tenor of the legislation is generally more severe than the actual law of Athens at that time. "Their effect, on the one hand, is to give greater authority to masters in the exercise of rule over slaves, and on the other hand to accentuate the distinction between slave and free man."[30] Paradoxically, neither were the believers in the brotherhood of man (whether Cynic, Stoic, or early Christian) opponents of slavery. In their eyes, all material concerns, including status, were a matter of essential indifference. Diogenes, it is said, was once seized by pirates and taken to Crete to be sold. At the auction, he pointed to a certain Corinthian among the buyers and said: "Sell me to him; he needs a master."[31]

The question must then be faced, how much relevance has all this for the majority of Greeks, for those who were neither philosophers nor wealthy men of leisure? What did the little man think about slavery? It is no answer to argue that we must not take "the political theorists of the philosophical schools too seriously as having established 'the main line of Greek thought concerning slavery.'"[32] No one pretends that Plato and Aristotle speak for all Greeks. But, equally, no one should pretend that lower-class Greeks necessarily rejected everything which we read

[30] Glenn R. Morrow, Plato's Law of Slavery in Its Relation to Greek Law (Univ. of Illinois Press 1939), 11 and 127. Morrow effectively disproves the view that "Plato at heart disapproved of slavery and in introducing it into the *Laws* was simply accommodating himself to his age" (pp. 129–30). Cf. G. Vlastos, "Slavery in Plato's Thought," Philos. Rev. L (1941), 293: "There is not the slightest indication, either in the *Republic,* or anywhere else, that Plato means to obliterate or relax in any way" the distinction between slave and free labour.

[31] Diogenes Laertius 6.74. On the Cynics, Stoics, and Christians, see Westermann, op. cit., pp. 24–25, 39–40, 116–17, 149–59.

[32] Westermann, op. cit., p. 14 n. 48.

in Greek literature and philosophy, simply because, with virtually no exceptions, the poets and philosophers were men of the leisure class. The history of ideology and belief is not so simple. It
is a commonplace that the little man shares the ideals and aspira-
tions of his betters—in his dreams if not in the hard reality of his
daily life. By and large, the vast majority in all periods of history
have always taken the basic institutions of society for granted.
Men do not, as a rule, ask themselves whether monogamous
marriage or a police force or machine production is necessary to
their way of life. They accept them as facts, as self-evident. Only
when there is a challenge from one source or another—from outside or from catastrophic famine or plague—do such facts become questions.

A large section of the Greek population was always on the
edge of marginal subsistence. They worked hard for their livelihood and could not look forward to economic advancement as a
reward for their labours; on the contrary, if they moved at all, it
was likely to be downward. Famines, plagues, wars, political
struggles, all were a threat, and social crisis was a common
enough phenomenon in Greek history. Yet through the centuries
no ideology of labour appeared, nothing that can in any sense be
counterpoised to the negative judgments with which the writings
of the leisure class are filled. There was neither a word in the
Greek language with which to express the general notion of "labour," nor the concept of labour "as a general social
function."[33] There was plenty of grumbling, of course, and there
was pride of craftmanship. Men could not survive psychologically without them. But neither developed into a belief: grumbling
was not turned into a punishment for sin—"In the sweat of thy
face shalt thou eat bread"—nor pride of craftsmanship into the
virtue of labour, into the doctrine of the calling or anything comparable. The nearest to either will be found in Hesiod's *Works
and Days,* and in this context the decisive fact about Hesiod is
his unquestioning assumption that the farmer will have proper
slave labour.

[33] See J.-P. Vernant, "Prométhée et la fonction technique," J. de Psych.
XLV (1952), 419–29; "Travail et nature dans la Grèce ancienne," J. de Psych.
LII (1955), 18–38.

That was all there was to the poor man's counter-ideology: we live in the iron age when "men never rest from toil and sorrow by day, and from perishing by night"; therefore it is better to toil than to idle and perish—but if we can we too will turn to the labour of slaves. Hesiod may not have been able, even in his imagination, to think beyond slavery as *supplementary* to his own labour, but that was the seventh century, still the early days of slavery. About 400 B.C., however, Lysias' cripple could make the serious argument in the Athenian *boule* that he required a dole because he could not afford a slave as a *replacement*.[34] And half a century later Xenophon put forth a scheme whereby every citizen could be maintained by the state, chiefly from revenues to be derived from publicly owned slaves working in the mines.[35]

When talk turned to action, even when crisis turned into civil war and revolution, slavery remained unchallenged. With absolute regularity, all through Greek history, the demand was "Cancel debts and redistribute the land." Never, to my knowledge, do we hear a protest from the free poor, not even in the deepest crises, against slave competition. There are no complaints—as there might well have been—that slaves deprive free men of a livelihood, or compel free men to work for lower wages and longer hours.[36] There is nothing remotely resembling a workers' programme, no wage demands, no talk of working conditions or government employment measures or the like. In a city like Athens there was ample opportunity. The *demos* had power, enough

[34] Lys. 24.6: τον διαδεξομενον δ'αυτην ουπω δυναμαι χτησασθαι.

[35] Xen. Poroi 4.33; cf. 6.1. The best examples of Utopian dreaming in this direction are, of course, provided by Aristophanes, in Eccl. 651–61 and Plut. 510–26, but I refrain from stressing them because I wish to avoid the long argument about slavery in Attic comedy.

[36] This generalization stands despite an isolated (and confused) passage like Timaeus 566 F 11, ap. Athen. 6.264D, 272B, about Aristotle's friend Mnason. Periander's prohibition of slave ownership (Nicolaus of Damascus 90 F 58) sounds like another of the traditional tyrant's measures designed (as Nicolaus suggests) to keep the citizens of Corinth occupied. If there is any truth in it, the "slaves" may actually have been debt-bondsmen, for the background of Periander's programme was an archaic rural one; see Édouard Will, Korinthiaka (Paris 1955), 510–12.

of them were poor, and they had leaders. But economic assistance took the form of pay for public office and for rowing in the
fleet, free admission to the theatre (the so-called theoric fund),
and various doles; while economic legislation was restricted to
imports and exports, weights and measures, price controls.[37]
Not even the wildest of the accusations against the demagogues
—and they were wholly unrestrained as every reader of Aristophanes or Plato knows—ever suggested anything which would
hint at a working-class interest, or an anti-slavery bias. No issue
of free versus slave appears in this field of public activity.[38]

Nor did the free poor take the other possible tack of joining
with the slaves in a common struggle on a principled basis. The
Solonic revolution in Athens at the beginning of the sixth century B.C., for example, brought an end to debt bondage and the return of Athenians who had been sold into slavery abroad, but
not the emancipation of others, non-Athenians, who were in
slavery in Athens. Centuries later, when the great wave of slave
revolts came after 140 B.C., starting in the Roman west and
spreading to the Greek east, the free poor on the whole simply
stood apart. It was no issue of theirs, they seem to have thought;
correctly so, for the outcome of the revolts promised them nothing one way or the other. Numbers of free men may have taken
advantage of the chaos to enrich themselves personally, by loot-
ing or otherwise. Essentially that is what they did, when the opportunity arose, in a military campaign, nothing more. The

---

[37] There is, of course, the argument of Plutarch, Pericles 12.4–5, that the
great temple-building activity in fifth-century Athens was a calculated make-
work programme. I know of no similar statement in contemporary sources,
and the notion is significantly missing in Aristotle, Ath. Pol. 24.3. But even if
Plutarch is right, public works at best provided supplementary income (see n.
13) and they made use of slave labour, thus serving as further evidence for
my argument. Nor could Plutarch's thesis be applied to many cities (if any)
other than Athens.

[38] I doubt if any point can be made in this context of the fact that citizens
and slaves worked side by side in the fields and workshops and on public
works, or that they sometimes belonged to the same cult associations. Such
phenomena are widespread wherever slavery existed, including the American
South.

slaves were, in a basic sense, irrelevant to their behaviour at that moment.[39]

In 464 B.C. a great helot revolt broke out, and in 462 Athens dispatched a hoplite force under Cimon to help the Spartans suppress it. When the revolt ended, after nearly five years, a group of the rebels were permitted to escape, and it was Athens which provided them refuge, settling them in Naupactus. A comparable shift took place in the first phase of the Peloponnesian War. In 425 the Athenians seized Pylos, a harbour on the west coast of the Peloponnese. The garrison was a small one and Pylos was by no means an important port. Nevertheless, Sparta was so frightened that she soon sued for peace, because the Athenian foothold was a dangerous centre of infection, inviting desertion and eventual revolt among the Messenian helots. Athens finally agreed to peace in 421, and immediately afterwards concluded an alliance with Sparta, one of the terms of which was: "Should the slave-class rise in rebellion, the Athenians will assist the Lacedaemonians with all their might, according to their power."[40]

Obviously the attitude of one city to the slaves of another lies largely outside our problem. Athens agreed to help suppress helots when she and Sparta were allies; she encouraged helot revolts when they were at war. That reflects elementary tactics, not a judgment about slavery. Much the same kind of distinction must be made in the instances, recurring in Spartan history, when helots were freed as pawns in an internal power struggle. So, too, of the instances which were apparently not uncommon in fourth-century Greece, but about which nothing concrete is known other than the clause in the agreement between Alexander and the Hellenic League, binding the members to guarantee that "there shall be no killing or banishment contrary to the laws of each

[39] See Joseph Vogt, Struktur der antiken Sklavenkriege (Mainz Abh. 1957, no. 1), 53–57; cf. E. A. Thompson, "Peasant Revolts in Late Roman Gaul and Spain," Past & Present, no. 2 (1952), 11–23.

[40] The relevant passages in Thucydides are 4.41, 55, 80; 5.14; 5.23.3; 7.26.2. The "slave-class" ($\eta\ \delta o \upsilon \lambda \epsilon \iota \alpha$) here meant the helots, of course. In my text in the pages which follow immediately (on slaves in war), I also say "slaves" to include the helots, ignoring for the moment the distinction between them.

city, no confiscation of property, no redistribution of land, no cancellation of debts, no freeing of slaves for purposes of revolution."[41] These were mere tactics again. Slaves were resources, and they could be useful in a particular situation. But only a number of specific slaves, those who were available at the precise moment; not slaves in general, or all slaves, and surely not slaves in the future. Some slaves were freed, but slavery remained untouched. Exactly the same behaviour can be found in the reverse case, when a state (or ruling class) called upon its slaves to help protect it. Often enough in a military crisis, slaves were freed, conscripted into the army or navy, and called upon to fight.[42] And again the result was that some slaves were freed while the institution continued exactly as before.

In sum, under certain conditions of crisis and tension the society (or a sector of it) was faced with a conflict within its system of values and beliefs. It was sometimes necessary, in the interest of national safety or of a political programme, to surrender the normal use of, and approach to, slaves. When this happened, the institution itself survived without any noticeable weakening. The fact that it happened is not without significance; it suggests that among the Greeks, even in Sparta, there was not that deep-rooted and often neurotic horror of the slaves known in some other societies, which would have made the freeing and arming of slaves en masse, for whatever purpose, a virtual impossibility. It suggests, further, something about the slaves themselves. Some did fight for their masters, and that is not unimportant.

Nothing is more elusive than the psychology of the slave. Even when, as in the American South, there seems to be a lot of material—autobiographies of ex-slaves, impressions of travellers from non-slaveholding societies, and the like—no reliable pic-

[41] Ps.-Demosthenes 17.15. For earlier periods, cf. Herod. 7.155 on Syracuse and Thuc. 3.73 on Corcyra (and note that Thucydides does not return to the point or generalize about it in his final peroration on *stasis* and its evils).

[42] See the material assembled by Louis Robert, Etudes épigraphiques et philologiques (Bibl. Éc. Hautes Ét. 272, Paris 1938), 118–26. Xenophon, Poroi 4.42, uses the potential value of slaves as military and naval manpower as an argument in favour of his proposal to have the state buy thousands of slaves to be hired out in the mines. Cf. Hypereides' proposal after Chaeronea to free all the Athenian slaves and arm them (see fragments of his speech against Aristogeiton, Blass no. 18, and Ps.-Plut., Hyper. 848F–849A).

ture emerges.[43] For antiquity there is scarcely any evidence at all, and the bits are indirect and tangential, and far from easy to interpret. Thus, a favourite apology is to invoke the fact that, apart from very special instances as in Sparta, the record shows neither revolts of slaves nor a fear of uprisings. Even if the facts are granted—and the nature of our sources warrants a little scepticism—the rosy conclusion does not follow. Slaves have scarcely ever revolted, even in the southern states.[44] A large-scale rebellion is impossible to organize and carry through except under very unusual circumstances. The right combination appeared but once in ancient history, during two generations of the late Roman Republic, when there were great concentrations of slaves in Italy and Sicily, many of them almost completely unattended and unguarded, many others professional fighters (gladiators), and when the whole society was in turmoil, with a very marked breakdown of social and moral values.[45]

At this point it is necessary to recall that helots differed in certain key respects from chattel slaves. First, they had the necessary ties of solidarity that come from kinship and nationhood, intensified by the fact, not to be underestimated, that they were not foreigners but a subject people working their own lands in a state of servitude. This complex was lacking among the slaves of the Greek world. The Peripatetic author of the *Oeconomica* made the sensible recommendation that neither an individual nor a city should have many slaves of the same nationality.[46] Second, the helots had property rights of a kind: the law, at least, permitted them to retain everything they produced beyond the fixed deliveries to their masters. Third, they outnumbered the free population on a scale without parallel in other Greek communities. These are the peculiar factors, in my opinion, which explain the revolts of the helots and the persistent Spartan concern with the question, more than Spartan cruelty.[47] It is a falla-

[43] See Stampp, op. cit., pp. 86–88.
[44] Ibid., pp. 132–40.
[45] Vogt, Sklavenkrieg.
[46] Ps.-Arist., Oec. 1.5,1344b18; cf. Plato, Laws 6.777C–D; Arist., Pol. 7.9.9, 1330a 25–28.
[47] Note that Thucydides 8.40.2 makes the disproportionately large number of Chian slaves the key to their ill-treatment and their readiness to desert to the Athenians.

cy to think that the threat of rebellion increases automatically with an increase in misery and oppression. Hunger and torture destroy the spirit; at most they stimulate efforts at flight or other forms of purely individual behaviour (including betrayal of fellow-victims), whereas revolt requires organization and courage and persistence. Frederick Douglass, who in 1855 wrote the most penetrating analysis to come from an ex-slave, summed up the psychology in these words:

"Beat and cuff your slave, keep him hungry and spiritless, and he will follow the chain of his master like a dog; but feed and clothe him well,—work him moderately—surround him with physical comfort,—and dreams of freedom intrude. Give him a *bad* master, and he aspires to a *good* master; give him a good master, and he wishes to become his *own* master."[48]

There are many ways, other than revolt, in which slaves can protest.[49] In particular they can flee, and though we have no figures whatsoever, it seems safe to say that the fugitive slave was a chronic and sufficiently numerous phenomenon in the Greek cities.[50] Thucydides estimated that more than 20,000 Athenian slaves fled in the final decade of the Peloponnesian War. In this they were openly encouraged by the Spartan garrison established in Decelea, and Thucydides makes quite a point of the operation. Obviously he thought the harm to Athens was serious, intensified by the fact that many were skilled workers.[51] My immediate concern is with the slaves themselves, not with Athens, and I should stress very heavily that so many skilled slaves (who must be presumed to have been, on the average, among the best treated) took the risk and tried to flee. The risk was no light one, at least for the barbarians among them: no Thracian or Carian wandering about the Greek countryside without credentials could

[48] My Bondage and My Freedom (New York 1855), 263–64, quoted from Stampp, op. cit., p. 89.

[49] Stampp, op. cit., ch. III: "A Troublesome Property," should be required reading on this subject.

[50] I am prepared to say this despite the fact that the evidence is scrappy and has not, to my knowledge, been properly assembled. For mass flights in time of war, see e.g. Thuc. 7.75.5; 8.40.2.

[51] Note how Thucydides stressed the loss of anticipation (1.142.4; 6.91.7) before actually reporting it in 7.27.5.

be sure of what lay ahead in Boeotia or Thessaly. Indeed, there is a hint that these particular 20,000 and more may have been very badly treated after escaping under Spartan promise. A reliable fourth-century historian attributed the great Theban prosperity at the end of the fifth century to their having purchased very cheaply the slaves and other booty seized from the Athenians during the Spartan occupation of Decelea.[52] Although there is no way to determine whether this is a reference to the 20,000, the suspicion is obvious. Ethics aside, there was no power, within or without the law, which could have prevented the re-enslavement of fugitive slaves even if they had been promised their freedom.

The *Oeconomica* sums up the life of the slave as consisting of three elements: work, punishment, and food.[53] And there are more than enough floggings, and even tortures, in Greek literature, from one end to the other. Apart from psychological quirks (sadism and the like), flogging means simply that the slave, as slave, must be goaded into performing the function assigned to him. So, too, do the various incentive plans which were frequently adopted. The efficient, skilled, reliable slave could look forward to managerial status. In the cities, in particular, he could often achieve a curious sort of quasi-independence, living and working on his own, paying a kind of rental to his owner, and accumulating earnings with which, ultimately, to purchase his freedom. Manumission was, of course, the greatest incentive of all. Again we are baffled by the absence of numbers, but it is undisputed that manumission was a common phenomenon in most of the Greek world. This is an important difference between the Greek slave on the one hand, and the helot or American slave on the other. It is also important evidence about the degree of the slave's alleged "acceptance" of his status.[54]

[52] Hellenica Oxyrhynchia 12.4.

[53] Ps.-Arist., Oec. 1.5,1344a35.

[54] The technical and aesthetic excellence of much work performed by slaves is, of course, visible in innumerable museums and archaeological sites. This is part of the complexity and ambiguity of the institution (discussed in the following section), which extended to the slaves themselves as well as to their masters.

IV

It is now time to try to add all this up and form some judgment about the institution. This would be difficult enough to do under ordinary circumstances; it has become almost impossible because of two extraneous factors imposed by modern society. The first is the confusion of the historical study with moral judgments about slavery. We condemn slavery, and we are embarrassed for the Greeks, whom we admire so much; therefore we tend either to underestimate its role in their life, or we ignore it altogether, hoping that somehow it will quietly go away. The second factor is more political, and it goes back at least to 1848, when the *Communist Manifesto* declared that "The history of all hitherto existing society is the history of class struggles. Free man and slave, patrician and plebeian, lord and serf, guild-master and journeyman, in a word, oppressor and oppressed, stood in constant opposition to one another. . . ." Ever since, ancient slavery has been a battleground between Marxists and non-Marxists, a political issue rather than a historical phenomenon.

Now we observe that a sizable fraction of the population of the Greek world consisted of slaves, or other kinds of dependent labour, many of them barbarians; that by and large the elite in each city-state were men of leisure, completely free from any preoccupation with economic matters, thanks to a labour force which they bought and sold, over whom they had extensive property rights, and, equally important, what we may call physical rights; that the condition of servitude was one which no man, woman, or child, regardless of status or wealth, could be sure to escape in case of war or some other unpredictable and uncontrollable emergency. It seems to me that, seeing all this, if we could emancipate ourselves from the despotism of extraneous moral, intellectual, and political pressures, we would conclude, without hesitation, that slavery was a basic element in Greek civilization.

Such a conclusion, however, should be the starting-point of analysis, not the end of an argument, as it is so often at present. Perhaps it would be best to avoid the word "basic" altogether, because it has been preempted as a technical term by the Marxist theory of history. Anyone else who uses it in such a question as the one which is the title of this paper, is compelled, by the intellectual (and political) situation in which we work, to qualify the term at once, to distinguish between *a* basic institution and *the* basic institution. In effect what has happened is that, in the guise of a discussion of ancient slavery, there has been a desultory discussion of Marxist theory, none of it, on either side, particularly illuminating about either Marxism or slavery. Neither our understanding of the historical process nor our knowledge of ancient society is significantly advanced by these repeated statements and counter-statements, affirmations and denials of the proposition, "Ancient society was based on slave labour." Nor have we gained much from the persistent debate about causes. Was slavery the cause of the decline of Greek science? or of loose sexual morality? or of the widespread contempt for gainful employment? These are essentially false questions, imposed by a naive kind of pseudo-scientific thinking.

The most fruitful approach, I suggest, is to think in terms of purpose, in Immanuel Kant's sense, or of function, as the social anthropologists use that concept. The question which is most promising for systematic investigation is not whether slavery was the basic element, or whether it caused this or that, but how it functioned.[55] This eliminates the sterile attempts to decide which was historically prior, slavery or something else; it avoids imposing moral judgments on, and prior to, the historical analysis; and it should avoid the trap which I shall call the free-will error. There is a maxim of Emile Durkheim's that "The voluntary character of a practice or an institution should never be assumed beforehand."[56] Given the existence of slavery—and it is given, for our sources do not permit us to go back to a stage in Greek history when it did not exist—the choice facing individual Greeks was socially and psychologically imposed. In the *Memorabilia* Xenophon says that "those who can do so buy slaves so

[55] Cf. Vogt, "Wege zur Menschlichkeit," pp. 19–20: "What we lack is a clear picture of the functions maintained by slavery in the organism of ancient society, and a critical evaluation of its role in the rise, development, and decline of the culture."

[56] E. Durkheim, The Rules of Sociological Method, transl. from 8th ed. (repr. Glencoe, Ill., 1950), 28.

that they may have fellow workers."[57] That sentence is often quoted to prove that some Greeks owned no slaves, which needs no proof. It is much better cited to prove that *those who can*, buy slaves—Xenophon clearly places this whole phenomenon squarely in the realm of necessity.

The question of function permits no single answer. There are as many answers as there are contexts: function in relation to what? And when? And where? Buckland begins his work on the Roman law of slavery by noting that there "is scarcely a problem which can present itself, in any branch of law, the solution of which may not be affected by the fact that one of the parties to the transaction is a slave."[58] That sums up the situation in its simplest, most naked form, and it is as correct a statement for Greek law as for Roman. Beyond that, I would argue, there is no problem or practice in any branch of Greek life which was not affected, in some fashion, by the fact that many people in that society, even if not in the specific situation under consideration, were (or had been slaves). The connection was not always simple or direct, nor was the impact necessarily "bad" (or "good"). The historian's problem is precisely to uncover what the connections were, in all their concreteness and complexity, their goodness or badness or moral neutrality.

I think we will find that, more often than not, the institution of slavery turned out to be ambiguous in its function. Certainly the Greek attitudes to it were shot through with ambiguity, and not rarely with tension. To the Greeks, Nietzsche said, both labour and slavery were "a necessary disgrace, of which one feels *ashamed*, as a disgrace and as a necessity at the same time."[59] There was a lot of discussion: that is clear from the literature which has survived, and it was neither easy nor unequivocally one-sided, even though it did not end in abolitionism. In Roman law "slavery is the only case in which, in the extant sources . . ., a conflict is declared to exist between the *Ius Gentium* and the

[57] Xen., Mem. 2.3.3.

[58] Op. cit., p. v.

[59] The Greek State: Preface to an Unwritten Book, in Early Greek Philosophy & Other Essays, transl. by M. A. Mügge (London & Edinburgh 1911), 6.

Ius Naturale."[60] In a sense, that was an academic conflict, since slavery went right on; but no society can carry such a conflict within it, around so important a set of beliefs and institutions, without the stresses erupting in some fashion, no matter how remote and extended the lines and connections may be from the original stimulus. Perhaps the most interesting sign among the Greeks can be found in the proposals, and to an extent the practice in the fourth century B.C., to give up the enslavement of Greeks.[61] They all came to nought in the Hellenistic world, and I suggest that this one fact reveals much about Greek civilization after Alexander.[62]

It is worth calling attention to two examples pregnant with ambiguity, neither of which has received the attention it deserves. The first comes from Locris, the Greek colony in southern Italy, where descent was matrilineal, an anomaly which Aristotle explained historically. The reason, he said, was that the colony was originally founded by slaves and their children by free women. Timaeus wrote a violent protest against this insulting account, and Polybius, in turn, defended Aristotle in a long digression, of which unfortunately only fragments survive. One of his remarks is particularly worth quoting: "To suppose, with Timaeus, that it was unlikely that man, who had been the slaves of the allies of the Lacedaemonians, would continue the kindly feelings and adopt the friendships of their late masters is foolish. For when they have had the good fortune to recover their freedom, and a certain time has elapsed, men, who have been slaves, not only endeavour to adopt the friendships of their late masters, but also their ties of hospitality and blood; in fact, their aim is to keep them up even more than the ties of nature, for the express

[60] Buckland, op. cit., p. 1.

[61] See F. Kiechle, "Zur Humanität in der Kriegführung der griechischen Staaten," Historia VII (1958), 129–56, for a useful collection of materials, often vitiated by a confusion between a fact and a moralizing statement; and even more by special pleading of a familiar tendency, as in the argument (p. 140 n. 1) that reports of mass enslavement or massacre must not be taken too literally because some always managed to escape, or in the pointless discussion (pp. 150–53) of the supposed significance of Polybius' use of ἀναγχ αξουσιν instead of χελευο υσιν in 5.11.3.

[62] See Rostovtzeff, op. cit. I 201–08.

purpose of thereby wiping out the remembrance of their former degradation and humble position, because they wish to pose as the descendants of their masters rather than as their freedmen."[63]

In the course of his polemic Timaeus had said that "it was not customary for the Greeks of early times to be served by bought slaves."[64] This distinction, between slaves who were bought and slaves who were captured (or bred from captives), had severe moral overtones. Inevitably, as was their habit, the Greeks found a historical origin for the practice of buying slaves—in the island of Chios. The historian Theopompus, a native of the island, phrased it this way: "The Chians were the first of the Greeks, after the Thessalians and Lacedaemonians, who used slaves. But they did not acquire them in the same manner as the latter; for the Lacedaemonians and Thessalians will be found to have derived their slaves from the Greeks who formerly inhabited the territory which they now possess, . . . calling them helots and penestae, respectively. But the Chians possessed barbarian slaves, for whom they paid a price."[65] This quotation is preserved by Athenaeus, whose floruit was about 200 A.D. and who went on to comment that the Chians ultimately received divine punishment for their innovation. The stories he then tells, as evidence, are curious and interesting, but I cannot take time for them.

This is not very good history, but that does not make it any less important. By a remarkable coincidence Chios provides us with the earliest contemporary evidence of democratic institutions in the Greek world. In a Chian inscription dated, most probably, to the years 575–550 B.C., there is unmistakable reference to a popular council and to the "laws (or ordinances) of the demos."[66] I do not wish to assign any significance other than symbolic to this coincidence, but it is a symbol with enormous implications. I have already made the point that, the more advanced the Greek city-state, the more it will be found to have had true slavery rather than the "hybrid" types like helotage. More bluntly put, the cities in which individual freedom reached

---

[63] Polyb. 12.6a (transl. by E. S. Shuckburgh).

[64] 566 F 11, ap. Athen. 6.264C; cf. 272 A–B.

[65] 115 F 122, ap. Athen. 6.265B–C.

[66] For the most recent discussion of this text, see L. H. Jeffery in Annual of the Brit. Sch. Athens, LI (1956), 157–67.

its highest expression—most obviously Athens—were cities in which chattel slavery flourished. The Greeks, it is well known, discovered both the idea of individual freedom and the institutional framework in which it could be realized.[67] The pre-Greek world—the world of the Sumerians, Babylonians, Egyptians, and Assyrians; and I cannot refrain from adding the Mycenaeans—was, in a very profound sense, a world without free men, in the sense in which the west has come to understand that concept. It was equally a world in which chattel slavery played no role of any consequence. That, too, was a Greek discovery. One aspect of Greek history, in short, is the advance, hand in hand, of freedom *and* slavery.

[67] It is hardly necessary to add that "freedom" is a term which, in the Greek context, was restricted to the members of the *koinonia,* always a fraction, and often a minor fraction, of the total male population.

3   *Max Weber*

The Social Causes of the Decay of Ancient Civilization[1]

The Roman Empire was not destroyed from without; its destruction was not caused by the numerical superiority of its opponents nor by the inadequacy of its political leaders. In the last century of its existence Rome had her iron chancellors: heroic figures, like Stilicho, men who combined Teutonic boldness with the art of cunning diplomacy, were at the head of the state. Why could they not accomplish what the illiterate princes of the Merovingian, Carolingian, and Saxon houses were able to achieve

SOURCE. Max Weber, *Journal of General Education,* Vol. V (October 1950), 75–88. Reprinted by permission of Pennsylvania State University Press.

[1] A public lecture delivered before the Academic Society of Freiburg in 1896. The German title is "Die sozialen Gründe des Untergangs der antiken Kultur." Published in the magazine *Die Warheit* (Stuttgart, 1896), reprinted in Weber's *Gesammelte Aufsätze zur Sozial- und Wirtschaftsgeschichte* ["Collected Essays on Social and Economic History"] (Tübingen, 1924), pp. 289–311. Translated by Christian Mackauer.

and to defend against Saracens and Huns? The Empire had, long before, undergone a change in its very essence; when it disintegrated, it did not suddenly collapse under one powerful blow. The Teutonic invaders brought to its logical climax a development that had been long in the making.

But most important: the decay of ancient *civilization* was not caused by the destruction of the Roman *Empire*. The Empire as a political structure survived by the centuries the acme of Roman culture. This culture had vanished much earlier. As early as the beginning of the third century Roman literature had come to an end. The art of the jurists decayed together with their schools. Greek and Roman poetry were dead. Historiography languished and almost disappeared. The Latin Language was soon in a state of full degeneration. When, one and a half centuries later, with the extinction of the office of the emperor in the West, the books were closed, it becomes obvious that barbarism, long ago, has conquered the Empire from within. The barbarian invaders, moreover, are far from establishing completely new conditions on the soil of the demolished Empire; the Merovingian kingdom, in Gaul at least, continues for some time the pattern of the Roman province. The problem, therefore, arises for us: What has caused the decline of ancient civilization?

Quite a few different explanations have been offered by different scholars, some missing the point completely, others getting off to a good start, but making a wrong use of correct premises.

Some authors maintain that despotism necessarily strangled the soul of the ancient Romans and so destroyed their state and their civilization. But the despotism of Frederick the Great was, on the contrary, a powerful force of growth.

Others assert that the alleged luxury and the undeniable decline of morality in the highest social ranks called forth the revenge of History. But both phenomena are symptoms themselves. We shall see that much more powerful factors than the guilt of individuals destroyed ancient civilization.

Still others believe that the foundations of society were dissolved by the emancipation of the Roman woman and the loosening of the ties of marriage in the ruling classes. The fables told by a biased reactionary like Tacitus about the Germanic woman, that miserable slave of a peasant-warrior, are repeated by modern reactionaries. In fact, the ubiquitous "German woman" decided the victory of the Germanic invaders as little as the ubiquitous "Prussian schoolmaster" decided the battle of Königgrätz. On the contrary, we shall see that the *re-establishment* of the family among the *lower* classes of society was connected with the decay of ancient civilization.

Pliny, an eye-witness, assures us: *Latifundia perdidere Italiam* ["the large estates have ruined Italy"]: "Here you see it," one school among the moderns says, "it was the Junkers who ruined Rome." "Yes," their opponents reply, "but only because they were ruined themselves by grain imports from foreign countries." If the Romans had protected their agriculture with high tariff walls, the Caesars, apparently, would still be on their throne today. But we shall see that the destruction of ancient civilization was a first step on the way towards the *re-establishment* of a *peasant* class.

There is even what people call a "Darwinistic" hypothesis: a quite recent author contends that the process of selection by which the strongest men were drafted into the army and so condemned to celibacy led to the degeneration of the Roman race. We shall rather see that increasing recruiting of the army from its own ranks was a symptom of the decay of the Roman Empire.

But enough of these examples. Only one more remark before we take up our proper subject:

The interest in a story is always keener when the audience has the feeling: *de te narratur fabula,* and when the story-teller can conclude his yarn with a *discite moniti!* Unfortunately, the discussion which follows does not fall into this enviable category. We can learn little or nothing for our contemporary social problems from ancient history. A modern proletarian and a Roman slave would be as unable to understand one another as a European and a Chinese. Our problems are of a completely different character. The drama we are going to study has only an *historical* interest; but it presents one of the most singular historical phenomena, indeed, the internal dissolution of an old civilization.

Our first task will be to understand those peculiarities of the social structure of ancient society that we have just mentioned.

We shall see how they determined the cycle of ancient civilization.

The civilization of classical antiquity is, in its essence, first of all an urban civilization. The city is the foundation of political life as well as of art and literature. With regard to its economic system, also, the ancient world, at least during its earlier period, represents what we call today a "city economy." The ancient city, during the Greek period, is not essentially different from the medieval city. As far as differences exist, they can be explained by the differences between the climate and race of the Mediterranean, on the one hand, and those of Central Europe, on the other, just as even today English workers are different from Italian workers and German craftsmen from Italian ones. Originally, the economic basis of the ancient, just as of the medieval city, is the exchange in the urban market of the products of urban craftsmanship for those of its immediate rural neighborhood. Almost the whole demand is satisfied by this direct exchange between producer and consumer, without any importation from outside. Aristotle's ideal of urban autarchy had been realized in the majority of Greek cities.

To be sure, since very ancient times, an international trade has been built on these local foundations; it comprises a vast area and numerous objects. Our historical reports are almost exclusively concerned with those cities whose ships are engaged in this trade; but because we hear just about them, we are prone to forget how insignificant, quantitatively, this trade was. In the first place, the civilization of European antiquity is a *coastal* civilization, just as European ancient history remains for a long time the history of coastal towns. Side by side with the technically highly developed urban exchange economy, and in sharp contrast to it, there presents itself the "natural economy" of the barbaric peasants of the inland regions, entrammeled in tribal communities or bent under the rule of feudal patriarchs. A steady and regular international traffic is carried on only by sea or on large rivers. No inland traffic comparable to that even of the Middle Ages existed in ancient Europe. The glorified Roman highways never carried a traffic even remotely reminiscent of modern conditions; the same applies to the Roman postal service. There is an immense difference in revenue between estates lying inland and those located on rivers or on the sea shore. To be close to a highway was generally considered not an advantage in Roman times but rather a nuisance because of billeting and of—vermin: Roman highways are military not commercial roads.

On the ground of such a still intact "natural economy" international exchange is unable to strike deep roots. Only a small number of high-priced articles such as precious metals, amber, valuable textiles, some iron ware and pottery, are objects of regular trade. Such a trade just cannot be compared to modern commerce. It would be the same as if today nothing but champagne and silk were exchanged, while all trade statistics show that *mass* demand alone accounts for the big figures in the balance of international trade. At some time or other, to be sure, cities like Athens and Rome become dependent on imports for their grain supply. But such conditions are highly abnormal; and in all these cases the *community* takes over the responsibility of supplying these goods. The citizens are not inclined to leave this task to uncontrolled private trade nor can they afford to do so.

Not the masses with their day-by-day needs, but a small group of well-to-do people are interested in international commerce. This has one implication: increasing differentiation of wealth is a prerequisite of the development of commerce in the ancient world. This differentiation—and here we reach a third, decisive point—takes a quite definite form and direction: ancient civilization is a *slave* civilization. From the very beginning, unfree labor in the countryside exists side by side with free labor in the city; unfree division of labor on the rural estate, producing for the master's own use, side by side with the free division of labor regulated by the conditions of exchange in the urban market, just as in the Middle Ages. And in the ancient world, as in the Middle Ages, these two forms of productive co-operation were naturally antagonistic. Progress is based on progressing division of labor. Under conditions of free labor, this progress is, in its beginnings, identical with a progressive growth of the market, extensively through geographical, intensively through personal extension of the area of exchange; the citizens of the towns, therefore, try to destroy the manorial estates and to include the serfs in the process of free exchange. Where unfree labor prevails, however, economic progress takes place through the progressive accumulation of human beings; the more slaves or serfs are combined on one estate, the higher the degree of specialization which can be attained with unfree workers. But while during the Middle Ages the development leads more and more to the victory of free labor and of free exchange, the outcome in the ancient world is exactly the opposite. What is the reason for this difference? It is the same reason which determines the limits of technological progress in antiquity: the "cheapness" of human beings resulting from the character of the uninterrupted warfare in the ancient world. Wars in ancient times are always slave raids; they continuously throw new supplies upon the slave market and so favor unfree labor and the accumulation of human beings as in no other period of history. The development of free handicraft, therefore, was arrested at the level of non-capitalistic wage-work for a narrowly defined local clientele. No competition arose between (capitalistic) free enterprisers and free (non-capitalistic) wage-work for supplying the market, and so the economic premium on labor-saving inventions was absent which has called forth such inventions in our modern epoch. In the ancient world, on the contrary, the economic importance of unfree labor in the *oikos* (the autarchic estate) is all the time on the increase. Only slave-owners are able to satisfy their economic needs by division of labor, through slave labor, and so to raise their standard of living. Only they can—in addition to satisfying their own needs—more and more produce for the market.

This determines the peculiar economic development of the ancient world and its difference from that of the Middle Ages. In medieval Europe, free division of labor first expands *intensively* within the economic area of the city, in the form of production for a clientele and for the local market. Later, increasing external trade on the basis of a geographical division of labor creates new forms of production for foreign markets; making use of free labor, it takes the form first of the putting-out system, then of manufacture. And the development of a *modern* system of economy is accompanied by the phenomenon that the masses increasingly satisfy their demand through interlocal and finally international exchange of goods. In the ancient world, as we see, devlopment of international commerce is accompanied, on the contrary, by the conglomeration of unfree labor on the big slave-estates. So, under the superstructure of the exchange economy one finds a ceaselessly expanding substructure of an economy without exchange (a "natural economy") : the slave-combines, constantly absorbing human beings and satisfying their demand essentially not in the market but by their own production. The higher the standard of living of the slave-owning top-stratum of society rises and the more, therefore, the *extensive* development of commerce increases, the more this commerce loses in *intensity;* it is transformed into a thin net spread out over a substructure of a "natural economy," a net whose meshes become finer while its thread becomes thinner and thinner all the time. During the Middle Ages, the transition from production for a local clientele to production for an interlocal market is prepared by the slow infiltration of (capitalistic) enterprise and the principle of competition from the circumference towards the center of the local economic community; during the ancient period, however, international commerce leads to the growth of the *oikoi* which stifle the *local* exchange economy.

This development has reached its most gigantic dimension in the Roman Empire. Rome is first—after the victory of the *plebs* —a conquering state of peasants or better: of townsmen cultivating their own land. Every war ends with the annexation of more land for colonization. The younger sons of land-owning citizens, who cannot expect to inherit their father's estate, fight in the army for an estate of their own and so, at the same time, for full citizenship. This is the secret of Rome's expansive strength. This development comes to an end with the extension of Roman conquests to territories overseas. Now, the peasants' interest in acquiring new land for settlement is no longer decisive, but rather the interest of the aristocracy in exploiting the newly conquered province. The purpose of these wars consists in slave raids and in the confiscation of land to be exploited by the farmer of state land or the tax-farmer. In addition, the Second Punic War decimated the peasantry in the homeland—the consequences of its decline are partly a belated triumph of Hannibal. The reaction following the Gracchan movement finally decides the victory of slave-labor in agriculture. From this time on, the slave-owners alone are the representatives of a rising standard of living, of an increase in buying-power, of the development of production for the market. This does not mean that free labor completely disappears; but the slave-using enterprises alone represent the *progressive* element. The Roman agricultural writers presuppose slave-labor as the natural basis of the labor system.

The cultural importance of unfree labor was finally decisively re-enforced through the inclusion of large inland areas—like Spain, Gaul, Illyria, the Danubian countries—into the Roman world. The center of gravity of the Roman Empire shifted into the inland regions. This means that ancient civilization made an attempt to change its scene of action, to turn from a coastal into an inland civilization. It expanded over an immense economic area which even in the course of centuries could not have been converted into an exchange and market economy similar to that existing along the coasts of the Mediterranean. Even in these coastal areas, as we have pointed out, interlocal exchange of commodities was only a superficial net, getting thinner all the time; in the inland regions, the meshes of the net of exchange were, of necessity, much looser still. In these inland regions, progress of civilization in the way of a free division of labor through the development of an *intensive* exchange of commodities was virtually *impossible*. Only through the rise of a landed aristocracy, based on slave-ownership and unfree division of labor (the *oikos*), could these regions gradually be drawn into the orbit of Mediterranean civilization. In the inland regions, to a higher degree still than along the coasts, the immensely more expensive commerce could serve only the luxury needs of the uppermost social stratum, the slave-owners; and, at the same time, the possibility of producing for the market was restricted to a small number of large slave-owning enterprises.

Thus the slave-owner became the economic representative of ancient civilization; the organization of slave-labor forms the indispensable basis of Roman society. We have to study, therefore, somewhat more closely its specific social character.

Our sources are mostly concerned with the *agricultural* enterprises of the late republican and early imperial periods. Large land-ownership constitutes, anyway, the main form of wealth; even wealth that is speculatively used rests on this basis: the large-scale Roman speculator is, as a rule, also a great landowner; if for no other reason, than because security in the form of landed property was legally required for the most lucrative kinds of speculation, tax-farming and contracting.

The typical large Roman land-owner is not a gentleman-farmer, supervising his own estate, but a man who lives in town, devotes his time to political activity, and is interested above all in receiving a money rent. The supervision of his estate is entrusted to unfree bailiffs *(villici)*. The methods of cultivation are influenced mainly by the following circumstances.

Production of grain for the market is, in most cases, not profitable. The market of the city of Rome, e.g., is closed to private producers because of public grain distributions; transportation of grain from inland estates to distant markets is impossible anyway because the price cannot support the costs. In addition, slave-labor is not suited to grain production, especially since the Roman agricultural technique requires scrupulous and intensive work and therefore presupposes a personal interest on the worker's part. For this reason, land for grain production is mostly, at least in part, leased to *coloni,* small tenants, the descendants of the free peasantry who are deprived of their former property. But such a *colonus* is, even in earlier times, not an independent tenant and self-responsible farmer. The owner provides the inventory, the *villicus* controls the cultivation. From the very beginning, apparently, it was a frequent practice that the tenant had to do a certain amount of work on the owner's estate, especially during harvest time. Leasing of land to *coloni* is considered a form of cultivation of the land by the *owner* "by means of" the tenants *(per colonos).*

The part of the estate under direct management by the owner produces for the market primarily high-priced products like olive-oil and wine, and secondarily garden vegetables, cattle-raising, poultry, and luxuries for the table of the highest stratum of Roman society, for the people who alone have the money to purchase them. By these products grain is pushed back to the less fertile land which is in the hands of the *coloni.* The master's own estate resembles a plantation, and the workers on it are slaves. *Coloni* and a herd of slaves (the *familia),* side by side, represent, under the Empire as well as during the late Republic, the normal population of a large estate.

We first turn to the slaves. What is their condition?

Let us look at the ideal pattern which the agricultural writers describe. The lodging of the "talking inventory" *(instrumentum vocale)*, i.e., the slave stable, is found close to that of the cattle *(instrumentum semi-vocale)*. It contains the dormitories, in addition a hospital *(valetudinarium)*, a lockup *(carcer)*, a workshop for the craftsmen *(ergastulum)*. Whoever has worn the king's colors will be reminded by this picture of a familiar experience: the barracks. And indeed, the life of a slave normally is a barracks life. The slaves sleep and eat together, under supervision of the *villicus;* their better piece of clothing is left at the store-room with the bailiff's wife *(villica)* who takes the place of the store-room sergeant; every month the clothing is inspected at a roll-call. The work is disciplined in a strictly military manner: squads *(decuriae)* are formed every morning; they march to work under supervision of the "drivers" *(monitores)*. This was absolutely necessary. It never has been possible to use unfree labor for market production on a permanent basis without resorting to the lash. For us one implication of this form of life is of special importance: the slave in his barracks is not only without property but without family as well. Only the *villicus* lives permanently together with his wife in his special cell in some form of slave-marriage *(contubernium)*, comparable to the married sergeant or staff-sergeant in modern barracks; according to the agricultural writers, this is even a "standing regulation" for the *villicus,* in the interest of the master. And as the institutions of private property and private family always go hand in hand, so it is here: the slave who owns property owns a family as well. The *villicus*—and only the *villicus,* as the agricultural writers seem to indicate—has a *peculium,* originally, as the name tells, his own cattle which he grazes on the master's pasture, just as the agricultural laborer does today on the large estates of eastern Germany. As the masses of the slaves have no *peculium,* they also do not live in monogamous sexual relations. Sexual intercourse for them is a kind of controlled prostitution with bounties awarded to female slaves for the raising of children—some masters granted them liberty when they had raised three children. This last practice already indicates what the consequences of the absence of monogamous marriage were. Human beings thrive only in the circle of the family. The slave barracks were unable to reproduce themselves, they depended for their recruitment on the continuous purchase of slaves, and the agricultural writers assume, indeed, that new slaves are bought regularly. The ancient slave estate devours human beings as the modern blast-furnace devours coal. A slave market and its regular and ample supply with human material is the indispensable presupposition of slave barracks producing for the market. The buyer looked for cheap ware: Varro recommends that one should choose criminals and similar cheap material; the reason he gives is characteristic: such rabble, he maintains, is mostly "sharper" (*velocior est animus hominum improborum*). So this form of enterprise depends on the regular supply of the slave market with human cattle. What would happen if this supply should collapse? The effect on the slave barracks must be the same as that of an exhaustion of the coal deposits on the blast-furnaces. And the time came when it happened. Here we have reached the turning-point in the development of ancient civilization.

When we are being asked from which event we should date the—first latent, soon manifest—decline of the Roman power and civilization, it is difficult, at least for a German, not to think of the battle in the Forest of Teutoburg. There is, indeed, a kernel of truth in this popular conception, although it seems to be contradicted by the obvious facts which show the Roman Empire at the zenith of its power at the time of Trajan. To be sure, the battle itself was not decisive—a reverse like this occurs in every war of expansion waged against barbarians; decisive was the aftermath: the suspension of offensive warfare on the Rhine by Tiberius. This brought to an end the expansive tendencies of the Roman Empire. With the internal and in the main also external pacification of the area of ancient civilization, the regular supply of the slave-markets with human cattle begins to shrink. As a result of this, an immense *acute* scarcity of labor seems to have developed already at the time of Tiberius. We are told that under his regime it was necessary to inspect the *ergastula* of the large estates because the large land-owners resorted to kidnapping; like the robber-barons of later times, it seems, they were lying in ambush along the highways, on the look-out, not for merchants' goods, but for hands to work on their deserted land. More important was the slow but steadily spreading *long-run* result: it became impossible to continue production on the basis of slave barracks. They presupposed a continuous supply of new slaves; they could not provide for their own needs. They were liable to break down when this supply came to a permanent stand-still. From later agricultural writers we get the impression that the decline is the "cheapness" of human cattle first led to an improvement in agricultural technique: one tried to raise the performance of the workers by careful training. But when the last offensive wars of the second century were over (they had already acquired the character of slave-raids), the large plantations with their celibate and propertyless slaves were bound to dwindle away.

That this really happened and how it happened we learn from a comparison of the conditions of the slaves on large estates as described by the Roman writers with the conditions prevailing on the estates of the Carolingian epoch about which we know from Charlemagne's regulations for the royal demesnes *(capitulare de villis imperialibus)* and from the surveys of monasteries of this time. In either epoch we find the slaves as agricultural laborers; in either case they are equally without rights, especially equally subject to the unlimited exploitation of their labor-power by their master. No change has occurred in this regard. In addition, numerous individual traits have been taken over from the Roman estate; even in the terminology used we rediscover, e.g., the women's house *(gynaikeion)* of the Romans under the name of *genitium*. But one thing has changed fundamentally: the Roman slaves live in "communistic" slave barracks, the *servus* of the Carolingian epoch has his own cottage *(mansus servilis)* on the land which he holds from his master; he is a small tenant, subject to service on the lord's demesne. He has a family, and with the family individual property has returned. This separation of the slave from the *oikos* occurred in late-Roman times; and it was bound to occur, indeed, as the result of the lacking self-recruitment of the slave barracks. By restoring the individual family and by making the slave his hereditary serf, the lord secured for himself the offspring and so a permanent labor supply which could not be provided any more through purchases in the shrinking slave market whose last remnants disappeared during the Carolingian epoch. The risk of the maintenance of the slave (which on the plantations the master had to carry) was now shifted to the slave himself. The impact of this slow but irreversible development was deep. We are faced here with a gigantic process of change in the lower strata of society: family and individual property were given back to them. I can only indicate with one word here how this development runs aparallel to the victory of Christianity: in the slave barracks Christian religion could hardly have taken roots, but the unfree African peasants of the time of St. Augustine already were supporters of a sectarian movement.

While in this way the slave advanced in his social status and became a serf, the *colonus,* at the same time, slides down into serfdom. The reason for this change in his social position was that his relation to the land-owner more and more took on the character of a *labor* relation. *Originally,* the lord is mainly interested in the *rent* which the tenant pays, although, as we have pointed out, there probably were some cases from the very beginning where he had to work on the lord's own land, in addition. But already early in the Empire the agricultural writers put the main emphasis on the *labor* of the *colonus,* and this interest was bound to increase as slave labor became scarcer. African inscriptions of the time of Commodus show that there the *colonus* already had become a kind of serf who, in return for the use of the land he held, was forced to render certain services. This *economic* change in the position of the *colonus* was followed soon by a *legal* change which expressed in legal terms his treatment as part of the *labor* force of the estate: he was tied to the soil. In order to understand how this happened we have to discuss in a few words some concepts of Roman public administration.

The basis of Roman public administration, at the end of the Republic and the beginning of the Empire, was the *city,* the *municipium,* just as the city was the *economic* basis of ancient civilization. The Romans had all the areas which they incorporated into their empire consistently organized in the form of urban communities (in various gradations of political dependence) and so had expanded the administrative form of the *municipium* over the whole empire. The city regularly was the lowest administrative unit. The city magistrates were responsible to the State for taxes and military recruitment. In the course of the imperial epoch, however, the development takes a new turn. The great estates successfully attempt to escape incorporation into the urban communities. The more the center of gravity of the empire moves inland (with the increase of population in the inland regions), the more the rural inland population supplies the recruits for the army. But these same circumstances more and more make the interests of the "agrarians" of Antiquity, of the great land-owners, the controlling factor in State politics. Whereas today we meet with strong resistance in our attempt to integrate the large estates of Eastern Germany in the rural communities, the government of the Roman Empire hardly resisted the tendency of the large estates to withdraw from the urban communities of which they formed a part. In great numbers the *saltus* and *territoria* appear side by side with the cities, administrative districts in which the landowner is the local government, just as the squire of Eastern Germany in the so-called "manorial districts." The landowner, in those districts, was responsible to the State for the taxes of the *territorium*—in some cases he advanced them for his "vassals" and then collected from them—and he supplied the contingent of recruits imposed upon his estate. Supplying recruits, therefore, was soon considered, like any other assessment, as an impost on the estate whose labor force—the *coloni*—were decimated by it.

Those developments paved the road for the legal fettering of the *colonus* to the estate.

The right of free movement never was legally guaranteed to all inhabitants of the Roman Empire. We all remember how familiar an idea it is to the author of the Gospel of Luke that, for the purpose of taxation, everybody can be ordered to return to his home community *(origo)*—to his "place of settlement," as we would say—as Christ's parents returned to Bethlehem. The *origo* of the *colonus,* however, is the estate of his lord.

Quite early we see it happen that a man is forced to return to his community for the performance of public duties. The senator, to be sure, who played truant all year long, was just fined. But the councilor of a provincial town, the *decurio,* who shirked his duties, did not escape so lightly; he was brought back if his community required it. Such a request was often enough necessary, for the position of the councilor—who was accountable for the tax arrears of his community—was not an enviable one. Later when, with the decay and mixture of all legal forms, these claims for return were resolved into the one concept of the claim for restitution (the old "real action": *vindicatio*), the communities chased their run-away councilors just like a run-away parish bull.

What was good for the *decurio* was good for the *colonus*. No distinction was made between his public obligations and the statute-labor he owed to his lord because lord and magistrate were the same person, and he was forced to return to his duties when he tried to escape. So, in the way of administrative practice, he became a real serf, permanently tied to the estate and therefore subject to the manorial rule of the landowner. In his relation to the State he was, so to speak, "mediatized." And above the ranks of these new serfs there arose the group of independent seigneurs (the *possessores*) which we meet, as a well established social type, in the later Roman Empire as well as in the Ostrogothian and Merovingian kingdoms. A *caste order* had taken the place of the old simple distinction of free and unfree. This was the result of an almost imperceptible development which was forced upon society by the change in economic conditions. The signs of *feudal society* were already apparent in the later Roman Empire.

So, on the late-imperial estate, two categories of tenants existed side by side: those who were unfree (*servi*) with "indefinite" service obligations, and those who were personally free (*coloni, tributarii*) with strictly defined money payments, payments in kind, later on more and more frequently payments in form of a fixed share of the produce, and, in addition—not always, but as a rule—regular labor duties. It is apparent that such an estate already represents the type of the medieval manor.

Under the economic conditions of the ancient world, production *for the market* could not be based on statute-labor of free or unfree tenants. Well-disciplined slave barracks were the precondition of any market production. Especially in the inland regions, market production disappeared as soon as the peasants' cottages took the place of the barracks; the thin threads of commerce which were spun over the substratum of a "natural economy" were bound to become looser still and finally to break. This is quite evident already in an argument of the last important agricultural writer, Palladius, who advises the owner to see to it that as far as possible the estate provides through its own labor for all its needs in order that any buying be made superfluous. Spinning and weaving as well as the grinding and baking of the grain had always been done by the women of the estate under the estate's own management; but now, smiths, joiners, stone masons, carpenters, and other unfree craftsmen were added, and they finally produced the total supply on the estate itself. By this development, the small group of urban craftsmen who mostly worked for wages plus board, lost still further in relative importance; the economically prominent households of the great landowners provided for their needs without any resort to exchange.

Supplying the landowner's own needs, on the basis of an internal division of labor, necessarily became the proper economic purpose of the *oikos*. The large estates dissociate themselves from the urban market. The majority of the medium-sized and small towns thereby more and more lose their economic basis, the exchange of services and commodities with the surrounding countryside, this very essence of the city economy. The resulting decay of the cities remains visible to us even through the dim and broken glass of late Roman legal sources. Again and again the emperors inveigh against the flight from the city, they especially take the *possessores* to task for giving up and tearing down their town residences and conveying wainscotting and furniture to their country seats.

This collapse of the cities is re-enforced by the financial policy of the government. As its financial needs increase, the state increasingly adopts the pattern of a "natural economy"; the exchequer becomes an *oikos*, it purchases as little as possible in the market and covers its needs as far as possible through its own production. This prevents the accumulation of private fortunes in money form. For the subjects it was a boon that one of the main forms of speculative enterprise, tax-farming, was abolished and tax collection by State officials took its place. Transporting the public grain supply on ships whose owners were rewarded by land grants was perhaps more efficient than leaving it to private enterprise. The increasing monopolization of numerous lucrative trades and management of the mines by the government brought certain financial advantages with it. But all these measures naturally hindered the accumulation of private capital and nipped in the bud the development of a social class comparable to our modern bourgeoisie. And such a financial system on a "natural economy" basis was increasingly emerging the more the Empire developed from a conglomeration of cities exploiting the countryside and having its economic point of gravity on the coast and in coastal traffic into a political system that tried to incorporate and to organize large inland regions which had not advanced beyond the stage of a "natural economy." This expansion led to an enormous increase in public expenses, and the shell of exchange was much too thin to make possible the satisfaction of the growing public needs by means of a money economy. Hence, the scope of "natural economy" within public finance was bound to expand.

The provinces always had paid their taxes largely in kind, especially in grain, which was stored in the public warehouses. During the Empire, even the manufactured products needed by the government were less and less frequently bought in the market or procured by contracts, but their supply was assured by forcing urban craftsmen to deliver them *in natura;* they were often forced, for this purpose, to form compulsory guilds. This development made of the wretched free craftsman actually a hereditary serf of his guild. This income in kind was used up by the exchequer through corresponding expenses in kind. In this way, especially the two main expense items in the budget were taken care of without resort to money payments: the bureaucracy and the army. But here the "natural economy" reached its limit.

A large inland state can be ruled permanently only by means of a salaried bureaucracy, an institution unknown to the ancient city states. Since Diocletian's time salaries of state officials are very largely paid in kind; they are somewhat similar—only on a much larger scale—to the emoluments of an agricultural laborer on a contemporary Mecklenburgian estate: a few thousand bushels of grain, so and so many heads of cattle, corresponding quantities of salt, olive oil, etc.; in short, whatever the official needs for his food, clothing, and other sustenance, he draws from the imperial warehouses, in addition to relatively modest pocket money in cash. But in spite of this unmistakable preference for direct satisfaction of material needs, the maintenance of a numerous bureaucracy made considerable money expenses unavoidable. This was true, to a still higher degree, of the military requirements of the Empire.

A continental state with neighbours threatening its frontiers cannot be without a standing army. Already at the end of the Republic, the old citizen militia, based on conscription and self-equipment of all landowners, had been replaced by an army recruited from the ranks of the proletariat and equipped by the state—the main pillar of the power of the Caesars. The emperors created what was, not only in fact but legally, a standing *professional* army. To maintain such an army two things are needed: recruits and money. The need for recruits was the reason why the mercantilist rulers during the epoch of "enlightened despotism" curbed big enterprise in agriculture and prevented enclosures. This was not done for humanitarian reasons and not out of sympathy with the peasants. Not the individual peasant was protected—the squire could drive him out without any scruples by putting another peasant in his place. But if, in the words of Frederick William I, "a surplus of peasant lads" was to be the source of soldiers, such a surplus had to *exist*. Therefore, any reduction in the number of peasants through enclosures was prevented because it would endanger the recruitment of soldiers and depopulate the countryside. For quite similar reasons, the Roman emperors regulated the status of the *coloni* and prohibited, e.g., an increase in the duties imposed on them. There is one difference, however. The mercantilist rulers of the 18th century strongly fostered the big manufacturers because they increased the population and, secondly, brought money into the country. Frederick the Great chased with warrants not only his deserting soldiers, but also his deserting workers and—manufacturers. This part of mercantilist policy the Caesars could not adopt since large industries using free labor and producing for the market did not exist and could not develop in the Roman Empire. On the contrary, with the decay of cities and commerce and with the relapse into a "natural economy," the country became more and more unable to pay the ever increasing taxes in cash. And under the prevailing scarcity of labor, which resulted from the drying up of the slave market, recruitment of the *coloni* for the army threatened the large estates with ruin, a menace from which they tried to escape by all possible means. The draftee flees from the decaying

city to the countryside into the safety of serfdom, because the
possessor—under the pressure of the existing scarcity of labor
—is interested in hiding him from the draft. The later Caesars
fight against the flight of townsmen to the countryside exactly as
the later Hohenstaufen fight against the flight of the serfs into the
cities.

The repercussions of this scarcity of recruits are distinctly reflected in the army of the imperial epoch. Since Vespasian, Italy
is no longer subject to the draft; since Hadrian, the units of the
army are no longer composed of contingents from different local
districts; in order to save money, one tries to recruit each army,
as far as possible, from the district in which it is stationed—the
first symptom of the decomposition of the Empire. But the process goes far beyond this: when we study the places of birth of the
soldiers as given in their discharge documents through the centuries, we discover that the number of those characterized as "natives of the camp" *(castrenses)* rises during the imperial epoch
from a few per cent of the total to almost one half—in other
words, the Roman army increasingly reproduces itself. Just as
the peasant with his individual family takes the place of the celibate barracks slave, so—partly at least—the professional and actually hereditary mercenary soldier, who enjoys a kind of substitute marriage, replaces the celibate barracks soldier, or rather,
camp soldier, of the earlier period. The increasing recruitment of
the army from the ranks of barbarians was dictated by the same
principal purpose: by the desire to preserve the labor force of
the country, especially of the large estates. Finally, for the defense of the frontiers, the Romans completely turn away from
the principles of money economy: landgrants are made to barbarians, carrying with them the obligation of military service,
and this device, the remote forerunner of the fief, is used with increasing frequency. In this way the army, which controls the
Empire, is changed into a horde of barbarians, maintaining
weaker and weaker ties with the native population. The victorious invasions by the barbarians *from without,* therefore, meant
for the inhabitants of the provinces, at first, nothing but a change
in the force billeted on them: even the Roman pattern of billeting was preserved. In some parts of Gaul, the barbarians, far
from being feared as conquerors, apparently were welcomed as

liberators from the pressure of the Roman administration. And this we can well understand.

For not only was it difficult for the aging Empire to recruit soldiers from the ranks of its own population, but the provinces, relapsing as they were into a "natural economy," virtually collapsed under the pressure of the money taxes without which a mercenary army cannot possibly be maintained. Raising of money increasingly becomes the sole aim of political administration; and it becomes more and more apparent that the *possessores*, now producing almost exclusively for their own needs, are economically unable to pay *money* taxes. It would have been a different story if the emperor had told them: "Well, gentlemen, make your *coloni* forge arms for yourselves, mount your horses, and protect with me the soil on which you live!" To *this* task they would have been economically equal. But this would have meant the beginning of the Middle Ages and of the feudal army. The feudal organization of the army was, indeed, like the feudal structure of society, the end towards which the late-Roman development was tending and which—after the short and only local reverse in favor of colonizing peasant armies during the Age of Migrations—was already attained, on the whole, in the Carolingian epoch. But although with feudal armies of knights one can conquer foreign crowns and defend a restricted territory, one cannot preserve with them the unity of a world empire nor hold hundreds of miles of frontiers against the attacks of land-hungry invaders. A transition, therefore, to that army pattern which would have conformed to the "natural economy" basis of society was impossible during the late-Roman epoch. This was the reason why Diocletian had to attempt the reorganization of public finances on the basis of uniform *money* taxes, and why, to the very end, the *city* officially remained the lowest cell of the State organism. But the *economic* basis of the great majority of Roman cities was withering away: in the interest of a money-hungry state administration they were sitting, like cupping-glasses, on a soil covered with a net of seigneuries. The fall of the Empire was the necessary political result of the gradual disappearance of commerce and the spread of a "natural economy." This fall essentially meant the abolition of that state administration and hence, of the political superstructure with its money economy character which was no longer adapted to its changed economic basis.

When, after half a millennium, the belated executor of Diocletian's will, Charlemagne, revived the political unity of the Occident, this development took place on the basis of a strictly "natural" economy. Whoever studies the instructions he gave to the administrators of his domains (the *villici*)—the famous *capitulare de villis,* in its practical sense and the tartness of its language reminiscent of the ukases of Frederick William I of Prussia—will find this fact most impressively illustrated. At the side of the king, the queen appears in a dominant position: the king's wife is his minister of finance. And justly so; "administration of finance" here principally is concerned with the needs of the royal table and household which is identical with the "state household." We read there what the bailiffs have to provide for the king's court: grain, meat, textiles, surprisingly large quantities of soap, etc.; in short whatever the king needs for his own use, for that of his companions, and for political functions, like horses and vehicles for warfare. The standing army has disappeared; so has the salaried bureaucracy and, with it, the very concept of taxation. The king feeds his officials on his own table or he endows them with land. The self-equipped army is about to become, for good, an army on horseback and so a military caste of landowning knights. Interlocal exchange of commodities has disappeared as well; the threads of commerce connecting the self-sufficient cells of economic life are broken, trade is reduced to peddling, carried on by foreigners, Greeks and Jews.

Above all, the *city* has disappeared; the Carolingian epoch does not know this term as a specific concept of administrative law. The seigneuries are the vehicles of civilization; they also form the basis of the monasteries. The seigneurs are the political officials; the king himself is a seigneur, the biggest of all—rural and illiterate. His castles are situated in the countryside; therefore he has no fixed residence: for the sake of his livelihood he travels even more than some modern monarchs do; for he continuously moves from castle to castle and eats up what has been stored for him. Civilization has become rural, indeed.

The cycle of the economic development of antiquity is now completed. The intellectual achievements of the ancients seem to be totally lost. Gone with commercial traffic is the marble splendor of the ancient cities and, with them, all the intellectual values based on them: art and literature, science and the elaborate forms of ancient commercial law. And on the estates of the *possessores* and seigneurs the songs of the troubadours are not yet heard. We hardly can suppress a feeling of sadness when we witness a culture that seems to aim at perfection lose its material foundation and collapse. But what is it actually that we are witnessing in this gigantic process? In the depth of society organic structural changes occur (and had to occur) which, if we look at them as a whole, must be interpreted as an immense process of recovery. Individual family life and private property were restored to the masses of unfree people; they themselves were raised again, from the position of "speaking inventory" up into the circle of human beings. The rise of Christianity surrounded their family life with firm moral guarantees: already late-Roman laws for the protection of the peasants recognize the unity of the unfree family to a degree not known before. To be sure, at the same time one sector of the free population was sinking down into actual serfdom, and the highly cultivated aristocracy of the ancient world declined into barbarism. As we have seen: the spread of unfree labor and the increasing differentiation of wealth based on slave-ownership had formed the foundation of the evolution of ancient civilization. But later, when the center of political gravity had shifted from the coast to the inland regions and when the supply of human cattle had dwindled away, this new system of "natural economy" as it had become established on the big estates had forced its own semi-feudal structure upon the exchange economy originally developed in the coastal cities. So, the threadbare wrap of ancient civilization disappeared, and the intellectual life of western man sank into a long night. But that fall reminds us of that giant in Greek mythology who gained new strength whenever he rested on the bosom of mother earth. If one of the old classical authors had arisen from his manuscript in Carolingian times and had examined the world through the window of the monk's cell in which he found himself, his surroundings would have looked strange to him, indeed: the dung-heap odor of the manor-yard would have hit his nostrils. But those classics were deep asleep now, as was all civilization, hidden away under the cover of an economic life which had returned to rural forms. Neither the songs nor the tournaments of feudal society roused it out of this sleep. Only when, on the basis of free division of labor and of commercial exchange the *city* had arisen again in the Middle Ages, when, later still, the transition to a national economy prepared the ground for civil liberty and broke the fetters imposed by the external and internal authorities of the feudal age, only then the old giant arose and carried with him the intellectual inheritance of antiquity up to the new light of our modern middle-class civilization.

PART TWO

African Ramifications of the Slave Trade

The rapid strides in African history have formed one of the more heartening intellectual developments in recent years. These selections were chosen to show the impact of the slave trade on the economic (and general) history of Africa and to suggest the vital differences between the precolonial socioeconomic system of most of West Africa and of Europe.

The opening selection, by Philip D. Curtin, is the concluding chapter of his indispensable book, *The Atlantic Slave Trade: A Census,* which replaces all other works concerning the measurement of the trade. As such, it provides the starting point for any demographic and economic study of the impact of the trade on either Africa or the Americas. The essays by Rosemary Arnold and Karl Polanyi, together with that of Basil Davidson, which has a different point of view, demonstrate the special character —as seen from a Euro-American vantage point—of African economy and society. The two brief selections from Davidson, rather arbitrarily combined here, give us a quick but penetrating look at the variety of effects that the slave trade and early contacts with Europe had on different parts of Africa. The selections by Polanyi and Arnold bring to the surface the dissolving effects that the economic forces generated by the expansion of European capitalism had on traditional societies. They suggest the profound differences between those societies in general and their economies in particular and those of an increasingly capitalist Europe. And they lead us toward a more specific understanding of the irresistible power of the expanding world market. As such, they demonstrate, from a decidedly non-Marxist point of view, Marx's argument for the irreversibility of the historical process inherent in the rise of capitalism, as well as the worldwide revolutionary role played by an increasingly imperialist European bourgeoisie. In so doing, they suggest, too, how the penetration of European capitalism transformed not merely the economic relations within traditional societies but the whole fabric of society: politics, ideology, psychology, religion—in a word, the culture.

Philip D. Curtin
Major Trends

It is now possible to look at the long-term movement of the Atlantic slave trade over a period of more than four centuries. Table 1 sums up the pattern of imports for each century, while Figure 1 shows the same data drawn as a graph to semi-logarithmic scale. Together, these data make it abundantly clear that the eighteenth century was a kind of plateau in the history of the trade—the period when the trade reached its height, but also a period of slackening growth and beginning decline. The period 1741–1810 marks the summit of the plateau, when the long-term annual average rates of delivery hung just above 60,000 a year. The edge of the plateau was reached, however, just after the Peace of Utrecht in 1713, when the annual deliveries began regularly to exceed 40,000 a year, and the permanent drop below 40,000 a year did not come again until after the 1840's. Thus about 60 per cent of all slaves delivered to the New World were transported during the century 1721–1820. Eighty per cent of the total were landed during the century and a half, 1701–1850.

The higher rates of growth, however, came at earlier phases of

SOURCE. From Philip D. Curtin, *The Atlantic Slave Trade, A Census* (Madison: The University of Wisconsin Press; (C) 1969 by the Regents of the University of Wisconsin), Chapter IX.

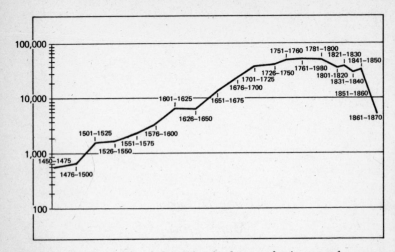

Figure 1. Major trends of the Atlantic slave trade, in annual average number of slaves imported (figure by UW Cartographic Laboratory).

the trade. The highest of all may have been an apparent growth at the rate of 3.3 per cent per year between the last quarter of the fifteenth century and the first quarter of the sixteenth, but the data for this early period are too uncertain for confidence in this figure. In the smoothed-out long-term annual averages of the graph, the growth of the trade was remarkably constant at a remarkably uniform rate over more than two centuries. Two periods of stability or possible decline occur, one between the first and second quarters of the sixteenth century and again between 1601–1625 and 1626–1650. Aside from these periods, the growth rate was an overall 2.2 per cent per year in the last half of the sixteenth century and the first quarter of the seventeenth, and at about the same rate during the equivalent period a century later. But during the first four decades of the eighteenth century, the growth rate was 0.7 per cent.

These trends are not surprising. They run parallel to the growth of the South Atlantic System traced in the literature on qualitative evidence. The nineteenth-century portion of the curve is less predictable from the present literature, but hardly surprising. The slave trade began to decline in the 1790's—not after 1808 with the legal abolition of the British trade. . . . One of the common older views of the slave trade holds that a last burst of imports took place between about 1802 and 1807, as planters sought to fill out their slave gangs before the trade became illegal. This pattern may be true of imports into the Anglo-Saxon territories, but not for the slave trade as a whole. Instead, the general trend shows a drop to the 1810's, then a rise in the 1820's. At first glance, the removal of British shipping from the trade in 1808 made no difference at all in the totals transported.

But this interpretation is probably mistaken. In the eighteenth century, warfare was the really important influence on the short-run rise and fall of the slave trade. There is no reason to expect this pattern to have changed at the end of the century. The drop of the 1790's seems to be accountable to the Napoleonic Wars, and it continued into the decade of the 1800's. After the wars, and especially after such a long period of warfare, an enormous backlog of demand would be expected, and the trade might well have shot up to meet that demand—had it not been for British abolition and the early work of the anti-slave-trade patrols at sea. The trade recovered somewhat in the 1820's, but the recovery was drastically dampened by the anti-slavery movement and by the shifts to new carriers (like Spain) and new sources (like Mozambique). In short, the quantitative impact of British abolition on the trade as a whole is obscured by other influences, but not completely missing.

The present projections also suggest a solution to some of the nineteenth-century controversies that still influence historical literature. Figure 1 shows a high and sustained level of annual average import from the 1810's through the 1840's—not a sharp drop as a result of abolition, nor yet a boom carrying the slave trade to new heights in the 1830's. Although an annual average export in excess of 135,000 a year is still mentioned by some authorities, it is clearly based on the Foreign Office estimate of 1848, apparently made without sufficient evidence and with a clear political interest in trying to show Parliament that the anti-slavery blockade had been effective. If the estimates here are correct, it *was* effective in diverting about 8 per cent of the trade, perhaps in keeping the trade from going even higher; but

Table 1. Estimated Slave Imports into the Americas, by Importing Region, 1451–1870 (000 Omitted)

Region and country	1451– 1600	1601– 1700	1701– 1810	1811– 1870	Total
British North America	—	—	*348.0*	*51.0*	*399.0*
Spanish America	75.0	292.5	*578.6*	*606.0*	*1,552.1*
British Caribbean	—	263.7	*1,401.3*	—	*1,665.0*
Jamaica	—	85.1	662.4	—	747.5
Barbados	—	134.5	252.5	—	387.0
Leeward Is.	—	44.1	301.9	—	346.0
St. Vincent, St. Lucia, Tobago, and Dominica	—	—	70.1	—	70.1
Trinidad	—	—	22.4	—	22.4
Grenada	—	—	67.0	—	67.0
Other BWI	—	—	25.0	—	25.0
French Caribbean	—	155.8	*1,348.4*	*96.0*	*1,600.2*
Saint Domingue	—	74.6	789.7	—	864.3
Martinique	—	66.5	258.3	41.0	365.8
Guadeloupe	—	12.7	237.1	41.0	290.8
Louisiana	—	—	28.3	—	28.3
French Guiana	—	2.0	35.0	14.0	51.0
Dutch Caribbean	—	40.0	*460.0*	—	*500.0*
Danish Caribbean	—	4.0	*24.0*	—	*28.0*
Brazil	50.0	560.0	*1,891.4*	*1,145.4*	*3,646.8*
Old World	149.9	25.1	—	—	*175.0*
Europe	48.8	1.2	—	—	50.0
São Thomé	76.1	23.9	—	—	100.0
Atlantic Is.	25.0	—	—	—	25.0
Total	274.9	1,341.1	6,051.7	1,898.4	9,566.1
Annual average	1.8	13.4	55.0	31.6	22.8
Mean annual rate of increase[a]	—	1.7%	1.8%	−0.1%	

[a] These figures represent the mean annual rates of increase from 1451–1475 to 1601–1625, from 1601–1625 to 1701–1720, and from 1701–1720 to 1811–1820.

the trade nevertheless continued, at a level about a third less than its eighteenth-century peak. It was sustained first by the postwar boom of the 1820's, then by the sugar boom in Cuba and the coffee boom in Brazil. Really significant decline came only with the 1850's, when Brazil, the largest single importer, dropped from the trade. Steep as the final decline of the 1850's and 1860's appears to have been, the rate of import in the 1860's, the last important decade of the trade, nevertheless exceeded the rate for any period before the seventeenth century.

It would be premature to generalize about the impact of the slave trade on African societies over these four centuries. On the other hand, historians have already begun to do so. The range of opinion runs the gamut from the view that the slave trade was responsible for virtually every unfavorable development in Africa over these centuries, to the opposite position that even the slave trade was better than no trade, that it was therefore a positive benefit to the African societies that participated. Since the results of this survey could be brought into the argument on either side, it is appropriate to enter a few caveats.

One conclusion that might be drawn is that, in reducing the estimated total export of slaves from about twenty million to about ten million, the harm done to African societies is also reduced by half. This is obvious nonsense. The demographic consequences of moving any number of people from any society can have meaning only in relation to the size of the society, the time-period concerned, the age and sex composition of the emigrants and of the society from which they depart. Until we know at least the size of the African population that supplied the slaves, the demographic implications of the ten-million estimate are just as indeterminate as those of the twenty-million estimate. As for the social or political consequences of the slave trade to African societies, these would not necessarily vary directly with the number exported.

For that matter, the slave trade—even in its demographic consequences—was merely one aspect of the tightening web of intercommunication which followed the maritime revolution in the Atlantic basin. The new intensity of contact between Africa and Europe began to be felt by the 1480's, with the Americas enter-

ing shortly after 1500. The slave trade constituted a movement
of people along these new lines of communication, but two other
demographically important migrations took place along these
same lines—the migration of diseases and the migration of food
crops.

It is well known that the Old-World diseases virtually wiped
out the American Indian populations of the tropical lowlands
and caused a very sharp drop among other New-World populations. Given our present lack of knowledge about the epidemiological history of Africa, it is impossible to say what European
(or even American) diseases were new to the tropical African
disease environment—and hence what demographic consequences they may have had. For southern Africa, it seems clear
that newly imported strains of smallpox and perhaps some other
diseases effectively destroyed the integrity of the San or "Hot-
tentot" community at the Cape. What similar events may have
taken place in tropical Africa during the sixteenth and seventeenth centuries is not yet known.

As for the migration of food crops, at least two New-World
crops were introduced into Africa by the sixteenth century: man-
ioc and maize spread very widely and came to be two of the
most important sources of food on that continent. If other factors
affecting population size had remained constant, the predictable
result would have been population growth wherever these crops
replaced less efficient cultigens. Since this process took place
over very large areas, it seems possible and even probable that
population growth resulting from new food crops exceeded population losses through the slave trade. Whatever population loss
may have followed the introduction of new diseases would have
been temporary, while more efficient food crops tend to make
possible a permanently higher level of population. It is even possible that, for sub-Saharan Africa as a whole, the net demographic effect of the three Atlantic migrations was population
growth, not decline. Only further research in demographic and
epidemiological history can give a firm answer.

But even if a firm answer were available, it would not solve
the problem of assessing the impact of the slave trade on African
societies. For statistics, "sub-Saharan Africa as a whole" is a
useful entity, but not for this historical problem. People did not

live in "sub-Saharan Africa as a whole." They lived in a series of
particular African societies. The incidence of the slave trade was
extremely variable, seriously affecting some regions while leaving others completely untouched. Useful analysis will therefore
have to begin with particular societies, looking far beyond the
narrowly demographic trends and seeing each society in its
broader context. Only a systematic comparative study of the variety of different African responses to the European demand for
slaves can expose the relevant evidence. The kind of quantitative
evidence about the slave trade presented here is not completely
irrelevant, but neither is it crucial.

One of the key questions to be answered, for example, is the
possible role of the slave trade in social and political change.
One model frequently found in the historical literature depicts
the transformation of a previously peaceful peasant community
into a militarized slave-catching society, where slave-raiding becomes an economic activity consciously pursued for the sake of
the European imports that could be bought with slaves, and
slaves alone. If the European demand for slaves did indeed force
this kind of adaptation on African societies, the slave trade can
be shown to have had disastrous consequences for the hunters as
well as for the hunted. Alongside the destruction and death
caused by the raids themselves, human resources and creative effort among the hunters must have been diverted from the pursuit
of innovation and progress in other fields.

But another possibility, or model, is conceivable. African societies, like those of other people in other places, settled disputes
by military means. Warfare produces prisoners-of-war, who can
be killed, enslaved, or exchanged—but they may be a by-product of war, not its original cause. The African adaptation to the
demand for slaves might be to change military tactics and strategy to maximize the number of prisoners, without actually increasing the incidence or destructiveness of warfare. In that case,
the slave trade might have done little serious damage to the
well-being of the African society.

Between these two extreme models, many mixed cases are obviously possible, and several of them appear to have existed historically. The crucial question is one of degree—which model
was most common, or which tendency was dominant? The ques-

tion asks for measurement, but the number of slaves exported (or even the ratio of slave exports to population) is no evidence of the way they were acquired. It tells even less about what might have happened if they had not been exported at all.

At best, the export data of the slave trade can be suggestive. If the dominant African pattern at the height of the slave trade was that of the militarized, slave-catching society, systematically preying on its neighbors, the export projections should show a relatively large and continuous supply of slaves from these hunter societies; and the slaves themselves should have been mainly from the less organized neighbors. This pattern does not emerge clearly from the slave-export data of eighteenth-century Africa. Some ports, notably the city-states of the Bight of Biafra, did produce a continuous supply that may imply slave-catching as an economic enterprise. Elsewhere, the rapid shift in sources of supply from one region to another suggests that by-product enslavement was the dominant feature, or that, if systematic slave-hunting were tried, it could not be maintained.

These weaknesses of quantitative evidence are important to keep in mind, if only because of a popular tendency to regard numbers as more "scientific" and reliable than other kinds of data. A great deal more could nevertheless be profitably done with the quantitative study of the slave trade. More and better samples of slave origins and better data on the numbers carried by the trade at particular times should make it possible to project the annual flow of slaves from particular societies, to take only one example. Even if the dimensions of the slave trade outlined here were as accurate as limited sources will ever allow—and they are not—still other dimensions of far greater significance for African and Atlantic history remain to be explored.

5   *Karl Polanyi*[1]
          The Challenge of the Slave Trade

The historical event that subjected Dahomean society to great strain reached it from outside and happened in the economic sphere. The explosion of the slave trade which resulted from overseas plantations of sugar cane hit the Guinea Coast in the immediate vicinity of Dahomey with a unique impact.

In the last resort a geographical fact, the Gap of Benin, frustrated the inherent intent of historic Dahomey to organize as an inland state, for any sudden massive development on the coast was certain to burst the thin partition of marshy ground that separated Dahomey from the strip of small maritime states, and to make inevitable a Dahomean move to the south. The peripety brought about by the onrush of the slave trade eventually sharpened the crisis of the new state and called forth an exceptional performance on the part of the monarchy.

An epochal event as specific as the invention of the steam engine by James Watt some 130 years later had happened in the Antilles—sugar cane had been introduced into Barbados in 1640. Less than twenty years after it "had overtaken tobacco and accounted for nearly half of London's imports from the Plantations" (Davies, 1957:14–15). A dramatic transformation in Atlantic trade was set in train. Within twenty-five years the whole edifice of what came to be called the Old Colonial system was erected. The French trading company, founded in 1664, was government-financed and directed by Colbert himself.

The widely held belief that the new pattern of Afro-American commerce simply followed in the wake of the Age of Discoveries is erroneous. Actually, for another century and a half, until the rise of the sugar plantations, nothing of the sort was in sight. Only by 1683 were African Negroes—3,000 of them having

SOURCE. From *Dahomey and the Slave Trade: An Analysis of an Archaic Economy* by Karl Polanyi. Copyright (C) 1966 by the University of Washington Press. Chapter II.
[1] In collaboration with Abraham Rotstein.

been acquired in Africa for use in the colony—found in Bahia, then the capital of the overseas empire of the Portuguese. Nor were there yet significant changes in evidence on the Guinea Coast itself. Until 1664 the Guinea trade, according to Mme Berbain, "was restricted to pepper, gold and ivory" (1942:34). In England the corresponding date was 1660, the year in which the company of "Adventurers of London trading into Africa" was founded. "Its principal objective was the search for gold" (Davies, 1957:41). Only twelve years later the Royal African Company was launched, of which its historian comments that "the new company was to deal chiefly in negroes for which there appeared to be an expanding demand in the English colonies' (ibid.:60). The modern slave trade can be regarded as having started in 1672.

The plantations were enormously profitable and the West Indies had become the private possession of royalty and the highest ranks of the aristocracy. The procurement of slaves was now recognized as an "absolute necessity" (ibid.:277). The planter's interest was given teeth through legislation. The private trader was permitted to participate in plantation profits on condition that he undertake to procure the slave labor on which that rich harvest depended. In the France of Louis XIV a government bounty was paid on every African slave exported to the Americas.

A shift in the international economy had caused a tidal wave to cross the Atlantic and to hurl itself against a twenty-mile stretch of the West African coast. This was not the usual kind of exchange of goods which by its nature enriches the people who are engaged in it. The trade that within less than a century was to sweep millions of Africans from their villages into slavery overseas was of a peculiar kind. It bore more similarity to the Black Death than to peaceful barter. The ruling strata of powerful white empires had been mesmerized by the prospect of great riches, if only they were able to provide a labor force from tropical climates for the rapidly spreading sugar plantations. The outcome was the modern slave trade.

Doubts might arise whether the new variant was really very different from the earlier; slavery being an old institution, so must the slave trade be, one might think. This would be like arguing that the Industrial Revolution of the eighteenth century could not have specific consequences, since machines had been invented and employed in production before. When all is said, the Afro-American slave trade of the eighteenth century was a unique event in social history. John Hawkins had been no more than a colorful episode. As late as 1620 an English explorer in the upper waters of the Gambia River was offered slaves by an African merchant. He replied that, "We were a people who do not deal in any such commodities, nor did we buy or sell one another, or any that had our own shapes" (Jobson, 1904:112 q. Davies, 1957:15).

The purposeful support accorded by Western governments to the slave trade was soon to produce a new configuration of commerce on the Guinea Coast. Up to the 1670's beaches from Senegambia to the Gold Coast were visited by traders; farther on they called only at Benin, the Calabars, and Angola. What was to become the Slave Coast was bypassed. Between Ardra and the Calabars no gold was found, and slaves were not yet in demand. An early English skipper's bill of lading on his return trip from Benin showed no slaves among the wares (Dunglas, 1957–58:111–12).

After 1670 the word "Guinea" in the language of trade took on an altered meaning. Formerly it stretched from the Senegal to Ardra and the Volta River—now it started there. At the same time it changed its politico-social character.

Traders had visited the northern Guinea Coast since the middle of the fifteenth century, yet no regular slave trade developed. On the off-chance of purchasing a stray fugitive from crime, a straggler or panyarred Negro shackled by an African to whom a debt was owed by the man's villagers or kinsmen, no dealings with African brokers, even less a searching of the beaches, would pay a skipper otherwise engaged in regular trade. Yet his acquisition of two or three slaves on the coast depended on just such a dribble or seepage of slaves, or tribal warfare carried on reasonably close to the shore might offer a windfall. For no African community would sell its own members into slavery except as a punishment for a very few capital crimes. Hence the beginnings of eighteenth-century slave trade tell of surprise raids perpetrated by white traders, intruding by stealth into villages off the coast. The Africans, taken in their sleep, were dragged into captivity unless they resisted, in which event they were slaughtered alongside the aged and infirm. Such a fiendish foray occurred only a few hours distant from the Ivory Coast (Smith, 1744). This was neither war nor trade. Rather, it was the sport and business of the adventuring skipper and his crew. Such manhunts could grow into a scourge to whole countrysides, either in the neighborhood of the coast or even far inland, if rivers or caravan roads offered means of transportation which stimulated the sale of captives. Unprotected bush and forest regions on which the razzias concentrated were sometimes fated to depopulation. Nevertheless, in the absence of an overseas demand requiring a regular flow of supply, the ravages of slave trading had been confined within narrow limits. Hence the organized hinterland state was fairly safe until the modern slave trade—that "enormity," to use Toynbee's term—got under way.

The beaches of Senegambia traditionally were in the hands of the Africans. No permanent relations between the foreign trader and the political sovereign were required. For orderly transactions no particular establishment on the beaches nor even treaty arrangements between the local chiefs and the white trader were needed. Gold, pepper, and ivory were regular objects of trading but no specialized slave trade developed alongside them. Even when mercantilist notions induced European governments to establish some personnel on the shore, the white man still claimed only tenant's status, not owner's. The Negro kingdoms of the hinterland jealously guarded their territory against penetration; they never ceded land. Dahomey's subsequent offer that England take over Whydah permanently was indeed a desperate step of statesmanship born of an impasse.

With the advent of sugar cane in the West Indies the rush for Negro slaves was on. Ardra was the first and most important slave trading state on the Upper Guinea Coast. Since the end of the 1660's Ardra and its tributaries, the Popos, Djekin, Lampe, Offra, Glehoue (the later Whydah), Adjache (Porto Novo) were places where inland slaves were regularly traded, most of them having passed through the territory of Ardra. By the turn of the seventeenth century the French, who had a lodge in the neighborhood, achieved permanent settlement in the coastal area of Whydah (so named after the Houeda people) and entry into the slave trade of that tribe. The Royal African Company, which previously favored the neighboring Offra, also moved its principal settlement there, "while the Portuguese became increasingly frequent visitors" (Davies, 1957:229). In 1705 the English Agent-General at Capo Corso wrote to the London office that the Whydah trade would be lost if a stop was not put to the new French settlement. Next year the English factor of the Royal African Company informed London of his intention "to enter into articles with the French," and two years later that he was renewing these articles, "The Dutch having already done so" (ibid.:279). (The terms of the agreement are still not known.) K. G. Davies adds that "by the early years of the eighteenth century all four of the leading slaving nations had acknowledged the advantages of Whydah as a slave-mart" (ibid.:229). And in a survey of prices "from the northern to the southern extremities of the company's trade," he asserts truly that they were "cheapest of all at Whydah" (ibid.:237).

When, in the first decade of the eighteenth century, Whydah emerged as the pre-eminent center of this new branch of world trade, the history of Dahomey took a decisive turn. The event in her close proximity was a challenge which brought the latent contradictions of her position to a head. She was now compelled to come to terms with her geographical and strategic dependence upon the coast.

The unexpected localization of the slave trade and the economic pressure of slavers' fleets off the coast undermined the inland status of Dahomey. Never before had the slave trade forced itself on an inland state of West Africa as a concern dominating its total existence. Internally and externally the supply situation was unprecedented in regard both to the numbers involved and the social wreckage caused. Not a few scores of slaves at the most were brought up annually from stray *slattees* (chained groups of slaves for sale in a market place), but many thousands of slaves were channeled in spurts of hundreds of organized *coffilas* (slave *coffles* or chain gangs). This would not have been possible without fortified lodges erected against local pillagers, even though such settlements would still be at the mercy of the concerted action of African rulers (Davies, 1957:6). Other requirements of the trade were procedures and manipulations of transporting, keeping, barracooning, subsisting, and branding adult human beings in the mass. A *modus vivendi* with the authorities of the large African states had to be found, and occasional meddling with the intricate politics of the region was inevitable (Davies, 1957:278). Benin, Oyo, and Ashanti could remain militarily aloof from the coast, with small buffer states located between them and the more densely wooded approach to the shore. The Gap of Benin, narrowing toward the south, deprived Dahomey of such a zone of insulation.

The rationale of Dahomey's policy was stringent. In her precarious military position, defense and slave trading were inseparable. Admittedly, the slave trade was also a source of very considerable revenue to the king, yet there was scarcely any room for private gain in a royal household which comprised the total expenses of army and civil service, not excluding the heavy cost of annual campaigns. Dahomey was surrounded by militarily prepared states. Acquiring slaves through intensified raiding against the weaker neighbors was impracticable. Large-scale slave wars and preventive action against over-powerful neighbors went together. Slave trading by the state, which, apart from Ardra, Dahomey alone practiced in that region, grew into a convolute of incessant wars which raised the heat of the country's devotion to the warrior's way of life beyond all normal standards. Add to this the European slavers' mercenary intent, stiffened by mercantilist bounties and bureaucratic incentives. The demand for slaves was insistent, the forts and settlements reached out for them with their ships and incited, bribed, and pressured the coastal chieftains to provide them. Dahomey, the slaver state, and the white slavers were in spite of passing differences mutual customers.

Returning to the vicious circle of Dahomean wars: three patterns of campaigns can be distinguished. Annual wars were carried on as a national institution: first, for the supply of foreign trade; to a smaller extent for the refilling of royal plantations; last, but not least, for the regular upkeep of half the male population engaged in the campaigns. Forbes called *all* soldiers traders, since the king bought from them either the head of an enemy

or the live person of at least one prisoner (1851[II]:90). Every
soldier to whom powder had been issued was expected to live up
to this requirement or suffer punishment. To water the graves of
the ancestors many hundreds of prisoners were put to death.
Apart from the sacrifices at the Annual Customs, massacres of
prisoners were the rule. This was a requirement of ancestor worship, the national religion. Functionally it spread fear of the king
in the "bush" and helped to maintain discipline through terror.

The wars were launched under trivial pretexts or with no reasons being given. Ceremonies of mobilization heralded the event,
yet the actual attack was launched in the deepest secrecy. Absence of means of rapid communication made surprise not only a
part of good tactics but even of sound strategy.

A permanent constellation of power potentials underlay Dahomean wars and war threats almost all through the two and one-
half centuries of the country's existence. It was fully effective in
the eighteenth century, less so in the seventeenth and nineteenth.
Cardinal points were: Oyo, the great power, in the northeast; a
middle state, Ardra, in the south and southwest; and territorially
minute Whydah, with its seaport due south. A disgruntled vassal
of Oyo, Dahomey thus faced the problem of Whydah, with Oyo
in the back and Oyo's ally Ardra on the flank. The power pattern did not altogether cease to operate even after Dahomey's
conquest of Allada, the chief town of Ardra, in 1724. For Ardra's coastal tributaries, the Popos, and the other tribal allies remained a very real force. A campaign against Whydah had to
reckon with this hostile potential, and even after Whydah was
conquered the shadow of their surf pirogues haunted Dahomey's
precarious tenure of the port. Moreover, the white forts and factories were always prepared to conspire with the beaten Houedas
and Popos against Dahomey, the northern inland state whose
supplies of slaves were exhausted time and time again owing to
its excessive involvement in power politics. The Dutch, the
French, and even the English commanders occasionally instigat-
ed the coastal natives to stand together to throw off the Dahomean yoke.

The national enemy was, of course, Oyo. This became an established fact in 1708, when, after a twenty-three years' effort,
Dahomey succeeded in destroying the Wemenou. These were

mainly a Yoruba people, densely settled along the banks of the Weme on the Dahomean side of the boundary. The disappearance of this long-stretched buffer state which separated the might of Oyo from rapidly growing Dahomey brought the power play into action. From that time onward Oyo was every ready to crush Abomey in a preventive move. Oyo's irresistible cavalry compelled King Agadja to flee from his capital and in 1712 forced Dahomey into a condition of abject vassalage, bound to send its forces at any time against a neighbor at Oyo's bid. Dahomey was burdened with a heavy annual tribute. One item to be delivered was significant: forty-one sets of forty-one guns each (Dunglas, 1957–1958:170). Oyo procured its mounts from the north but lacked firearms, which were just coming in through the southern ports.

Dahomey possessed, to our knowledge, nothing to offer the European trader in exchange for guns except slaves, who, however, had to be captured in expensive wars on its neighbors. Only in 1818, with Oyo in decline, did King Gezo succeed in freeing Abomey from a heavy tribute and strict subservience to the formidable taskmaster. For more than a century Oyo had kept watch on the influx of arms for Dahomey by way of Whydah. Ardra, as a friendly buffer, had been on the whole an asset to Oyo. Dahomey needed safe access to the coast to deliver slaves for guns and powder. In an authenticated instance Whydensian port authorities passed on a big consignment of foreign firearms to Abomey having first, as a matter of precaution, removed the flints from the hammers (Dunglas, 1957–1958:152). Every Dahomean soldier had to be accompanied in battle by another man with a fusee to light the powder in the pan. Access to the port was therefore vital to Dahomey, to say nothing of the heavy cuts in revenue it suffered from Ardran tolls and customs. With Ardra eliminated, ways of running trade through the port of Whydah under Dahomey's supervision could be devised, without exposing the person of the king to the contagion of the coastal snake religion or the white man's intimacy.

Dahomey had a strong reluctance to establish itself on the coast by force of arms or to make itself the ruler of Whydah. The king of Dahomey never to our knowledge had himself released, as part of his inauguration ceremony, from the tabu of

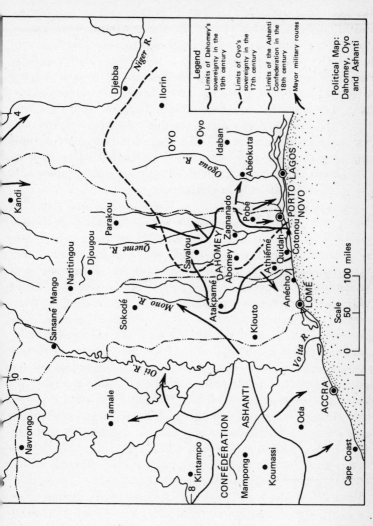

Figure 1. Slightly enlarged fragments of Map. No. 3 (Paul Mercier, *Cartes Ethno-démo-graphiques de L'Afrique Occidentale*, Feuilles No. 5, I.F.A.N. Dakar, 1954).

the sea, as had his cousins who occupied the golden *katakle* at
Porto Novo. In Part II [*of Dahomey and the Slave Trade: An
Analysis of an Archaic Economy*], "Patterns of the Economy,"
institutional evidence is sought for the reluctance that had its
roots in the impossibility for Dahomey to incorporate a conquered Houeda kingdom. Bosman (1814) and Barbot (1732),
who knew both Whydah and Ardra, insisted on the near identity
in language and culture of these two politically antagonistic kingdoms. The opposite would be true of Dahomey and its ruling
group, the Fon. Yet why accept in this case language and religion as absolute barriers to political incorporation, seeing how
empire-building in these parts often proceeded irrespective of
such obstacles? Those patterns reflected the internalization of a
way of life which forbade amalgamation.

The attack proceeded by stages. The seizure of Ardra in 1724
(Smith, 1744:169) was followed by a move against Savi, the political capital of the Houeda kingdom. The conquest of Whydah,
the economic capital, followed only after the European factors
were advised and requested to stay neutral. But abandonment of
the enterprise, or even a temporary retreat, would have meant
giving up hope of emancipation from the humiliating subservience to Oyo. Even the European traders were hard put to brook
the indignities to which the sudden wealth of the coastal buffer
states exposed them. The Royal African Company's agent was
retained in Porto Novo two years and was made to do slave labor under pretense that his company owed the king a debt (Snelgrave, 1734:66–68). Porto Novo, together with Ardra and Whydah,
enjoyed the privileges of compulsory intermediaries between the
white traders and Dahomey. Customs were inordinately raised by
Porto Novo as well as by Whydah, which also claimed the right to
"first refusal" from imports and over and above arbitrarily cut off
Dahomey from European prestige goods.

Symbolic of the broad logic of challenge and response were
the distressing circumstances that gave rise to some of Dahomey's great achievements. The conquest of Whydah in February,
1727, was far from final. The Houedan King Huffon had fled
with a part of his army into the marshes of Atheme and Great
Popo, where the landbound Dahomeans were unable to follow
them. His caboceer, Assu, courageously fought his way back to

Whydah, setting up camp between the French and the English settlements, Saint-Louis and Fort William's, but was chased away by a Dahomean counterattack (*ibid.*:116). The Houeda succeeded in letting Oyo have word of their plight. Oyo cavalry descended upon Abomey, sending King Agadja into the bush for refuge. Trade was hard hit, enough to make the European factors regret the change. The English governor, the unfortunate Testefole, persuaded the Houedas to join with the Popos and recapture Whydah. The Dahomeans had withdrawn their garrison from Savi and were amazed to learn that a convoy of slaves sent to Whydah found the port in the hands of a Houedan army 15,000 strong, which they believed dispersed in the marshes.

In this extremity Agadja decided to arm a company of female elephant hunters he had inherited from his father. They had hitherto served only as a bodyguard, but were now to form a regiment to make up the rear and—at least visually—swell the ranks. The daring experiment culminated in the justly famed institution of the "Amazons." This large elite force of a volunteer army of virgins was domiciled around the court, and its veterans were pensionable. This inventiveness of the Alladoxonu dynasty was an asset to the new state in its struggle for survival under arduous circumstances, but the secret source of success was the moral cohesion uniting the state and nonstate factors in Dahomean society.

If, in a general way, Dahomey's history might be regarded as a manifold response to the challenge of the Gap of Benin, this is undoubtedly true of the economy of Dahomean Whydah. A noncommercial inland nation was to adapt this port to a trading task of extraordinary magnitude and complexity. There is no need to enlarge on the technicalities of transacting the intricate business of the slave trade with many European countries and with brokers from numerous inland peoples. The entrance of foreign goods had to be technically and financially administered; weights and measures concerted; cultural contacts controlled while insulating internal trade from all avenues of unwanted external influences, particularly those which accompany the penetrative effects of foreign currencies. We will see how the port of trade organization admirably answered these apparently conflicting requirements.

Consider the currency situation. Whydah was a small kingdom with the two hinterland regions of Dahomey and, somewhat further to the northwest, Ashanti for neighbors. The statesmanship of Dahomey and Ashanti was, we should assume, aware of the importance of maintaining separate and distinct systems of currencies for the sake of the political and cultural integrity of their countries. Coastal Whydah, even after its political subjection by Dahomey, which always kept it culturally at arm's length, remained a *corpus separatum*. European company officials and African traders of various extraction intermingled freely. Many of the latter were of Afro-American background, Portuguese mulattoes, and repatriated African slaves. This was a place of multiple currencies, while Dahomey and Ashanti had succeeded in keeping their monetary systems separate in the face of what must appear to the modern mind as almost insuperable obstacles. Dahomey used cowrie exclusively, in elaborate, never-changing division, maintained at an unvarying exchange rate of 32,000 cowries to one ounce of gold—an amazing feat. Ashanti used gold dust as a currency, nuggets being appropriated by the king; cowries were banned in Ashanti as was gold dust in Dahomey. In Whydah under Dahomean rule both were current. Silver, the domestic currency of the various European nations, was of small account in Whydah since no coins were current, but it was commonly melted down to serve for ornaments.

Again, in foreign relations the onrush of the slave trade called forth an unprecedented expedient on the part of the Alladoxonu. West African hinterland states never relinquished any of their territory to the European powers. This was more than keeping jealous guard over sovereign rights. Dahomean religion dedicated the soil of the country to the gods and denied to the king the right of alienating any part of it. This policy was reversed by the Alladoxonu rulers and the reversal was steadfastly adhered to. The traditional attitude would have committed Dahomey to hold on to the possession of Whydah at all cost and, as a consequence, doomed the country to vassalage to Oyo, while all that Dahomey needed was the assurance of a free import of arms. Her solution was to seek close cooperation with the great power that owned the strongest fleet.

There is documentary evidence of Agadja's endeavors to co-operate with the English, even prior to his attack on Whydah. His contacts dating from Bulfinch Lambe, the first white man to visit Abomey, can be reconstructed from documents (cf. Bulfinch Lambe's letter in Smith, 1744 : 171–89). Captain William Snelgrave arrived in desolated Whydah only a few weeks after it was sacked and was promptly met in neighboring Djekin by Agadja's messenger with the king's invitation to proceed to Allada for consultation. Eventually Dahomean policy matured to the grand decision of offering to cede the sovereignty over Whydah to the English on sole condition of a guaranteed supply of arms to Dahomey. Bulfinch Lambe, after a two years' enforced visit at Agadja's court, was allowed to leave, laden with presents, having promised to return with a whole colony of Englishmen. Unavailing efforts to persuade the London government to accept Whydah continued under successive rulers (cf. Commodore Wilmot in Burton, 1893 [II] : 252). Indeed, this perseverance appeared not unreasonable under the circumstances, but the Colonial Office refused even to consider the king of Dahomey's offer.

By the first half of the nineteenth century Oyo was in decline. Fulbe cavalry had pushed back the frontiers of the Yoruba kingdoms, and the seceding Egba had set up the fortress of Abeokouta. King Gezo of Dahomey freed his country from the shameful burden of the tribute and the military overlordship of the Oyo. Dahomey could now feel secure within its frontiers, and with the falling off of the slave trade could shift her economy to the export of palm oil. Eventually Abomey fell to French artillery, though defended by an Amazon army still possessed of all the soldierly virtues. Superior technology was victorious over a nation of great gifts exercised on an exceptional institutional level.

REFERENCES

John Barbot, *A Description of the Coasts of North and South Guinea, and of Ethipia inferior, vulgarly Angola*, Vol. V (London, 1732).
Simone Berbain, *Le Comptoir Français de Juda (Ouida) au XVIII° Siècle* (Paris, 1942).

Willem Bosman, *A New and Accurate Description of the Coast of Guinea*. In John Pinkerton, ed., *A General Collection of the Best and Most Interesting Voyages and Travels in All Parts of the World*, XVI (London, 1808–1814).

Capt. Sir Richard F. Burton, *A Mission to Gelele, King of Dahomey* (2 vols.; London, 1893).

Kenneth Gordon Davies, *The Royal African Company* (New York, 1957).

Edouard Dunglas, *Contribution à l'histoire du Moyen-Dahomey* (Paris, 1957–1958).

Frederick E. Forbes, *Dahomey and the Dahomans, Being the Journal of Two Missions to Dahomey, and Residence at His Capital in 1849 and 1850* (London, 1851).

Richard Jobson, *The Golden Trade, or a Discovery of the River Gambia and the Golden Trade of the Aethipians (1620–1621)* (Teignmouth, 1904).

William Smith, *A New Voyage to Guinea* (London, 1744).

Capt. William Snelgrave, *A New Account of Some Parts of Guinea and the Slave Trade* (London, 1744).

6   *Rosemary Arnold*

A Port of Trade: Whydah on the Guinea Coast

It was in the course of inquiring into the commercial organization of eighteenth-century Whydah, historically known as the slave port of the Negro kingdom of Dahomey, that attention was first drawn to the subject of this chapter—the port of trade.[1] Whydah was an organ of administered trade, a way of trading which appears as general from antiquity almost to the threshold of modern times. The capacity of the port of trade for outlasting the millennia reflected the positive role played by that institution in resolving some of the less obvious problems of statecraft under archaic conditions, such as military requirements and protection against undesirable culture contact.

SOURCE. "A Port of Trade: Whydah on the Guinea Coast" by Rosemary Arnold, Reprinted with permission of The MacMillan Company from *Trade and Market in the Early Empires: Economics in History and Theory* edited by Karl Polanyi, Conrad M. Arensberg and Harry W. Pearson. © by The Free Press, A Corporation, 1957, pp. 154–175.

In the institution of the port of trade, therefore, many strands meet, some deriving from the early state, some from even earlier primitive conditions. Apart from the military and cultural considerations which made the inland empires shun the coast, there was the position of the foreign trader, who refused to venture for the sake of commerce onto a strange and distant shore unless the safety of his person and goods was fairly assured. No one but the armed pirate could feel secure on a beach. Hence the combination of pirate and trader famed from the Odyssey. It was a long time before the neutrality of the trading place was ensured not by native weakness, as in silent trade, or around the mariners' altars on secluded beaches, but by the deliberate neutrality with which law and order enforced equal justice to all comers at the hand of port authorities. Fear would drive out traffic.

The international status of the port of trade thus ran the gamut from a free port "in weak hands," as Whydah originally was, to a mere port-town of an inland power administered from the distant capital as Whydah became under Dahoman rule after the conquest, in 1727.

Since the last quarter of the seventeenth century Whydah was famed in the Western world as the port of call of the African slave trade. In the beginning of the eighteenth century the small coastal kingdom that formed Whydah's immediate neighborhood was overrun by the powerful inland state of Dahomey, which thus appeared in the limelight of history. Whydah was incorporated in Dahomey, the capital of which, Abomey, was some 150 miles removed from the coast. While Whydah was frequented by the crews of the White slavers of many nations, Abomey, secluded in the Dark Continent, remained inaccessible to foreigners. Whydah, a flourishing port town, renowned in distant countries, was never deemed worthy of the King of Dahomey's personal presence. Although a commercial emporium, no native class interested in trade was in evidence. European observers were sometimes baffled by the ambiguous status which this trading place held in Dahomey. An inquiry into the organization of trade in Whydah may then well start from the history of Dahomey, and the reasons which made it seize Whydah, and having done so, keep it at arm's length.

Dahomey was one of the great Negro states of West Africa, an inland kingdom of some 300,000 population, heir to a political tradition stemming from the empire-builders of the Western Sudan. For several hundred years, from the foundation of the kingdom, which legend places around 1625, until its conquest by the French in 1892, Dahomey was governed by the same dynasty of Negro kings and maintained its independence until borne down by overwhelming military forces.

Eighteenth-century Dahomey had produced a planned economy of an advanced type, using trade, money and markets with sophistication. Viewed in historical perspective, this planned economy was a method of coping with the massive pressures which the external situation, the danger of foreign conquest, brought to bear upon Dahomey. Planning was a technique for survival, and the monarchy, the central planning organ, performed functions without which the society could not have maintained its independent existence. Given Dahomey's situation, the organs of a tribal society would have been powerless. No loose tribal formation could have organized a sustained military effort on the scale required nor dealt effectively with the outside world through trade nor assured internal peace under the stresses and strains of permanent mobilization. A power transcending the tribal organs had to be called into being to meet the threat to the communal existence.

The kings of the Alladoxonou dynasty created such a power and succeeded in welding the Dahoman peoples into an empire. Out of disunity and impotence, a military organization was created which Dahomey's neighbors were compelled to respect. Despite the strain which an annual war placed upon the resources of the country and its institutions, the well-being of the population was assured by an unquestionably efficient administration of the economy. And out of diverse traditions, a common tradition was forged, so deeprooted that it lives on among the people of Dahomey even today despite military conquest and a couple of generations of foreign rule.[2]

Yet Dahomey under the monarchy retained its tribal base—it was an empire built on tribal foundations. The traditions of the clan were the core values of Dahoman life, constitutive of the political community as of the tribal community. Far from disintegrating under the pressure of the throne, the clans of Dahomey remained as the basic social units and exercised indispensable functions in economic and political life. Even the monarchy appeared in the guise of the clan. The royal house ranked as the highest of the clans and the ancestors of the royal house were regarded as the ancestors of all Dahomans. As mediator between the living and the dead, the king's relationship to his people was that of head of a clan to its members—he was the link with the ancestors, high priest and chief magistrate, first among warriors, and guardian of the people's livelihood. While the king embodied the aristocratic virtues of a tribal chief, the democratic traditions of the tribal society were likewise perpetuated in the rights enjoyed by the clans, the villages, the gilds, and the innumerable voluntary associations—a charter of freedoms which was the keystone of Dahoman society.

In adapting tribal institutions and traditions to the new circumstances created by political expansion, Dahomey produced that singular combination of centralization and decentralization, of authority and flexibility, of controls and freedoms, which characterized its redistributive economy.

WAR AND TRADE IN NATIVE DAHOMEY

If a military policy was forced upon Dahomey in self-defense, this was no less true of its trade policy. The Dahomans were anything but a trading people. Their geographical position isolated them from trade. A glance at the map reveals that Dahomey stood well below the 12th parallel which marks the southernmost extension of the great trade routes of Africa. These well-worn tracks link the west-east flow of the middle Niger exclusively with the Moorish north and the Haussa country in the east. No roads whatsoever lead from the middle Niger to the western or southern coast.[3]

Though sheltered from the main approaches of the trade, the Niger to the north and Guinea coast to the south, Dahomey could not remain entirely aloof from trade. Like the other Negro peoples of the interior, Dahomey was accustomed to fight only with bow and arrow. But once the Moors from the north had introduced firearms into the Sudan, and once the Europeans on the Guinea Coast were arming the coastal natives of the south with

European muskets, those who knew only the bow and arrow were doomed to extinction or unending flight. Dahomey was caught between two fires. Trade with the Europeans at Whydah had become essential since it was this trade, as the Dahomans themselves said, which "brings guns and powder to Dahomey." So crucial was the control of the trade that Dahomey permitted guns and powder to move inland only to those border peoples who had certified their friendship by alliance with Dahomey. "The Mahee," Duncan says of the northern neighbors of Dahomey, "use the bow and arrow, the King of Dahomey forbidding the transport of firearms through his kingdom from the coast."[4]

Yet trade with the Europeans at Whydah—literally a condition for survival—raised at the same time the gravest threat to Dahomey's security. Dahomey was a passive trader, maintaining, herself, no organization for active trade over long distances. While there are a few reports of trading parties sent into the interior, the meagerness of these reports suggests that active trade was the exception rather than the rule. As a passive trader, however, dependent upon supplies brought by others from afar, Dahomey would be exposed to all the dangers involved in letting down the gates to the foreigner. Without a counter-organization for trade, by which the movements of foreigners and their goods could be regulated in conformity with the requirements of state, Dahomey would stand defenseless before a dual enemy: her hostile neighbors, and the strangers come to trade.

Herein lies the explanation of Dahomey's policy toward Whydah. So long as Dahomey's access to the port was secure, Dahomey was content to leave Whydah in the hands of the Whydasians. Dahoman traders, it seems, had been accustomed to come freely to Whydah for some time before 1727 when Whydah passed to Dahomey.[5] Such a relationship permitted Dahomey to secure the essential trade goods and yet remain aloof from the foreigner in her inland retreat.

What, then, prompted Dahomey to change her policy and take Whydah by force in 1727?

This question was the subject of considerable controversy among the Europeans who witnessed the event. Norris, upholding the viewpoint that Dahomey's commercial interests were the motivating factor, commented as follows:

"I knew many of the old Whydasians as well as Dahomans who were present when Trudo attacked that kingdom. They attributed his enterprize solely to the desire of extending his dominions, and of enjoying at first hand, those commodities which he had been used to purchase of the Whydasians. . . ."[6]

Herskovits follows this interpretation, affirming

"that the principal reason why Agadja was eager to conquer his way to the sea-coast was that . . . the transportation of goods through the kingdoms of Whydah and Ardra took from him a large proportion of his profits from slaving, and greatly increased the price of European goods which he received in exchange for the proceeds from slaves."[7]

And, further, that the conquest of Whydah

"gained for Agadja the right to sell his slaves directly to the captains of the slave vessels who called at the port, and from them to get, without paying the duties imposed by an intervening power, the European goods he valued so highly."[8]

These views are hardly consistent with the facts. Whatever their varying interpretations of the event, contemporary witnesses agreed as to the facts, and the most significant fact was that the king of Whydah had closed the port to traders from Dahomey. Norris says that the Dahoman king, Trudo,

"had solicited permission from the king of Whydah to enjoy free commercial passage through his country to the sea side, on condition of paying the usual custom upon slaves exported; this was peremptorily refused by the king of Whydah; and in consequence of this refusal, Trudo determined to obtain his purpose by force of arms. . . ."[9]

Likewise, Snelgrave confirms that Dahomey

"sent an Ambassador to the King of Whidaw, requesting to have an open Traffick to the Sea side, and offering to pay him his usual Customs on Negroes exported: which being refused, he from that time resolved to resent it, when Opportunity offered."

Furthermore, the king of Whydah, after refusing Dahomey's request, told Snelgrave that "if the King of Dahome should offer to invade him, he would not use him when taken according to their Custom, that is, cut off his Head, but would keep him for a Slave to do the vilest Offices."[10]

Atkins suggests that there were further provocations against Dahomey. "The king of Dahomey," he says,

"was probably incited to the Conquest from the generous Motive of redeeming his own, and the neighbouring Country People from those cruel Wars, and Slavery that was continually imposed on them by these Snakes (Whydasians) and the King of Ardra; . . . against those in particular, his Resentments were fired: First, on account of their public Robberies, and Manstealing, even to his Dominions; and Secondly, That Contempt the King of Whydah had expressed towards him. . . ."[11]

There is, then, no question of Dahomey's attempting to evade payment of the duties upon the trade since the king offers to pay Whydah "his usual Customs on Negroes exported." And indeed, the first step taken by Dahomey after its capture of Whydah was to reduce the customs to one half those fixed previously by the king of Whydah.[12] Instead, there was a security problem of the first order. Dahomey was being denied access to the Coast and the opportunity to secure firearms, while the public insult to Dahomey proffered by the king of Whydah could not be overlooked without grave damage to Dahomey's position. We may recall, moreover, that Dahomey was at this time under tremendous pressure from the Oyo, having suffered one invasion and standing in dread of another. Indeed, it seems likely that the taking of Whydah was regarded by Dahomey as a counter-move against the Oyo. During the first Oyo invasion, according to Snelgrave, the Dahomans had "comforted themselves with this Thought," that, in the event of a second invasion

"they might save their Persons, by flying to the Sea Coast, to which the J-oes durst not follow them. For as their national Fetiche was the Sea, they were prohibited by their Priests from ever seeing it, under no less a Penalty than Death."[13]

It may well be, then, that an outlet to the seaside was contemplated as an avenue of retreat from the Oyo. For the ultimate preserve of the "fugitive" peoples were the lagoons of the tropical coast.

Under these circumstances, it was only by placing Whydah in its own hands that Dahomey could secure access to the coast and guarantee the neutrality of the place of trade. The compelling urgency of such a move is underlined by the subsequent difficulties which it encountered in holding the port. The intrigues of the coastal peoples, spurred on intermittently by various European governors, were, for a time, a recurring threat to Dahomey's hold upon the trade—all the more since Oyo was also seeking to establish trade relationships with the coast. At any rate, by the end of the century, Oyo had succeeded in wresting control from Dahomey of the neighboring kingdom of Ardra and its port, Jaquin, or Porto Novo, so that the Oyo were in a position to close off the coast entirely unless Dahomey was securely in possession of its own port. The threat was a very real one. At one time, Dalzel says,

"The King of Ardrah . . . stopped all communication with Whydah. The messengers from Porto Novo were no longer seen at the King of Dahomey's Customs; and the Dahoman traders, who had been accustomed to visit Ardrah, were no more allowed that liberty."[14]

When Dahomey protested this action, even sending an expedition against Porto Novo, the king of Oyo replied with the warning that Dahomey should undertake no further offensive actions against Ardra, since "Ardra was Eyeo's callabash, out of which nobody should be permitted to eat but himself.[15]

Far from looking upon Whydah as a source of commercial gain, then, Dahomey regarded the acquisition of Whydah as a security measure. The Dahoman attitude toward Whydah was that of an inland people who abhor the foreigner-infected coast and its cosmopolitan activities, but who are forced to maintain contact because of imperative military considerations.[16] In short, the port of trade was a liability, not a source of profit.

Only this interpretation is consistent with the well attested massive fact that Dahomey, on more than one occasion, offered to cede Whydah to the British. The most complete account of such negotiations is that given by Duncan to whom the king "expressed his earnest desire to give up Whydah to the English Government, with full powers to exercise our own laws and customs; . . . [and] to afford us every necessary assistance and protection, and to give us any . . . quantity of land in the vicinity of that settlement we might require for agricultural purposes."[17]

Nothing could more definitely indicate Dahomey's noncommercial interests in Whydah than this offer to turn it over to the English crown. Moreover, this offer explicitly commits the king to the abolition of the slave traffic as well. "When we (i.e., the English) should have obtained possession of Whydah," the king goes on to say to Duncan, "we should have power to use our own discretion respecting the Slavetrade; and that . . . we could with much more propriety exert our authority to prevent slave traffic than he himself." And again, "He said he should be ready and very glad to make any reasonable arrangement with the English Government for the abolition of slavery, and the establishment of another trade."[18]

The king is evidently concerned to place the port of trade in the hands of a superlatively strong power. "He had, he said, refused possession of Whydah to the Prince de Joinville, stating his determination to treat with none but the Queen of England, who was the greatest of all white sovereigns."[19] The port of trade must be in the hands of a power strong enough to guarantee its neutrality even against the other powers and itself a power that is friendly to Dahomey and committed by treaty to respect her interests. This would be a solution to the vexing problem of the port of trade. There can be no doubt that the king regarded such a solution as preferable to continued possession of the port by Dahomey herself.

This offer, surprising as it may seem, represents Dahoman policy at the highest level. When the discussion with Duncan is concluded, Duncan reports, the king himself "dictated to me a letter to the Secretary of State for the Colonies, in which he formally ceded Whydah to the English Government . . . and when he found it satisfactory, he held the upper end of the pen while I signed his name."[20]

Again, some twenty years later, Commander Wilmot, meeting with the king in 1863, remarks "the friendly disposition evinced by the King towards the English," and quotes the monarch as saying:

" 'From hence forth the King of Dahomey and the Queen of England are one; you shall hold the tail of the kingdom, and I will take the head': meaning that we should have possession of Whydah for trading purposes, and supply him with everything."[21]

For Dahomey, then, war and trade were not commerical activities but conditions for survival. It is only in these terms that the economy and the society become intelligible. To misread war and trade as commercial activities is to distort beyond recognition the organs and techniques which Dahomey developed to cope with the conditions of existence imposed by its environment.

REMOTE CONTROL OF WHYDAH

For Dahomey, the creation of the port of trade at Whydah was the solution to a problem that might well have seemed insoluble. Here was Aristotle's dilemma concerning the Piraeus aggravated by manifold complications.[22] If neutrality demanded the admittance of all comers to the port of trade, it also demanded the isolation of the port, else how were the foreigners, both European and African, to be prevented from intriguing against Dahomey and interfering in Dahoman affairs? At the same time isolation could not signify a hands-off policy. There was need for a strong hand at Whydah to keep the flotsam and jetsam population of a port town in check and to compel respect for life and property so that trade would be secure. Yet how was Dahomey, supremely indifferent as she was to maritime commerce and its concerns, to exercise a strong hand and achieve an efficient administration of the port without shifting the very axis of her existence?

The dilemma was all the more complex in that trade and war imposed incompatible conditions, yet both were essential to Dahomey's survival. A regular trade was impossible except under peaceful conditions, yet war was no less a necessary condition for trade, since it provided the captives without which Dahomey could not trade at all. One aspect of the matter is revealed in the comments of those experienced Guinea traders, Snelgrave and Barbot. Snelgrave observes that for some time after the capture of Whydah by Dahomey, "the Trade . . . is almost ruined; for the far Inland People having now no Markets to carry their Slaves to, as formerly, and the Dahomes using no Trade but that of War, few Negroes are now brought down to be sold to the Europeans." This war between Dahomey and Whydah had not only disorganized the ordinary channels of trade and closed off the trade routes, but there was as well a "great Destruction of the Inhabitants of the neighbouring Countries, who used to carry on a regular Trade with the far Inland People."[23] Obviously, trade could not operate under such disturbed conditions. On thes other hand, peace might be equally disruptive of trade in so far as it cut off the supply of slaves. As Barbot complains: "In the year 1682, I could get but very few (slaves) because there was at that time almost a general peace among the Blacks along the coast."[24] Certainly Dahomey would have to find a way of separating war and trade so that the captives could be supplied to Whydah without embroiling the traders in military affairs and disrupting the peace of the port of trade.

Small wonder that Dahomey desired to avoid the problem of Whydah altogether. It was this attitude which explains, as we have seen, the repeated offers by the kings of Dahomey to cede Whydah to the English and thus to be relieved of the responsibility for its administration. Certainly it is striking that none of the kings of Dahomey was ever known to set foot in Whydah, even the conquest of Whydah being accomplished with the king remaining at a distance, in war encampment some miles outside of the town. Whydah was beyond the pale, and the Whydasians themselves an irritant in the body politic. On numerous occasions, the king displayed his contempt for these coastal people —a people of different stock, professing a strange religion, and worst of all, corrupted by trade with the foreigner.[25] To Norris, who pleaded with the king to spare the lives of the Whydasians taken by the Dahomans, in the assault upon Whydah, the king replied as follows:

". . . it would be setting a bad example, and keeping people in the country, who might hold seditious language; that his was a peculiar government, and that *these strangers* [my italics] might prejudice his people against it, and infect them with sentiments incompatible with it."[26]

And, Duncan, setting off for the Kong Mountains, found that his Whydah carriers were put under the Dahoman captain of the guard, to whom the king had given "strict orders to watch them narrowly, on account of their thievish propensities."

Yet the problem of Whydah could not be avoided. The trade was essential to Dahomey and the hostility of the Whydasians left no alternative but to take over the port. Dahomey's conflict of interests was reconciled by an indirect administration of the port, a system of remote control as it were, which protected the trade while keeping trade and traders at a safe distance.

FOREIGNERS' ENCLAVE

It was the distinctive characteristic of the port of trade that trade was open to all comers from the European side. It was an alien enclave. In contrast with the trading settlements of the European companies which sought to exclude the interlopers, Whydah ". . . was a free Port of all the Guinea Coast for the Slave Trade."[27] While the French, Portuguese, and English maintained permanent factories at Whydah, the king gave permission to trade to all ships: "Chaque navire qui arrive ici pour faire le commerce, ouvre une factorie et fait ses affaires lui-même. Pour ce privilege, il paie au roi. . . ."[28] Such a policy of "free trade" would seem to serve Dahomey's trade advantage, yet there was more than this involved. A grant of exclusive privileges to one European nation carried grave risks, as is hinted in Barbot's remarks about Bissos:

"I took notice of a grant made by the Black king of Bissos to the Portuguese, to trade and settle there, exclusive of all other Europeans; but not long after, the natives observing, that the Portuguese had built a fort with eight guns, oppos'd their design of ingrossing the whole trade of their island, and laid it open to all strangers resorting to their ports; who may carry on their commerce there with all imaginable safety, and without apprehending any insult, if they offer none."[29]

Opening the port to all comers was thus the only way to keep the peace and void the disastrous trade rivalries among the Europeans which, at other points along the Coast where the Europeans were settled, had ruined the trade and involved the natives in sanguinary wars.[30] From the standpoint of Dahomey's strategic political interests, the neutrality of the port of trade had to be assured, and Dahomey sought safety in numbers.

The inland position of Whydah made it possible to regulate the trade more effectively than at other places on the Guinea Coast where trade was conducted in the coastal settlements of the chartered companies or on board ship.

With the first sighting of a vessel off Whydah, the port authorities went into action. As soon as ships were sighted in the road, porters were sent from the town to assist in the landing. No goods or men could be disembarked in that forbidding surf without assistance, and not a move could be made by the traders without the full glare of publicity. As each ship arrived, an official party from the town, consisting of the Viceroy of Whydah, the local lords, and their armed escort, greeted the traders at the famous place of reception outside the town, the "Captain's Tree." Since the town of Whydah was some two miles from the beach, goods were stored temporarily in buildings on the beach and porters were appointed by the authorities to haul the goods inland to the factories or to other places in town set aside for the foreigners. Carrying was completely in the hands of the natives and no goods moved inland until the terms of trade were negotiated with the authorities—"This regulation being agreed on by the king and the factors," as Barbot relates, "the goods are brought ashore, and carried on men's backs to the French house. . . ."[31] While residing in the town, the traders were provided with servants, carriers, and other attendants by the native "head men" who had the disposal over labor. Fresh provisions for ships' crews and the daily table were procured on the local market at Whydah; at other places along the Coast provisions might likewise be secured in the markets, or, as was often the case, supplied to the traders by the natives under treaty arrangements.

These physical facilities provided for the foreigners by the port authority served a dual purpose: they safeguarded the traders' person and property, while at the same time making any evasion of the regulations well-nigh impossible.

Whydah was administered as a "White Man's Town," sealed off from Dahomey proper, and under the jurisdiction of resident officials. The immediate administration of Whydah was left in the hands of the Viceroy of Whydah appointed by the king—the Yevogan or "White Man's Captain," a title stemming from the pre-Dahoman period. In accordance with the customary Dahoman policy toward territories incorporated into the kingdom, Whydah was permitted to retain many of its previous customs, including the indigenous snake worship, and the traditions of administration stemming from the days of Whydasian rule were carried over under the Dahoman regime. The administrative personnel was changed, however, since the Whydasians had resisted Dahoman authority, although in other cases where submission to Dahomey was voluntarily tendered, local rulers were permitted to continue in power. The affairs of Whydah were conducted by the Viceroy and his staff, with trade matters directly under the supervision of the Chacha and the other trade officials appointed by the king.

The Europeans at Whydah enjoyed certain extraterritorial privileges. Each of the European factories, with its surrounding native settlement, constituted a separate quarter of Whydah. Each quarter had its own governor, usually of European nationality, though under the general supervision of the Viceroy of Whydah, and the natives of the settlement were placed at the service of the Europeans. In Burton's time, there were four such European quarters: French Town; Brazilian Town; English Town; and Portuguese Town.[32]

The European traders at Whydah were the "King's Men" and their factories the "King's Houses" so that any offense against the person of the traders or their places of trade constituted an affront to the monarch himself. Any native caught stealing from them would be put to death. If the king "were requested to take cognizance of any case of robbery of a white man, the robber would certainly lose his head," Duncan comments, adding, however, that ". . . the King of Dahomey not wishing to interfere with white people's affairs, and the merchants being too humane to urge the King's interference," the law might not be strictly enforced.[33] While the Europeans enjoyed the rights to practice their own religion, their factories were protected by native fetishes, the English fort, as Burton observed, having two fetishes, called the "Defenders of White Men."[34] While Burton was scandalized that native fetish ceremonies were performed at the factory, it is obvious that the fetish put the peace of the place of trade under sacral sanctions The purpose to be served was the same that made Alexander the Great enjoin Cleomenes to have two temples to deified Hephaistion erected in the confines of the future Alexandria, prospective port of trade of the Hellenic *oecumene*.

Whydah enjoyed considerable autonomy so long as the law was observed. The king rarely interfered with the local administration, yet if any bad report should reach the capital, a royal messenger forthwith descended upon the town and the local authorities trembled. While the Viceroy was "judge and jury" in Whydah, only the king wielded the power of life and death, and all cases involving the death penalty were handled by the king's court at Abomey. The dual sets of officials, here as elsewhere throughout Dahomey, provided a check upon illegitimate extensions of power. The Chacha and the superintendents of trade "attended all conferences," Forbes says, "reporting directly to the king any infringement of the royal prerogative," and acting as "political spies" upon the Viceroy and the local administration.[35]

The Europeans were left to their own affairs so long as they did not violate the regulations, but the king's justice was swiftly visited upon those who infringed the law. Twice, the governors of the French forts were expelled from Whydah, in one case "upon the charge of having sold contraband articles to the enemies of Dahomey," and the governor of the English fort, in the days of Trudo, was put to death by the king for insults to Dahomey.[36]

The royal justice, severe as it might be, was effective in maintaining law and order in Whydah. In pre-Dahoman Whydah, the white traders had often complained of the "impositions of great Men" and the thievery of the natives, while the common people of Whydah, as elsewhere throughout the kingdom, might find the

king their only succor against the oppression of their native lords
or the Europeans. Upon first meeting with the king of Dahomey
immediately after the conquest of Whydah, Snelgrave urged the
king

"That the best way to make Trade flourish, was to impose easy
Customs, and to protect us from the Thievery of the Natives, and
the impositions of great Men which the King of Whidaw not
doing, greatly hurt the Trade. For the ill usage the Europeans
had met with of late from him and his People, had caused them
to send fewer Ships than formerly they did."

The king responded sympathetically, saying that

"He designed to make Trade flourish; and I might depend upon
it, he would prevent all Impositions, and Thievery, and protect
the Europeans that came to his Country. . . ."[37]

Duncan testifies to the king's justice when he remarks that

"During my stay at Abomey, I was never asked by any individual for an article of even the most trifling value, nor ever lost anything, except what was stolen by my people from the coast. The
Dahoman laws are certainly severe, but they have the desired
effect."[38]

How necessary these safeguards were to the security of the
realm, and how real the threat of oppression by upstart local
lords is illustrated by the story of Tanga, Viceroy of Whydah,
which is related by Norris.[39] Tanga, appointed by the king to his
post, was an ambitious man and sought to make himself king of
Whydah. He acquired a large body of retainers, "attached to his
person by his liberality" and by the protection he afforded them
"in their villainies" against the king's law. "His oppressions ren-
dered him odious to the garrison at the fort" as well, Norris
adds. The European governors at Whydah, on the way to Abomey to lodge a protest with the king against the exactions of the
Viceroy, were intercepted by Tanga and imprisoned. Learning of
Tanga's attempt to take the English fort by stratagem, the king
declared him a traitor, set a price upon his head, and sent troops
against him. Besieged in the house, which he had fortified against

the king's troops, and surrounded by his hundreds of wives and the retainers whose loyalty he had secured by a reckless distribution of treasure, Tanga finally met his death.

ADMINISTERED TRADE

In pre-Dahoman Whydah, prices, as well as all other terms, had been negotiated with the king before any transactions could take place. The king "fixes the price of every sort of European goods, as also of slaves," Barbot tells us, "which is to stand betwixt his subjects and foreigners; and therefore no European must go there to trade, without waiting on him before he presumes to buy or sell." After the terms were agreed upon and the king's customs paid, Barbot goes on to say, "the factor has full liberty to trade, which is proclaimed throughout the country by the king's cryer."[40] Under Dahoman rule, the same principles applied but general administrative regulations replaced separate treaty negotiations. Equivalences were fixed by law and administered by the king's officials resident at Whydah. "The cha-cha is the principal agent to the king in all matters of trade," Forbes says,

"and to him must be subjected all commerce, whether in slaves or palm-oil, that he may have the refusal. The price is laid down by law, subject to his alteration if concurred in by the viceroy and six traders or superintendents of trade appointed by the king. . . . One or the other of these must be present at all sales to take the royal duty. . . ."[41]

This indirect administration of Whydah provided the necessary safeguards for trade while at the same time serving to isolate Whydah and its affairs from Dahomey proper. The policy of isolation was carried further in a series of measures which barred foreigners and their trade from the interior of the country and placed the organization of internal trade exclusively in Dahoman hands.

In laying drastic restrictions upon the movements of the European traders, Dahoman policy was animated by considerations

similar to those reported of the neighboring kingdom of Ardra:
". . . we commonly travel only by night," Barbot says of Ardra,

"unless we be in company of the prince, or of some very notable
men of the court, when we can travel by day; but the political
Blacks carry us then along by-roads, and never through any
town or village . . . and alledge, that it is a positive order from
the government so to do, that no strangers may observe the disposition of the country, and the nature and situation of
places."[42]

Traders, of course, were always regarded as spies, and it was
standard procedure for a native kingdom, contemplating a military operation, to send spies into the territory of the enemy disguised as traders. Even without these policy deterrents, however,
the Europeans could not get very far inland. Of the Gold Coast,
Barbot says:

"None of the Europeans dwelling along the coast [have] even
ventured far up the land . . . what account can be given of it, is
taken from the most intelligent Blacks, particularly as to the re-
motest countries, it being extraordinarily difficult and dangerous,
if not altogether impossible, for Europeans to venture so far into
such wild savage countries."[43]

As for Whydah, no movements outside the town could be made
without the permission of the authorities. Along the lagoons
which ring the town, ferrymen were stationed, as Duncan reports,

"to inspect all passes or permits obtained from the [king's
minister] of Whydah to persons leaving the port, specifying the
number of people wishing to proceed by canoe for any other
place on the lagoon."[44]

The efficiency of the system was remarkable; in one instance, a
whole party was turned back because *one* person had been included for whom no authorization had been received from the
Viceroy. Europeans might go inland only with the permission of
the king—"I say permission," Forbes remarks, "for such it is, as
travelling is not allowed in Dahomey without a passport, in the

shape of his Majesty's stick." Such permission was usually granted on state occasions, as for example, when the invitations were
issued to the Europeans to attend the Annual Customs at Abomey. All travelers moved under escorts provided by the king and
under the protection of the "King's Stick."[45] As the "King's
Strangers," they were isolated from the local population and hos-
teled in special way-stations provided for travelers along the road
to Abomey. There was another reason, of course, for the safeguards surrounding the traveler. As a foreigner, he stood under
the protection of the king, and any accident would be a fateful
matter, as Burton suggests in the following comment:

"The late king relaxed the usual Dahoman severity in matter of
ingress, giving escorts to Dr. Dickson . . . and to Mr. Duncan.
. . . His son, on the contrary, has shut up all the roads. . . . He
promised that, on my return, I should penetrate into the moun-
tain-land; pleaded want of time and troops, and consoled me by
the suggestion that I was too important a personage to be risked
in the bush. This was not wholly 'blarney'; any accident to the
'King's Stranger' would be looked upon as a dire and portentous
occurrence."[46]

If the Europeans were barred from the interior as a security
measure, similar considerations prompted restrictions on the
movements of native traders from neighboring states. While the
king of Whydah in pre-Dahoman times had admitted the Mahee,
Nagoes, Oyo, and other traders from inland countries to the
port, Dahomey apparently reversed this policy. Under the Dahoman regime, these traders from inland were refused passage
through Dahoman territory, the port of trade was closed to them,
and the European traders at Whydah were permitted to deal directly only with the Dahomans themselves. Snelgrave visited
Whydah immediately after its capture by Dahomey and observed
that "the far Inland People [have] now no Markets to carry
their Slaves to, as formerly."[47] And Norris remarks that the
slaves offered for sale by the Mahee and other inland traders
"are disposed of to the factors of Dahomey."[48] The reasons for
such a policy are implied in the account given by Dalzel of the
actions of Adahoonzou:

"In consequence of the failure of some of his expeditions, the King took it into his head, that it was owing to the intrigues of aliens residing in his dominions. He therefore ordered the Gongong to be beat; giving warning to all strangers, Eyeos excepted, immediately to quit the kingdom; alledging, that whenever any expedition was on foot, his designs were by them communicated to the enemy. . . ."

An additional reason for precautionary measures against foreigners of course was the danger of military supplies falling into their hands, "guns, powder, and iron [being] articles forbidden to be dealt in by strangers in Dahomey." As a result of the king's decree, Dalzel adds, "the Mahees, Nagoes, and other inland merchants . . . [came] no more through the Dahoman dominions."[49]

The interior was thus closed off, both to the native traders on Dahomey's borders and to the Europeans at Whydah. In contrast with the situation elsewhere along the Coast, Dahomey did not permit the Europeans settled on the Coast to send agents to inland places of trade, or even to meet face-to-face with caravans of traders from the interior coming to the Coast to trade, as was the case on the Gold Coast. The Europeans were completely excluded from trade within Dahomey proper and from any direct trade relations with the countries farther inland. They were permitted to meet face-to-face in trade only with the Dahoman traders and within the confines of the port of trade at Whydah.

By such measures, Dahomey was sealed off from the foreigner and the handling of trade goods within the country was kept entirely in Dahoman hands. Such a policy was clearly not dictated by considerations of "monopoly profit" but by vital political interests. If we take a look at the character of Dahomey's trade goods, we see clearly the political interest which motivated trade policy and made necessary the rigorous restrictions on the movement of goods in trade.

Dahomey's exports were slaves and palm-oil, the latter becoming of importance, however, only with the decline of the slave trade in the nineteenth century. Since slaves were enemies taken captive in war or criminals condemned by law, they constituted a menace to domestic security and it was inconceivable that they should be permitted to move throughout the country without adequate safeguards. As the king protested to Governor Abson, should these enemies be left free "to cut the throats of my subjects?" Slaves were elite goods, moreover, and their movements were restricted on this account as well. In principle all slaves belonged to the king, as was the case with all property in Dahomey, and the king's subjects held slaves only by his leave. To own slaves was a privilege limited to persons of rank and to trade in slaves was a prerogative of status, "licence to trade" being in effect contingent upon receiving an endowment in slaves from the hand of the king. As elite goods, slaves carried high political significance. Dahomey paid tribute in slaves to the king of Oyo, and slaves were frequently presented by the king of Dahomey to visiting foreign emissaries as a matter of diplomatic etiquette, as well as to the nobles of his own court.

From start to finish, then, the handling of slaves was an operation subject to meticulous controls and one from which outsiders were completely barred. Slaves were "collected" in war, obviously an operation at the highest levels of state in which strangers had no part. Or, if slaves were "collected" by purchase from inland merchants, they passed at once into Dahoman custody, as we have seen. All dispositions or transfers of slaves were matters of public record. The captives taken in war were ceremonially presented to the king at the Annual Customs, a count being kept in cowries of the number of captives thus presented, and thereafter the king might have a ceremonial award of some of the captives to the nobles of his court or to soldiers who distinguished themselves in combat. Such awards were acts of state and immediately publicized. A witness who was present when the Dahoman army returned from a campaign with prisoners of war reports that:

"As soon as any person had a Slave presented to them, a proper Officer made Proclamation of it, which was immediately echoed by the Populace, who were waiting in great numbers at the King's Gate for the Sacrifices."[50]

The slaves received as gifts from the king's hand could be disposed of thereafter by the owners only with the royal permission. While the caboceers who led their own armies into the field were entitled to keep the captives taken by their soldiers, "the cabceers always pay a nominal duty upon all slaves taken in war when sold."[51] Such a tax must have served as a device for keeping record as well as a source of revenue for the king.

When the slaves were turned over to the Europeans at Whydah, the transfer was subject to rigorous supervision. The confinement of the Europeans to Whydah made it easier to exercise control since all transactions between natives and Europeans could take place only in the authorized trading places in the European quarters where full publicity attended transactions and a close watch was kept on the handling of goods. Here is how the slaves passed from native hands to European hands:

"When these slaves come to Fida, they are put in Prison all together, and when we treat concerning buying them, they are all brought out together in a large Plain; . . . When we have agreed with the Owners of the Slaves, they are returned to their Prison; where from that time forwards they are kept at our charge. . . . So that to save Charges we send them on Board our Ships with the very first Opportunity."[52]

Procedures had changed somewhat a hundred years later but the safeguards were no less rigorous:

"Les courtiers, vont tous les matins par toute la ville, demander à chaque negociant, s'il lui est arrivé des esclaves. Ils le font savoir au facteur qui va avec eux, la measure à la main, dans la maison de ces negocians noirs, voi les esclaves, & s'ils lui conviennent, il les achète, donne une specification des marchandises d'échange dont ils sont convenus, & imprime sa marque à feu sur le corps des esclaves. Ceux-ci, s'ils ne sont point esclaves du roi, sont transporté dès le soir même au fort ou dans la factorie; mais si ce sont des Nègres du roi, il doivent demeurer chez le marchand, jusqu'à ce qu'ils puissent être transportés de suite à bord."[53]

With trading carried on only at these specified places of trade and under official scrutiny, it is clear that any private "street-corner" dealings were out of the question.

As for imports, they were similarly affected with a public interest. Goods imported were for the most part war material or elite goods which circulated only among the dignitaries of the kingdom. Foreign cloth, umbrellas, shoes, and other imported goods were regarded as attributes of status; special safeguards surrounded dealings in such goods and sumptuary laws banned their possession by the common people. Guns, powder, iron, and coral could not be sold except to the king or his officials, and the king forbade the transit of firearms through his kingdom, in order to prevent war material from falling into the hands of his enemies. That coral should be included in this list seems at first glance strange, but coral was treasure, and clearly a "security" item since it was demanded of Dahomey as tribute by the neighboring kings of Oyo. Dalzel relates an incident involving a woman trader at Whydah, by the name of Paussie, who had sold coral illicitly to the French traders.[54] This action precipitated a diplomatic crisis. When word of this reached the King of Oyo, he lodged official protest with the king of Dahomey, accusing Dahomey of deception in withholding the customary tribute of coral on the false plea that no ships had brought coral to Whydah recently. The woman Paussie, was seized by the king's messengers and taken to Abomey for punishment as a traitor, her residence in Whydah leveled to the ground and all her possessions confiscated by the king.

As in collecting slaves for export, so in distributing imported goods, foreigners were completely excluded. Imported cloth, rum, and cowries were distributed to the people from the hand of the king himself at the Annual Customs, and high-ranking dignitaries of the kingdom made similar distributions to their retainers on ceremonial occasions. Small quantities of imported goods were also made available to the general population in local markets throughout the country. The right to dispose of European goods on local markets was awarded by the king as a monopoly privilege to certain of his officials. This interesting arrangement was observed at first hand by Duncan, who was the only European ever allowed to penetrate through Dahomey and to the border countries beyond. He has left us descriptions of the trading arrangements in the various villages at which he stopped. At each town, he observed there were customs houses "for collecting the duties upon all goods carried through it, from whatever part they come." Moreover:

"The customs are bestowed by the king as rewards of conquest upon his caboceers . . . ; when a war takes place, and the Dahomans prove victorious, the town taken is considered as belonging to the minister or caboceer whose soldiers capture the town; or rather, his right of monopolizing the trade of the town is established, so far as to supply it himself with all goods of British manufacture or produce, with the exception of such traders as have obtained permits, as a proof of their having paid the duty. The trade is entrusted to the most confidential or head men belonging to the caboceer owning the trade. . . . The King also imposes on each caboceer a slight duty, according to the amount of their trade."[55]

Dahomey's vital interests were thus protected by an organization of internal and external trade which lodged control exclusively in Dahoman hands. In establishing an autonomous organization for trade, Dahomey made certain of isolating the foreign trader and securing the inviolability of the internal community. Without such an organization, surrender to the foreigner would have been inevitable.

The dilemma of war and trade was also resolved—at least to the degree permitted by the inherent limitations of the situation—by a drastic institutional separation of the trading organization and the military organization. By this administrative technique, Dahomey succeeded in severing trade affairs from military affairs and assuring the neutrality of the port of trade. The traders formed a separate class of officials, completely distinct in personnel and function from the military. The Akhi'sino, or "great traders," ranked fourth in the Dahoman hierarchy, just below the Ahwan-gan, or military officials, and thus set apart from them. Of these "great traders," Burton remarks, scornfully as usual, that they "certainly lead a more useful life than the Ahwangan, or military class, which will do nothing but eat and drink, dance, make war, and attend Customs."[56] Whatever one's opinion of the usefulness of the military—and the Dahomans certainly held a more balanced view than Burton's—it is evident from this account that the warriors of the kingdom washed their hands of trade, while the traders had nothing to do with military affairs. The Viceroy of Whydah never went to war, since he was expected to concern himself exclusively with the affairs of trade at Whydah, but the sub-Viceroy represented him at all military campaigns. Similarly at Benin, Barbot reports, the trade officials "are forbid under heavy mulots, or bodily punishment, to intermeddle in any manner of affairs relating to war."[57] Thus Whydah could live at peace, her trading organization intact, and her residents unmolested by the wars which took place at a safe distance inland, while Dahomey was free to manage her military affairs without intervention from the traders, whether European or Dahoman.

NOTES*

1. This and the following chapter result from research carried on under the auspices of the Council for Research in the Social Sciences, Columbia University, 1948–1952.
2. Compare the intimate picture of Dahoman culture in Professor Herskovits' classic, on which we have been leaning heavily.
3. Bovill, p. 254.
4. Duncan, II, 11–12.
5. Snelgrave, granted an audience with the King of Dahomey immediately after his armies had taken Whydah, met with a royal official by the name of Zunglar, "a cunning Fellow, who had formerly been the King's Agent for several Years at Whidaw; where I had seen him in my former Voyages." (61)
6. Norris, XIII–XIV.
7. Herskovits, I, 109.
8. *Ibid.*, I, 17.
9. Norris, X.
10. Snelgrave, pp. 5–6.
11. Atkins, p. 120.
12. Snelgrave, p. 64.
13. *Ibid.*, pp. 58–59.
14. Dalzel, p. 207.
15. *Ibid.*, p. 196.
16. See chapter IV [of *Trade and Market in the Early Empires*].
17. Duncan, II, 268–69.
18. *Ibid.*, 269–70.
19. *Ibid.*, 269–70.

*See Bibliography on p. 131.

20. *Ibid.*, 270–71.
21. Burton, II, 361.
22. The dominance of the import interest required such a practice (Arist. Pol., Bk. VI).
23. Snelgrave, pp. 130 and 136.
24. Barbot, p. 261.
25. The Whydasians had, after the conquest by Dahomey the status of metics in the Dahoman empire. Cf. on this problem *Arist. Pol.*, 1327a 11.
26. Norris, p. 135.
27. Snelgrave, pp. 2–3.
28. Isert, pp. 134–35.
29. Barbot, p. 428.
30. Trading peoples' traditional policy is to be at peace with all.
31. Barbot, p. 326.
32. Burton, I, 64–65.
33. Duncan, I, 198.
34. Burton, I, 64.
35. Forbes, I, 111.
36. Dalzel, pp. 228–29, and 58.
37. Snelgrave, p. 60 ff.
38. Duncan, II, 276.
39. Norris, p. 40 ff.
40. Barbot, p. 326.
41. Forbes, I, 110–1.
42. Barbot, p. 351.
43. *Ibid.*, p. 186.
44. Duncan, I, 110–12.
45. Forbes, II, 3.
46. Burton, II, 265–66.
47. Snelgrave, p. 130.
48. Norris, p. 138.
49. Dalzel, p. 213 ff.
50. Snelgrave, p. 39.
51. Duncan II, 263–64.
52. Bosman, p. 363 ff.
53. Isert, p. 136.
54. Dalzel, p. 208 ff.
55. Duncan, I, 282–83.
56. Burton, I, 226.
57. Barbot, p. 360.

7 FROM   *Rosemary Arnold*
Separation of Trade and Market: Great Market of Whydah

ZOBEME, THE NATIVE MARKET

One of the showplaces of Whydah was the Zobeme or Great Market. "The lions of Whydah are the snake fetish house and the market," Forbes remarks. The market, he adds, is the finest he has seen in Africa.[1]

As the reader may have noted in the previous chapter, we had no need to refer to markets in order to explain the conduct of trade. From start to finish, the trading operation is an affair of state, administered from the palace, and conducted by the dignitaries of the land under terms of treaty. The presence or absence of markets makes no difference to the trading operations described there. That a market exists in the port of trade itself is, then, striking confirmation of the independence of trade from market.

But what needs does this market serve in the port of trade? Whose needs does it serve? And how is it set apart from trade?

A composite picture of the Great Market at Whydah can be drawn from several authors.

Southwest of the Boa temple is the Zobeme, or market place. It covers an area of about fourteen acres, and is divided into several principal sections by cross streets. Each section is exclusively appointed to the sale of one class of articles, such as pottery, hardware, fetish charms, oil, and so forth. The meat, fish, corn, flour, vegetable, fruit, and foreign goods all have separate markets.

SOURCE. "Separation of Trade and Market: Great Market of Whydah" by Rosemary Arnold. Reprinted with permission of The Macmillan Company from *Trade and Market in the Early Empires: Economics in History and Theory* edited by Karl Polanyi, Conrad M. Arensberg and Harry W. Pearson. © by The Free Press, A Corporation, 1957, pp. 177–188.

The market shops are low booths, about ten feet by six, raised upon banks of clay, beaten hard, and are thatched with palm leaves, and the floor is usually smeared with cow dung. Each shop stands upon its own "islet," as they may be called, for in the rain the footpaths are not infrequently six inches deep in water. The vendor squats at the side of her booth, a black clay pipe stuck between her lips, sometimes a babe at her breast. The medium of exchange is the cowrie, although large purchases may be paid for in coin.

The market is held daily. It is well supplied with every article of native consumption and many articles of European manufacture.

Primarily it is a food market for the sale of cooked victuals. Half the shops contain either raw or cooked provisions, Burton says, and many a "working man" breakfasts and dines in the alley, or quenches his thirst at the "gin palace" where liquor is dispensed.

Numerous huts were devoted to the sale of cooked provisions, such as eggs, fried fish from the lagoons, smoked shrimps, baked ground nuts, yams, sweet potatoes. Others were vendors of ready-cooked meats. These generally affected a conical extinguisher shaped hut, and squatted on a low stool behind a circular table, with a broad rim and a depression in the centre. Set out to the best advantage on the rim were joints of roast and boiled pork, goat, fowls, ducks, etc. Of these for two cowries about a mouthful could be purchased, the butcher dexterously carving Vauxhall slices from the joint; slapping the morsel on a plantain leaf, he sprinkled some pounded chillies upon it, and handed it to the customer with all the airs of a London stall-keeper.

Marketing is in full sway about 4 P.M., when a scene that baffles description is to be witnessed. Swarms of people, especially women, meet to buy and sell. Here an old beldame, with shrivelled breasts hanging down to her waist, will be haggling with a child four years old for a farthing's-worth of fetish. It is a curious contrast, the placidity and the impassiveness with which the seller, hardly taking the trouble to remove her pipe, drawls out the price of her two-cowrie lots, and the noisy excitement of the buyers, who know that they must purchase and pay the demand.

Such was the Great Market of Whydah. Certainly nothing

could be more remote from the world of trade than this bustling market scene. Here is not a place of audience with kings, but a meeting place for the multitude. Not slaves, gold, ivory, and fine cloth are on display here, but the joints of meat smoking on the butcher's tables, the farthing's-worth of fetish, or the two-cowrie mouthfuls dished up on a plantain leaf. Not the careful etiquette of court, the studied exchange of gifts, the diplomatic negotia-tion, but the merry confusion of a crowd enjoying the sport of berating the wares of the old beldames.

Craft products are there too, but mostly utility wares—pottery and hardware, and the poorer sorts of cloth. For the fine cloth —the umbrellas with appliqué designs, the ornaments of brass, gold, and silver—these are not for sale. The makers of these products serve the great houses of king and lords.

Foreign goods are in evidence, though not in such plenty as those the natives produce. Duncan lists the articles exposed for sale, and among them we can identify those which appear to be foreign goods, cotton cloth, native and English, he says, thread, beads, gun flints, flints and steel. This is a scanty array and the articles are all of a utilitarian character, sold in small quantities.

Two smaller markets, subsidiary to the Great Market, are found in other parts of the town. One of them is described by Skertchly as a small accessory of the Zobeme established for the convenience of the residents in the northwest of the town. Here groups of vendors, chiefly women, squabble in full chorus. The stock in trade of each person is but small, and in this market there are no booths, but each seller squats on a diminutive stool behind her collection. The principal wares are "raw or cooked provisions," beads, a few pieces of the commonest cotton cloth, water, and firewood. Provisions are cheap enough so that "suffi-cient food for a native's meal can be procured ready cooked for about three pence."[2]

These are markets "for the convenience of the residents," re-minding us, in modern terms, of the corner grocery or the all-night hamburger counter where one may pick up a late snack or the loaf of bread overlooked in the day's shopping. The foreign goods are missing here altogether. Foodstuffs, and the barest household necessities, water and firewood, are the stock in trade.

The market at Cape Corso affords much the same kind of picture. It is kept every day, except Tuesdays, Barbot says, in a large place at the end of the town, whither great numbers of all the neighboring people resort every morning very early, "with all sorts of goods and eatables the land affords: besides the European goods carried by us. They come thither by break of day, from five or six leagues around about, loaded like horses, with each of them, one, or more sorts of goods: as sugar-cane, bananas, figs, yams, lemons, oranges, rice, millet, Indian wheat, malaguette or Guinea pepper, bread, kankies, fowl, fish raw, boiled, roasted, and fried, palm-oil, eggs, . . . earthen-ware, beer . . . , wood for fuel, thatch for houses, tobacco of the growth of the country, etc. The Blacks of the coast also carry thither several sorts of European goods."

Here, as at Whydah, the market is primarily a goods market, supplying the townsfolk with provisions from the countryside. The vendors are mostly women, Barbot says, who are commonly employed to keep market, "being looked upon as fitter for it than the men. . . ." Here also there are "several sorts of European goods" brought to market by the "Blacks of the Coast."[3] Though Barbot speaks earlier in this passage of the European goods "carried by us," it is obvious from the context that the goods are carried to market by the Blacks, and that he uses the phrase to mean "carried by ship." But goods other than food seem to be of lesser importance. Barbot refers to "bartering with the market women, for garlick, pins, small looking-glasses, ribbands, flints and steels, and such like trifles."

Nowhere in this inventory of market goods—this should be noted—are the native export staples to be found. Slaves, gold, ivory, etc., are not up for sale in the market place. Palm-oil, to be sure, is sold in the market for household use, or ladled out to flavor a mouthful of cooked meat, but this is a far cry from the export trade in large quantities. Nor are there anywhere foreign goods exposed by white men (or, for that matter, by Blacks) otherwise than in small quantities, in retail.

Neither in the collection nor in the disposition of export staples does the market figure. Slaves are booty taken in war, or procured by trade with the native peoples of the continent. They move from the hands of the king and the war captains to the European traders without passing at any point through the market. It is inconceivable that a war lord of Dahomey should set up stall in the market place to dispose of his booty. Bosman reminds us of the safeguards observed in handling slaves. Speaking of the trade at Whydah, he says, "most of the Slaves that are offered to us are Prisoners of War, which are sold by the Victors as their Booty. When these Slaves come to Fida, they are put in Prison all together, and when we treat concerning buying them, they are all brought out together in a large Plain, where, by our Chirurgeons, . . . they are thoroughly examined. . . . The Invalides and the Maimed being thrown out, . . . the remainder are numbered, and it is entred who delivered them. In the mean while a burn-in Iron, with the Arms or Name of the Companies, lyes in the Fire; with which ours are marked on the Breast. This done that we may distinguish them from the Slaves of the English, French, or others; (which are also marked with their Mark) and to prevent the Negroes exchanging them for worse; at which they have a good Hand. . . . When we have agreed with the Owners of the Slaves, they are returned to their Prison; where from that time forwards they are kept at our charge. . . . So that to save Charges we send them on Board our Ships with the very first Opportunity. . . ."[4]

Nor does the European trader sit in the market place shouting his wares. Bosman, writing to his correspondent at home, takes care to disabuse him of any such notion. "I would not have you conceive," he says, "that we set up a Market with our Wares, or send any of them to be sold without our Forts: No, that is not our Business; but the Negroes come daily to our Castle, or Fort, with their Gold; for which, after it is weighed, essayed and purified, they receive our Commodities; none of which ever go out of our Ware-houses before they are paid for. . . ."[5] This passage refers to the gold trade at Elmina, the major settlement on the Gold Coast.

Export-import transactions, then, are conducted in separate places of trade completely removed from the market place. Trade negotiations with the authorities take place at court, in formal conversation, or in special places of audience. Disposition of goods is made at the European forts, and for those traders not attached to the chartered companies, in lodges appointed for their use by the authorities or on board ship.

How, then, do European goods reach the local market? Here, surely, is a crucial point of contact between trade and market. But nothing could more sharply emphasize the segregation of trade from market than the manner of appearance of trade goods on the local market in the port of trade itself. Since trade dealings between European and native are confined to the places of trade, and the European has access to the local market only as a purchaser of provisions and other necessaries, the distribution of imported goods within the country, whether through markets or otherwise, is entirely in native hands. At every point in the movement of goods throughout the interior, as likewise in the port of trade, the institutional separation of trade from market is safeguarded by administrative regulations and operational devices of an all-embracing character.

ADMINISTERED TRADE AND LOCAL FOOD DISTRIBUTION

At Whydah, the isolation of places of trade from market place is the basis for the administrative divisions of the town. Each of the European forts, with its surrounding native settlement, constitutes a separate town under administration. In Burton's time, there were four such European quarters: French Town, Brazilian Town, English Town, and Portuguese Town. The fifth section of Whydah, Zobeme or Market Town, taking its name from the Great Market, comprised the market and its environs. All of these separate quarters have their own governors, under the jurisdiction of the Viceroy of Whydah. While the governors of the European towns are usually of the respective European nationality, the caboceer of the Market Town is a native official.

These administrative divisions facilitate the regulation of trade. Access to trade at the European forts is permitted only to those natives authorized to trade. Since exports must be licensed, and an export duty paid by the seller, the royal officials who "exercise the refusal of all commerce" have the means to control dealings between natives and Europeans. Any indiscriminate traffic with the Europeans is out of the question. Infractions of the regulations by the Europeans brought immediate reprisal by the "closing of the roads" to the European fort, that is, the cutting off of trade with the fort in question.

This physical separation of trade and market emphasizes the difference in function. Trade stocks the palace, the army, and the houses of the great. The market caters to the common wants of the population. The great ones of the lands have no need to resort to the market place for their provisions. Their tables are supplied from their own plantations, and their cloth and military stores from the warehouses of the Europeans in return for slaves.

The market is for the common folk and, in the port of trade, also for the foreigner. It is the "working man" taking his breakfast and dinner "in the alley," or the women selling in the market place, who have need of the piece of firewood or the two-cowrie mouthful of cooked meat. The resident native population of Whydah, belonging to one or the other of the European forts and subject to labor service for their masters, are "hired out" in menial capacities to the traders and receive "subsistence," partly in kind and partly in cowries, with which they can feed themselves in the market.

There is also the large floating population of a port town to be supplied with food and necessaries, men with no hearth or kin to care for them in Whydah: canoemen and carriers from other points on the coast, temporarily beached in Whydah; fishermen from the rivers and lagoons; and, after Britain's abolition of the slave trade, the liberated slaves dumped in Sierra Leone and finding their way back by stages to their native countries.

The Europeans may also rely upon the market. Barbot says of the market at Cape Corso that "not only the neighboring inhabitants, but also the crews of European ships riding in the road are plentifully supplied with many necessaries and refreshments." Ships captains whose provisions are running low may stock up for the return voyage by purchasing grain, fresh vegetables, and casava for the slave cargo taken on board at the coast. In principle, provisions in wholesale quantities are provided by treaty arrangement, as is seen, for instance, at Great Bandy, and watering and wooding privileges for ships are almost always a matter of treaty. Anyway, the resident European traders have less need to resort to the market since their forts are provisioned from overseas, and gifts for their table from the Viceroy of Whydah are liberal, or were in earlier times. Fresh foods, however, are purchased in the market, and the lower ranks of the garrisons receive "board wages" with which they purchase food and necessaries in the local market, or from the warehouses of the company.

The social distance between trade and market can be measured by the difference in status between those who engage in trade and those who go to market. The vendors in the market place are women. But trade, like war, is the affair of men, and more particularly "the business of kings, rich men, and prime merchants, exclusive of the inferior sort of Blacks," as Barbot says. Only women go to market "loaded like horses" with the produce of the countryside, or the makers of common wares such as hoes and iron utensils, or slaves who traffic for their masters.

Trade and market are administered by separate bodies of officials. Among the officials appointed by the king of Whydah, Bosman records, there were the Captains, "of which there are a great number; and each of these hath a particular Character: He to whom the care of the Market is entrusted, is Captain of the Market; by the same rule another is Captain of the Slaves, a third of the Tronks or Prisons, another of the Shoar." And yet another is "the Captain to whom the European Affairs were all entrusted." There was no break with this tradition under Dahoman rule. Snelgrave, upon his first meeting with the king of Dahomey, reports that the king had in his entrourage one "Allegee, the English Cabocier . . . that is, the Person appointed to trade with them in particular," as well as other "great men" for each of the "different Nations." In a later period, according to Forbes, "The cha-cha is the principal agent to the king in all matters of trade; and to him must be subjected all commerce, whether in *slaves* or *palm-oil,* that he may have the refusal. The price is laid down by law, subject to his alteration if concurred in by the viceroy and six traders or superintendents of trade appointed by the king. . . . One or the other of these must be present at all sales to take the royal duty. . . ."

Slaves—or palm-oil! This, and nothing else, is trade. All other produce of the country goes through the market.

The market, on the other hand, is under the watchful eye of its own officials. "The market is presided over by an officer," Skertchly reports of the Great Market at Whydah, "who expects a toll from every vendor, and the safety of the articles exposed for sale, is guarded by the native police."[6] For every market throughout the country, the king appoints a market chief and a corps of assistants to keep order in the market and enforce the regulations. In addition, associations of vendors and craftsmen exercise jurisdiction over each separate quarter of the market. Skertchly tells us of the Whydah market that "each section is exclusively appointed for the sale of one class of articles"; and Forbes reports that "The meat, fish, corn, flour, vegetable, fruit, and foreign goods have all separate markets." Thus the sale of foreign goods, as well as native produce, is allocated a definite place in the market and becomes subject to the supervision of the association of vendors and of the market officials. These physical arrangements in the market place obviously assure full publicity for all transactions and facilitate the enforcement of regulations.

There is no unregulated buying and selling. There are no shops in Whydah, Forbes says, so that all such transactions must take place in the market. This is undoubtedly a normative regulation. By restricting sales to the market place, the legality of transactions is assured.

Similar arrangements obtain in the market at Cape Corso, according to Barbot. "It is rare to hear of any quarrels or disorder committed," he says, "by reason of the good government of the Caboceiros, or magistrates, during the market." And, as at Whydah, "This place is so disposed, and the rules prescrib'd for the more orderly keeping of the market so religiously observ'd, that all who are of one trade, or sell the same sort of things, sit in good order together."[7]

Access to the market is no less strictly controlled. Toll-houses are located at the entrances to Whydah, as to every market town throughout the kingdom. The collection of tolls on all persons carrying goods serves not only as a revenue measure but as a device to ensure control of entry into the market.

Most remarkable of all the devices and regulations which maintain the separation of trade and market is the dual market, one outside the town and one inside the town. These inner and outer markets are the usual arrangement throughout the interior of Dahomey.

The segregation of trade and market is a general feature of the port of trade organization. Measures similar to those at Whydah are reported for the kingdom of Benin. "There are four principal places where the Europeans trade," Barbot says of Benin. These "places of trade," though located inland, are ports of trade in the institutional sense. They are isolated from the capital of the kingdom which is out of bounds to foreigners. Barbot says that the inhabitants of the capital "must be all natives of the country, for no foreigners are allow'd to settle there."

In the ports of trade, lodges are set aside for the use of the European traders. At all these places, the merchants and brokers, called mercadors and veadors, are appointed by the government of Benin to deal with the Europeans. "None but the Veadors or brokers can deal with us, and even the greatest person of the nation dare not enter the Europeans factories or lodges, under severe fines." The Europeans, then, have no contact with the native population except through the brokers appointed by the king. The markets at which European goods are sold to the native population are out of bounds to the European traders. Barbot makes this situation quite clear. "Besides the above-mentioned trading places," he says, "which are properly for dealing with Europeans, the king of Benin has appointed publick markets in many provinces of his kingdom, for the subject to trade together, every three days in the week; they have one at Gotton, to which they bring . . . abundance of Benin cloths, . . . with all the various species of European goods, usually imported into this country, bought of the Whites at Arebo, by the Veadors and brokers." Arebo and Gotton are two of the "above-mentioned trading places which are properly for dealing with Europeans." At Gotton, a port of trade, there is also a "publick market," a situation closely analogous to Whydah. But these markets are only for "the subjects to trade together," and European imports reach these markets only through the hands of the brokers appointed to deal with European traders.

Trade with the native peoples further inland is not permitted to the Europeans but is reserved to the subjects of Benin. "They have also at certain times of the year," Barbot explains, "publick markets or fairs appointed, and kept in large open plains . . . near the high-way; to which a great number of people resort from all the neighbouring places, to buy and sell goods." These fairs are not for the Benin people only, as were the markets mentioned above, but for the peoples of "all the neighbouring places," and these fairs are held only at certain times of the year instead of every three days in the week. These fairs have other special features. "It is a custom there," Barbot continues, "for the king to send his proper officers to the said markets to keep the peace and good order amongst the people that come to it, appointing every merchant a proper place, according to the nature of the goods he deals in, etc., for the reason, during the market-time, the ordinary justices of the place have no manner of authority; but it is vested for that time only in the court-officers."

These inland fairs resemble, therefore, the port of trade. As in the port of trade, safeguards are set up in dealing with strangers and guarantees of neutrality are provided by political authority. The intent is clearly to regulate transactions with foreigners, whether these be Europeans from overseas, or native peoples from inland countries.

The separation of trade and market is the transcending principle in regard to either.

NOTES

1. Forbes, I, 108.
2. Skertchly, p. 27.
3. Barbot, pp. 268–69.
4. Bosman, pp. 363 ff.
5. *Ibid.,* p. 91.
6. Skertchly, p. 59.
7. Barbot, p. 269.

BIBLIOGRAPHY TO SELECTIONS 6 AND 7

Atkins, John, *A Voyage to Guinea*, London, 1735.

Barbot, John A., *A Description of the Coasts of North and South Guinea*, London, 1732.

Bosman, William, *A New and Accurate Description of the Coast of Guinea*, London, 1705.

Bovill, E. W., *Caravans of the Old Sahara*, Oxford, 1933.

Burton, Richard F., *A Mission to Gelele, King of Dahomey*, London, 1864.

Dalzel, Archibald, *The History of Dahomey*, London, 1793.

Duncan, John, *Travels in Western Africa*, London, 1847.

Forbes, Frederick E., *Dahomey and the Dahomans*, London, 1851.

Herskovits, Melville J., *Dahomey, an Ancient West African Kingdom*, New York, 1938.

Insert, Paul E., *Voyages en Guinée et dans les îles Caraibes en Amerique* Paris, 1793.

McLeod, John, *A Voyage to Africa*, London, 1820.

Nadel, S. F., *A Black Byzantium*, Oxford, 1942.

Norris, Robert, *Memoirs of the Reign of Bossa Ahadee, King of Dahomey*, London, 1789.

Skertchly, J. A., *Dahomey As It Is*, London, 1874.

Snelgrave, William, *A New Account of Some Parts of Guinea*, London, 1734.

Notes on Sources

The works listed above are the major sources for the internal economy.

We have relied heavily upon Herskovits. While Herskovits' direct observations were made in the modern period, his account of economic administration under the kings (including accounts of the Census, Taxation, Operational Devices) was obtained from informants who had lived under the monarchy. Wherever possible, this information has been checked against earlier observations.

8 FROM   *Basil Davidson*
                      The Vital Contrast

In their impact on Africa, threre was . . . a tremendous difference between the Atlantic Ocean trade and that of the Indian
Ocean in medieval times: contraction of wealth in the first and
expansion in the second. One clear pointer to the reason for this
difference will be found in the different nature of the two commercial systems.

The Indian Ocean trade was never slave-ridden in ancient or
medieval times. This is not, admittedly, the standard opinion of
European textbooks. There, as Freeman-Greenville has lately
pointed out in contesting it, "the main theme is that the slave
trade was the principal occupation of the coast until the British
asserted their hegemony" at the end of the nineteenth century.
But the evidence will not support this view.

True, there was oversea slaving on these coasts from the earliest times. Old Egypt took slaves from the land of Punt; and Punt
was probably the Horn of Africa, Somalia of today. Arabia did
the same. Negro slaves were known in Parthia and Persia. So
many had reached the northern Arab lands by the ninth century
that furious slave revolts are traditionally said to have cost the
lives of as many as half a million slaves. Many East African captives were taken to India. Others were carried as far as China.

A Chinese document of A.D. 1178, evidently referring to Madagascar, says that "there is an island in the sea on which there
are many savages. Their bodies are black and they have frizzled
hair. They are enticed by food and then captured" and sold "as
slaves to the Arab countries, where they fetch a very high price.
They are employed as gatekeepers, and it is said that they have
no longing for their kinsfolk." Thus may one see how the legend
of "African inferiority" was no monopoly of the West. In the

SOURCE. Copyright © 1961 by Basil Davidson. "The Vital Contrast," by
Basil Davidson from *Black Mother: The Years of the African Slave Trade*
(Boston: Little, Brown, 1961), pp. 179–185, 278–282.

East the slaves from Africa (for they came from the mainland as well as Madagascar) were said "to have no longing for home"; in the West they would be found "docile and therefore fit to be enslaved."

Slaves for the civilizations of the East came of course from all the borders of the Indian Ocean and not merely from East Africa. They were regularly imported into China, for example, over a long period. The same Chinese report of 1178 says that both male and female slaves were bought, "and the ships carry human beings as cargo." A Chinese inspector of maritime customs, writing fifty years later, notes that a slave boy was priced at three taels of gold or their equivalent in aromatic wood. He says that slaves were used during voyages for stopping leaks in the hull, even though they had to go outboard and under the waves as well. Many of these luckless victims must have come from Africa.

But there is nothing to show that slaving ever overwhelmed this eastern trade or became more than a secondary item of commerce. The available evidence, slight though it is, goes all the other way. "Slaves of the better sort" could be purchased, according to the *Periplus of the Erythraean Sea* in the first century A.D., at Opone; but Opone was Ras Hafun, almost the far northern extremity of the Horn of Africa. For the ports of East Africa to the south of Ras Hafun there is no mention of slaving in the *Periplus.* Nor is there much mention of it by the medieval Arab writers, and in no single case do these writers place any emphasis on East African slaving. On the contrary, they speak of the importance of East Africa as a provider of ivory and gold and other raw materials.

Sofala, for El Mas'udi, who wrote in the tenth century, was the land of gold. He mentions ivory as a principal export from "the land of the Zanj," the Negroes of East Africa. This ivory was taken to India and China by way of Oman in southern Arabia, and "were this not the case, there would be an abundance of ivory in the Muslim countries." For Edrisi, two centuries later, iron was the most valued export of the East African coast. The iron of Sofala, he thought, was much superior to that of India, both in quantity and quality; and the Indians were accustomed to make from it the "best swords in the world." There is nowhere here any reference to an East African export trade in slaves. This does not mean, of course, that no slaves were sent abroad. But it certainly suggests that this part of commerce was an insignificant side line.

Evidence from the Swahili cities of the coast points the same way. The key trades of Kilwa in medieval times were undoubtedly the export of gold and ivory obtained from the states of the interior. Pate Island is said to have dealt in silver as well as ivory. Others are known to have exported, or collected for the export trade of their more important sister-settlements, a varied range of natural products: copal, ambergris, tortoise shell, copra, coconut oil, and mangroves. All this was the body of Swahili trade and the core of its prosperity.

One can reach the same conclusion from the other end. Where in the East were the vast plantations and many mines that required great armies of slave labor? They simply did not exist, just as they did not exist in the West until the crossing of the Atlantic. Where, again, can one find massive African minorities in the East that are comparable to the African minorities of America? They, too, do not exist. The notion that the old trades of the Indian Ocean dealt in slaves on the same scale as the later Atlantic trade is a pure illusion, the product of an uneasy European conscience and the fact of large-scale Arab slaving in the nineteenth century. What really occurred here was slaving on the same persistent but small scale as between many of the states of the medieval world—a miserable but secondary trade, rarely important in the general balance of wealth and enterprise.

The contrast with the Atlantic seaboard is very sharp. A thousand years of Indian Ocean contact, with slaving never of importance, could raise the peoples of the eastern seaboard to full membership in the family of eastern civilization, and send its fructifying influence far into the hinterland. But less than half a thousand years of Atlantic Ocean contact, with slaving of the highest importance, would reduce the peoples of the western seaboard to a condition of inferiority that even now weighs heavy on the conscience of the world.

These cities of the eastern coast vanished or dwindled through no fault of their own. They were ravaged by the Portuguese.

Loot was the key to the discoverers' ambition. Reflecting on da Gama's voyage of discovery, the king of Portugal wrote to the ambassador of Venice, then the most powerful city of the Mediterranean, that it would now profit Venetian galleys to come to Lisbon for their cargoes of goods from the East, instead of going to Alexandria. To his cousins of Castile, however, he was a little more forthcoming. Giving them news of da Gama's exploits, he explained that "we hope, with the help of God, that the great trade which now enriches the Moors of those parts"—that is, the Swahili Muslims and their oversea partners—"through whose hands it passes without the intervention of other persons or peoples, shall, in consequence of our dispositions, be diverted to the natives and ships of our own kingdom."

He took his dispositions without delay. Fleet after fleet was dispatched to the East, one almost every year for many years to come. Their orders were to seize the Indian Ocean trade, reduce the coastal cities to vassal status, exact tribute from them in gold, and establish Portuguese hegemony. They met with resistance. But the coastal cities, although they too believed that God was on their side, lacked cannon. And the cannon of the Portuguese, together with a ruthlessness and piratical determination never before witnessed in these seas, easily carried the day. Enmity and the threat of violence appeared with the earliest landfalls of da Gama. After 1501, by which time the Portuguese had taken the measure of their intended victims, there followed ten years of bloody invasion and assault. Kilwa, Mombasa, Zanzibar, Brava, and other cities were battered or bullied into submission.

Here and there, as in the Congo, the Portuguese were helped by calls for help from one African ruler against another. This led to the downfall, for example, of the lord of the Kerimba Islands, a long archipelago lying off the coast of northern Mozambique. In 1522 the Portuguese on Mozambique Island, then their principal base on the East Coast, were approached by envoys from Zanzibar and Pemba, far to the north. These envoys explained that their rulers had formerly paid tribute to the lords of the Kerimba Islands, but now that Pemba and Zanzibar had to pay tribute to the Portuguese they had stopped paying it to the Kerimbas. This had involved them in war with the Kerimbas, and they now asked for Portuguese protection. Another Portuguese version, written somewhat earlier and possibly nearer the truth, offers a different explanation but confirms the picture of a closely woven system of political and economic power up and down this long coast. According to this second version, the Kerimba Islands had once been subject to Zanzibar and Pemba but had lately transferred their allegiance to Mombasa.

Whatever the truth of the matter, settlers and soldiers on the island of Mozambique saw a golden opportunity in this appeal for aid and alliance. Eighty of them embarked without delay in two *zambucos*—large lateen-rigged coastal vessels—together with "a skiff and a ship's boat." After sailing and rowing for five days, they landed on the principal island of the Kerimbas, overcame its ruler and his troops (he turned out to be a nephew of the lord of Mombasa), and took a vast spoil reckoned at 200,000 cruzados. Whether exaggerated in the records or not, this booty is fairly conclusive proof of wealthy settlements on the Kerimbas during medieval times. We may learn more of these settlements when archeology at last finds time and money to make even a preliminary survey there.[1]

Within fifty or sixty years of frenzied onslaught on the accumulated wealth of centuries, the Portuguese effort had almost spent itself. Spread-eagled across the world, imperial Portugal lay dying, not from lack of courage or ambition, but from a shortage of men and from an even graver incapacity to move with the times and learn new ways. The Dutch overhauled them. The French and English elbowed them aside. Here and there along the coast they continued to enjoy supreme power; here and there they pushed bravely into the lands behind the coast. But the world soon passed them by. And the cities of the coast, still enduring though often sorely harassed, inescapably shared this decline.

• • •

[1] Research on the Kerimbas would surely throw new light on the broad-ranging scope of the Indian Ocean trade. A British naval survey of 1823—carried out to sailing-ship requirements—found that the Kerimbas had excellent harbors affording "perfect security in the heaviest gales." These sheltered harbors must have been greatly used in previous times.

In spite of an undoubted improvement in food supplies (for the new crops were soon in cultivation by many African peoples), there can be no doubt that on balance the economic effects of European contact worked steady and decisive damage.

After about 1650, with diminishing exceptions, African production-for-export became a monoculture in human beings. This can be seen to have suffocated economic growth in coastal and near-coastal Africa as surely as the extension of European production-for-export of consumer goods gave the maritime nations of Europe, at the same time, their long lead in economic development.

The reasons for this suffocation were various. It was obviously an impoverishment to send away the very men and women who would otherwise produce wealth at home. In exporting slaves, African states exported their own capital without any possible return in interest or in the enlargement of their economic system. Slave exports differed radically in this respect from the more or less forced emigration of improverished men and women from nineteenth century Europe. Thus the millions who left Britain in those years were able to enter the mainstream of capitalist expansion, and thereby benefit the mother-country in many indirect ways. But the African slaves could contribute nothing except to the wealth of their masters—a wealth that never returned to Africa. Dealers in Africa undoubtedly received payment for the slaves they sold; but the nature of the payment was strictly nonproductive. The very conditions of the exchange prevented the kind of capital accumulation that could have led to a more advanced economy. Such "capital" as the kings and prime merchants could accumulate was in mere baubles or the weapons of war. From an economic standpoint, in short, European slaving may be rightly regarded as a primitive and particularly destructive form of colonialism: the sale of consumer goods for the raw material of slave labor.

Wherever towns grew strong there was, true enough, a shift to cash economies and capitalist savings and investment. This happened in the great market centers of the Western Sudan, trading across the Sahara, and perhaps still more in the cities of the medieval East Coast that enjoyed contact with India and Arabia.

But these developments occurred only where slaving did not dominate the trade. With the partial exception of the delta partnership, the European connection was powerless to reproduce such results—precisely because it was above all a slaving connection.

In face of an ever more pervasive demand for slaves, local industries dwindled or collapsed. Where the only produce that was readily marketable was the producer himself (or herself), handicrafts and cottage industries could barely survive, let alone expand. Cheap European textiles drove out the excellent cloths of the Guinea Coast. Pereira had spoken of these as early as 1506, noting that the Portuguese purchased these cloths and carried them to Europe. Benin was especially famous for its textiles. Yet by 1850 these had fallen to minor importance, although the textile output of Kano in northern Nigeria (produced in an economic system that was far beyond any direct influence of the oversea slave trade, and where the overland slave trade never dominated commerce) flourished and grew at the same time. Dahomey textiles met the same fate as those of Benin, even though Governor Dalzell could write as late as 1789 that Dahomey still manufactured "very pretty and durable cloths of cotton. . . . Their dyes stand washing very well, especially the blues, which are inferior to none." It speaks much for the quality of this manufacture that it could survive at all in face of massive European sale of cheap Lancashire and Indian cottons.

These local industries declined while chiefs and merchants fattened on the slave trade. Yet here too there was no real expansion of the economic system. For this new trading wealth became increasingly a matter of individual prestige and display. Consider how the king of Bonny responded in 1826 to the offer of a bride by the king of Warri.

"King Pepple having repeatedly sent presents by his canoes to the King of Warri, with whose nation he carries on an immense trade . . . [and] the latter hearing of his amazing wealth and extensive connexions with the Europeans, offered him his eldest daughter in marriage. . . . So great and unexpected an offer was received by Pepple with the greatest exaltation, and to convince his intended ally how deeply he appreciated the distinguished favour he had conferred upon him, he loaded canoe after canoe with rare and most valuable treasures: English, French, Spanish and Portuguese merchandise were extracted from his warehouses—gold and silver plate—costly silks and exquisitely fine cloths—with embroidered laces and other articles too numerous to mention."

A glittering display of Pepple's wealth awaited the king of Warri when he eventually brought his daughter for the marriage ceremony. Pepple himself described the scene to a visiting European in graphic "pidgin" that loses nothing by being left in the original:

"That time I first hear, Warri's canoe come for creek, I fire one gun from my house—then all Bonny fire—plenty powder blow away you no can hear one man speak. I stand for my house —all my house have fine cloth. Roof, walls, all round, he hung with proper fine silks. No possible to look one stick, one mat: all be covered.

"My Queen Father stand for beach. His foot no touch ground. He stand on cloth. All way he walk, he walk for cloth. . . . I give Wine, Brandy, plenty punchoen—pass twenty. I give for my people and Warri's. All Bonny glad too much. . . . Every man, every woman, for my town, I give cloth—pass one thousand piece I give that day. Pass twenty barrel powder I fire that day."

There in a nutshell lay the truth about "capital accumulation" during the high days of the delta trade. Merchants who were also monarchs spent their wealth as traditional rulers must: to glorify their name and reputation and enlarge their power by winning allies from among their peers. The system was stable within its limits, but its limits stopped short of the economic growth that could have led to systematic investment. And the slave trade continually fortified those limits by enhancing the power of kings and prime merchants, while siphoning off those pressures of population or political dissent which had pressed, elsewhere, towards economic change and expansion.

After the ending of the slave trade, the powerful men of the delta went in for palm-oil production on a large plantation scale; Pepple, like Ja Ja, owed his wealth to oil exports rather than to slaving. Would this new form of production have developed rapidly into a West African capitalism? Perhaps. But it was never given the chance. Pressing on its heels, there followed colonial conquest; and the circumstances of invasion proved even more depressing to economic growth than the slave trade. These circumstances changed, yet even as late as the 1950's one may note that the many thriving merchants of West Africa had seldom developed into full-blown capitalists; more often than not, they remained trading middlemen who were content to sell African raw materials in exchange for non-African consumer imports. This was partly the reflection of subsistence economics persisting into modern times, but there is ground for thinking that it was also a consequence of the special trading systems of the past.

On the economic side, then, the slave trade exercised a serious and continuous effect in retarding and reducing African production. For this reason the European relationship generally failed to induce the social and cultural expansion that occurred among the trading cities of the "Saharan seaboard" or among those of the Indian Ocean littoral in pre-European times. The scale of this failure greatly varied. It was practically complete in the Congo and in East Africa. It was far from complete in some parts of Guinea. Yet even in Guinea the more favored areas paid a heavy price for their middleman prosperity in the social troubles that engulfed the lands behind them—and eventually themselves as well.

PART THREE

*New World Slavery in the
History of Capitalism*

Whatever slavery and the genesis of slave societies may have entailed, they constituted important elements in the rise and expansion of capitalism. The economic history of modern slavery is first and foremost a chapter in the economic history of a capitalist system that arose in Europe and conquered the world.

Eric J. Hobsbawm's essay on the sementeenth century is, at first glance, irrelevant to the question of slavery, but it constitutes a necessary starting point. The seventeenth century occupies decisive ground in the history of capitalism, and the colonial and plantation-slavery experiences must be related to the wider developments that Hobsbawm succinctly and impressively outlines.

Lewis Cecil Gray, an economist whose *History of Agriculture in the Southern United States to 1860* remains the indispensable introduction to the economic history of the Old South, lays out a now familiar and widely held thesis, which the historian Stuart Bruchey both supplements and implicitly criticizes. For Gray, the slave plantation constituted a specific form of capitalist enterprise within a worldwide capitalist system and, as such, represented an element in a particular stage of capitalist development. Eric Williams, a historian who later emerged as Prime Minister of Trinidad and Tobago, holds a similar view and relates the historical course of Caribbean slavery to the rise and fall of British mercantilism. Bruchey's essay, however, raises other questions and probes the role of slavery in strengthening and indeed creating impediments to capitalist development. C. L. R. James,

whose *Black Jacobins* ranks as a classic work of Marxian interpretation of a great revolution, agrees with Williams' viewpoint
in many respects but pushes it well beyond the economic level. It
remains a fair question whether or not, despite resemblances to
the work of Williams, his one-time protégé, James' work does
not in fact point in a fundamentally different direction.

The contribution of the young Marxist economist Jay R.
Mandle brings us back to the questions posed in Part One, but at
a much higher level of specificity. Mandle squarely faces the
contradictory nature of the plantation system as part of world
capitalist development and yet as a system in itself with powerful
tendencies antagonistic to that development. The possibilities inherent in his boldly innovative model remain to be developed,
but their exploration and testing ought to advance the discussion
significantly by forcing a confrontation with the contradictory
nature of the plantation experience.

E. J. Hobsbawm

The Seventeenth Century in the Development of Capitalism

It is now commonly admitted that there was, for several decades in the seventeenth century, a period of major economic and
social recession, crisis and secular readjustment, which contrasts
strikingly with the periods of economic expansion which preceded and followed it. Its effects were not confined to any single
country, but, with a few marginal exceptions, can be traced
throughout the entire range of the economic area dominated by
and from, western Europe, from the Americas to the China Seas;
nor were they confined to the economic field. The simultaneous
occurrence of revolutions or attempted revolutions in the middle
of the seventeenth century, in England, France, the Spanish Empire and the Ukraine have been plausibly connected with it.[1] In

SOURCE. Eric J. Hobsbawm, "The Seventeenth Century in the Development
of Capitalism," *Science & Society*, XXIV (Spring, 1960), pp. 97–112. Copyright
© 1960 by Science & Society.

[1] For the most convenient conspectus of the evidence for the "seventeenth
century crisis," *cf.* E. J. Hobsbawm, "The General Crisis of the European
Economy in the Seventeenth Century," *(Past & Present*, 4 and 5, 1954–1955).
For the possible relations between the crisis and the revolutions, "Seventeenth Century Revolutions" *(Past & Present*, 13, 1958) and H. R. Trevor-
Roper, "The General Crisis of the Seventeenth Century" *(Past & Present*, 16,
1959).

the present paper I want to consider the place of the seventeenth century crisis in the history of capitalist development, and especially in the genesis of the industrial revolution. This implies that the seventeenth century crisis was produced by the internal contradictions of the economy in which it occurred, and not by wholly extraneous factors. I have not space here to discuss this question at length, but it is possible briefly, and I think conclusively, to set aside the two principal "extraneous" explanations for the crisis which have been suggested. First, it cannot be put down to secular climatic changes. The suggestion has been specifically investigated and rejected.[2] Second, it cannot be ascribed to the effects of the Thirty Years' War, though nobody would wish to underestimate these. It is indeed tempting to make the Thirty Years' War responsible for the crisis, if only because its beginning coincides with the great collapse in the Baltic trade (the "slump of the 1620's") which initiates the crisis, and its end with the acute period of European revolutions.[3] However, a) at least one major component of the crisis, the collapse of the Spanish imperial economy in America, clearly begins some time before the Thirty Years' War and independently of it, and b) symptoms of the crisis are plainly visible in areas unaffected by the war. It is therefore legitimate to regard the wars as a complicating factor in the crisis rather than as a cause; except perhaps in its political aspect.

Two other possible objections to the following analysis may also be briefly dealt with before we go further. It has been argued that the present analysis pays too little attention to monetary factors, credit, movements of the price-level and other matters which, as experience has plainly shown, affect business decision.[4] Without arguing the case at length, I think it is rea-

[2] E. Le Roy Ladurie, "Histoire et Climat," (*Annales*, Janvier–Mars 1959) 31: "Inversement, la crise du xviie siècle, parfois présentée comme l'incidence humaine et historique du 'petit âge glaciaire," atteint en fait ses paroxysmes dans des périodes de rémission climatique."

[3] If, as is legitimate, we include the wars of the 1650's in the era of continuous European war which stretches from about 1620 to 1660, the coincidence becomes even more striking.

[4] *Cf.* F. Mauro, "Sur la crise du xviie siècle" (*Annales*, 1, 1959) 181–185; review of E. J. Hobsbawm, *loc. cit.* The Reviewer, perhaps not unjustly ascribes my suspicion of monetary etc. explanations to a "préjugé marxiste."

sonable, and in line with the general drift of economic theory on these matters, to regard such factors as secondary rather than primary in the long-term analysis of economic development, while in no sense denying their considerable importance in the short run. In any case, the general analysis here attempted can quite easily allow for a much greater autonomous effect of monetary factors (*e.g.*, the supply of American bullion, or the availability of suitable means of payment) than is here specifically considered. It may also be argued that autonomous movements of population are not allowed for in the study of a period when a fall, or at any rate a very considerable slowing down in population growth occurred, and clearly had important economic consequences. Here again it seems both more profitable, and more in line with the current trend of researches, to consider population not as an autonomous variable but as one dependent on the general movements of the economy in which it occurs. If the seventeenth century is one of widespread epidemics, it may well be argued that their capacity to kill people, if not their actual occurrence, depended on the economic and social factors which determined people's accessibility to infection and capacity to resist it. Poor men almost invariably die more frequently in epidemics than rich ones.

It is thus legitimate to regard the seventeenth century crisis as one generated by previous economic development. The problem facing us is how it fits into the economic evolution which, at the end of the eighteenth century, produced the industrial, agricultural and demographic revolutions which have ever since dominated the history of the world, or, in the current jargon phrase, the "take-off into self-sustained growth." There had been economic growth in previous ages. Indeed a tendency towards producing its conditions is fairly constant in the history of Europe from at least the tenth century onwards. But it will be accepted that everywhere and at all times before the end of the eighteenth century sooner or later this tendency came up against certain barriers and obstacles. The "feudal crisis" of the fourteenth and fifteenth centuries and the seventeenth century crisis are examples of what happened then: recession, relapse, breakdown, and within this setting, shifts and readjustments which eventually allowed the tendencies of growth to resume. The importance of the seventeenth century crisis is this. After it the barriers seem to have been permanently lifted. The march towards industrial revolution is no longer interrupted by secular breakdowns, though there are signs of certain difficulties of this kind in the eighteenth century. The world economy, as it were, taxis along the runway of its aerodrome, to become airborne in the 1780's. Since then, broadly speaking, it has been flying. Its internal difficulties and contradictions have been of a different kind.

I am not here concerned specifically with the reason why the economy took off into self-sustained growth. Theorists, starting with the classical economists and Marx, and in recent years once again, have analyzed under what conditions such growth becomes possible or inevitable, and every government planning economic development of its country acts on some such analysis, though only the socialist ones act effectively. The problem I am concerned with is how this happened under the peculiar historical conditions of Europe in the sixteenth to nineteenth centuries, *i.e.*, a) under conditions when nobody planned or knew enough to plan industrialization, and b) when the main dynamic force in the economy was private enterprise urged along by the motive to make and accumulate maximum profits. For the first (and therefore most difficult) industrial revolution, the initial breakthrough in world history, was achieved by and through capitalism, and could almost certainly, in seventeenth and eighteenth century conditions, not have been achieved in other ways, though today such other ways are available, and indeed preferable.[5] On the other hand we know that the actual process of the rise of industrial capitalism was a slow and tortuous process. It stretched over at least eight centuries—say from A.D. 1000 to A.D. 1800,

[5] Failure to observe that private enterprise industrialization must, by the nature of private enterprise, solve the technical problems of industrializing very differently from, say, socialist industrialization, makes W. W. Rostow's "The Stages of Economic Growth" largely useless. (*Cf. Economic History Review*, August 1959). Rostow's failure derives from a refusal—odd in a champion of private enterprise—to face the fact that entrepreneurs are in business for profit, or if they are not, will go bankrupt. It is understandable that businessmen like to pretend that their motives are more than just to make money, or that anti-Marxists should wish to deprive Marx of credit for everything, including his incidental demonstration of the historic achievements of capitalist enterprise in its early phases. But it makes for neither good history nor good economics.

and was interrupted by at least two major secular breakdowns, the fourteenth to fifteenth and the seventeenth century crises. That is to say, it included a number of demonstrably false starts.

This was natural, for private enterprise was and is blind. We know as a matter of fact that it did eventually produce industrial revolution, but that was not the object of entrepreneurs. Such men, acquisitive and anxious to accumulate the greatest profit, are not very rare—at any rate in Europe from the time of the crusades onward—nor is their behavior very recondite. It will advance economic development and industrial revolution if, and only if, greater profits are to be made by doing so than in other ways. If they are not, it will not. This simple and observable fact has created great difficulties for analysts, even though they (as usual with the shining exception of Marx) have not often been aware of their nature. Some have been tempted to assume that there are special kinds of entrepreneurs with a built-in tendency to innovate, as distinct from ordinary businessmen. (This seems to have been the position of Schumpeter). Others have assumed that industrialization comes about when entrepreneurs are combined with a "capitalist spirit" which produces the tendency to accumulate and innovate. (Calvinism has, since Max Weber, been most frequently cast for this role). Yet others prefer to make industrialization depend on the conjunction of entrepreneurs and some extraneously caused or unexplained "modern scientific attitude," as does Rostow. None of these explanations is either necessary or convincing. The Schumpeterian position is unconvincing because the argument is circular (the "right" kind of entrepreneur is always found and defined *ex post facto*). Moreover, it is quite clear that, say, the British industrial revolution was not made by specially innovating businessmen, but by businessmen who were no more and no less far-seeing, technologically progressive or original than any others. The Weberian position is unconvincing, because—within certain historical and institutional limits—ideology adapts itself to business as much as business follows ideology.[6] The reason why the (Catholic) finan-

---

[6] This is not to deny that some ideologies have shown themselves to be more favorable to capitalist enterprise than others—*e.g.* Calvinism than Catholicism—; or that, where the general social framework and ideology are highly hostile to capitalist enterprise, certain minority ideologies may be

ciers, merchants and manufacturers of fourteenth century Italy and Flanders failed to produce industrial revolution was not that they were not Calvinist. The Rostowian position, finally, is unconvincing, because the actual pioneer industrial revolution of the late eighteenth century depended hardly at all on any science and technology not already available by 1500. Technically speaking, it consisted above all of the application of a few simple empirical ideas well within the compass of intelligent working artisans.[7] This is no doubt a somewhat exaggerated statement, but it may stand. Modern science did not become *essential* to industrial development until the middle decades of the nineteenth century.

The difficulty which faces the analyst derives primarily from the fact that (as may still be observed in "underdeveloped" countries) in pre-capitalist economies the highest profits are rarely if ever found in business activities which advance economic development directly. What is needed for the preparation of industrial revolution is constant technological innovation and concentration on mass production, that is, on producing a constantly increasing range of goods turned out in constantly greater quantities at constantly cheaper prices, such as will create and maintain its own rhythm of economic expansion. What is needed is investment concentrating on those branches of production which will advance mass manufacture.[8] Thus, in the colonial en-

essential for the recruitment of a body of entrepreneurs. It is no accident that a disproportionately high number of Indian capitalists are Parsees or Jains. But in Western Europe—and notably in Italy and Germany—there was always a fair supply of potential entrepreneurs from the eleventh to twelfth century onwards.

[7] The one major exception to this generalization is the steam engine; but even this was a working proposition, though not yet a very efficient one, in France and England by 1700 or so; *i.e.*, several generations before the industrial revolution.

[8] *Cf*. Marx, *Capital*, Vol. III, (Berlin 1956 edn) 365, 369: "Der Weltmarkt bildet selbst die Basis dieser (d. kapitalistischen) Produktionsweise. . . . Sobald die Manufaktur einigermassen erstarkt, und noch mehr die grosse Industrie, schafft sie sich ihrerseits den Markt, erobert ihn durch ihre Waren. . . . Eine stets ausgedehntere Massenproduktion ueberschwemmt den vorhandenen Markt und arbeitet daher stets an Ausdehnung dieses Markts, an Durchbrechung seiner Schranken."

terprise of the sixteenth to eighteenth centuries, what was needed was not the spice trade, but sugar-plantations; for the pepper-merchant made and makes his money by cornering the scarce supply of a very expensive product and making a monopoly profit on each transaction, but the sugar-planter makes his money by producing increasing quantities of sugar at diminishing prices and thus by making a greater global profit out of a rapidly increasing market. What is needed, and for analogous reasons, is a cotton rather than a silk industry. In modern terms, what is needed is the technique of the makers of nylon stockings rather than that of Christian Dior. But this is a historians', or a planners' judgment. We cannot say that as a business enterprise Christian Dior is less desirable than the manufacture of standardized cheap textiles. (M. Boussac, who conducts both, expects to make good profits out of both). But under pre-capitalist conditions the Christian Dior type of enterprise would almost certainly have been *more* profitable, and therefore the natural tendency of private enterprise would have been to create it, rather than the nylon-type.

For in such societies the great bulk of the population, the peasantry, are virtually outside the range of the market, partly because they have and use very little money, partly because they live in a largely self-sufficient local or regional economy. The sections of the population which get their incomes in cash and habitually buy commodities with them—broadly speaking the townsmen—are small. The best markets are limited luxury markets. The biggest accumulations of wealth are in the hands of nobles or clergymen whose idea of how to spend or invest them—the latter mainly in different forms of building and decoration—happens not to be that best suited to economic progress. The fact that so large a proportion of the population is normally anchored to the land, makes the development of widespread or modern manufacture very difficult and sometimes imposes technical limits on it. In brief, we have a situation in which the intelligent entrepreneur will, if he has the choice, put his money first of all into finance or overseas trade, in which the biggest profits are to be made, second, into the production of relatively expensive goods for a relatively restricted market, and only lastly into mass production. There will thus be a marked tendency for all forms of capitalist enterprise to adjust themselves to life within what Marx called the pores of pre-capitalist society. Capital will therefore not create a capitalist mode of production and certainly not an industrial revolution, though undoubtedly contributing to disintegrate pre-capitalist modes of production.[9]

We are therefore faced with the paradox that capitalism can only develop in an economy which is already substantially capitalist, for in any which is not, the capitalist forces will tend to adapt themselves to the prevailing economy and society, and will therefore not be sufficiently revolutionary. But how then are the necessary conditions brought about?

In other words, the real problem of the seventeenth century is its outcome rather than its origin. I have elsewhere attempted to analyze its causes[10] and, while this analysis will no doubt be contested in detail by other students, it is safe to say that its general character will not. Any such analysis will have to demonstrate in one way or another how the barriers which the prevailing pre-capitalist economy imposed on economic development, prevented the economic expansion of the sixteenth century from reaching the point of "take-off into self-sustained growth," and most likely it will also show how the very process of economic expansion under such conditions produced the contradictions which generated the subsequent crisis.[11]

Thus we may point to the contradictions in East-West trade. The economic expansion of an urbanized sector in western Eu-

[9] Marx, who noted this effect clearly and discusses it fully, supposed it to apply only to mercantile and financial capital. I am inclined to believe that it applies more generally to all, including industrial capital, in pre-capitalist economies, at least until the capitalist or potentially capitalist sector of the economy has reached a certain critical size.

[10] E. J. Hobsbawm, *op. cit.*

[11] In this sense M. Mauro's criticisms of the view that "la structure 'féodal' de la société a gêné le développement capitaliste, l'a maintenu à l'intérieur de certaines limites," seem to me to be misconceived. (*Annales, loc. cit.*) It is clear that a "feudal" economy or society (or whatever else we choose to call it) is compatible with a certain amount of capitalist development, and may even, in certain ways, facilitate it. But the problem is not why Jacob Fugger was so like a nineteenth century tycoon in his business operations, but why, after all, sixteenth century Germany was economically so unlike mid-nineteenth century England.

rope was partly achieved by turning large areas of eastern Europe into a food and raw material-producing colony of the west.[12] But this was achieved by turning eastern Europe into a serf economy, dominated by landlords whose policy—free trade, de-industrialization, the increasing exploitation of the peasantry, and the sacrifices of the urban classes—eventually cut down the potential, and actual market for western goods in the east.

But the Baltic trade was the chief trade of northern Europe. The collapse of the Baltic market in the 1620's initiated the main period of general crisis. Furthermore the expansion of an extensive serf-estate economy in the Polish East produced the social tensions which led to the Ukrainian-Cossack revolution.

Again, we may trace the contradictions and deficiencies in the sixteenth century colonial system. Thus Spanish and Portuguese expansion, being based on robbery and monopoly, failed to stimulate European exports outwards which were at all equivalent to the flow of bullion and goods inwards, thus probably increasing European inflation and certainly making the European balance of trade with the outside world even more negative than it had always been. Moreover, once the initial grazing-off process had been completed, even the flow of wealth to Europe ceased or was offset by high costs. By the early seventeenth century the Spanish Empire, having virtually killed off all the Americans, relapsed into an extensive agrarian feudalism.[13] Or else, more generally, we may trace the effect of rapid economic expansion (including population growth) within an economic framework which did not at the same time produce a corresponding increase in agricultural productivity. It is fairly certain that the rise in agricultural output from all sources did not keep pace with the increase in demand, or in industrial output—as witness the price-scissors between agrarian and industrial prices in the later sixteenth century. A Malthusian situation thus tended to arise, and

[12] Cf. the writings of Polish historians on this point, especially of Prof. M. Malowist, e.g., in Econ. Hist. Rev. December 1959, Past & Present, 13,. April 1958.

[13] Cf. Woodrow Borah, New Spain's Century of Depression (Berkeley, 1954) for the depopulation, H. and P. Chaunu, Seville et l'Atlantique VII (1957) for the drop in trade after 1610, F. Chevalier, La formation des grandes domaines au Mexique (1952) for the relapse into agrarianism.

the demographic horrors of the seventeenth century, with their economic consequences, were being prepared. We can observe their approach as, for instance, an area like Holstein turns from a food-exporting to a food-importing area towards the end of the sixteenth century, and this at the very time when importing areas had to draw their food from increasingly distant or numerous exporters. We can watch its effect in an English village in the first third of the seventeenth century, as a permanent stratum of village poor arises in a steadily more crowded settlement, until population rise gives way, amid epidemics and sickness to population stagnation.[14] Any analyst could trace other, and perhaps equally significant self-contradictions in the economic expansion of the sixteenth century.

However, if the origins of the seventeenth century crisis are likely to yield to investigation, its results are much more difficult to analyze. For why, after all, did this breakdown produce what turned out to be satisfactory conditions for subsequent growth, and not yet another vicious circle? Here, I suggest, we must consider not only the gradually increasing disintegration of the precapitalist societies in Europe, but also three fundamental characteristics of our development: 1) that crises tended to weaken the "feudal" kinds of enterprise more than the "progressive"; 2) that the European economy and its colonies formed a single entity, and 3) "bourgeois revolution."

The first phenomenon is simple enough. Not all entrepreneurs can go into the most profitable business which (as we have seen) were likely to be the least revolutionary. Those who cannot take first choice must take second or third. And if a crisis knocks out the first choice, the second or third—which are likely to be less affected by it—may find themselves emerging into first place, thus revealing their economic potentialities. Thus, the decline of the expensive "old draperies" in England—a victim of the collapse of the Baltic market—may well reveal the advantages of

[14] Cf. W. Hoskins, *The Midland Peasant* (1957). Also: Phelps Brown and Hopkins in *Economica*, XXIV (1957), 289. The really appalling demographic ravages of the century are best indicated by an example from a peaceful area. Between 1660 and 1695 the population of the Essonnes valley (south of Paris) appears to have fallen in absolute terms by 25 per cent. Cf. M. Fontenay, "Paysans et Marchands Ruraux," in *Paris et Ile de France* IX, 1957–1958.

the cheaper "new draperies," which were capable not only of conquering new markets, but also of maintaining and expanding their hold in the old ones. Again, in the sixteenth century anyone out for American profits made straight for Eldorado. Only when gold and silver proved elusive, or were already monopolized by someone else, did venturers content themselves with such activities as sugar-planting, as in northeast Brazil. But these initially modest enterprises turned out to be excellent investments. Moreover, they turned out to be immensely stimulating to the economy in general, since they depended on a self-generated and constant expansion of markets all-round: more sugar sold at lower prices, more sales in Europe, more European goods sold in the colonies, more slaves needed for the plantations, more goods with which to buy slaves, and so on. Small wonder that the new colonial system which emerged in the middle of the seventeenth century became one of the chief elements and it may be argued the decisive element, in the preparation of industrial revolution. But—and this is the important point—the new colonial system only emerged fully in those countries which had no access to the old, and after the collapse of the old, *i.e.,* from the middle of the seventeenth century. The Dutch, who managed to capture the Portuguese system in the Indian Ocean, retained their economically unprogressive methods of colonial exploitation until well into the eighteenth century. Had the English been as successful as the Dutch, there is little doubt that they would have done much less to develop their methods of colonial exploitation, which turned out to be rather more useful for our subsequent industrialization.

The second phenomenon is more complex.[15] Briefly, the development of modern capitalism cannot be understood in terms of a single national economy or of the national economic histories taken separately, but only in terms of an international economy. (This is, of course, what Marx meant when emphasizing the "world market"). Broadly speaking, the capture of this entire world market—or most of it—by a *single* national economy or industry could produce the prospects of rapid and virtually un-

[15] It has lately been discussed more fully by K. Berrill in a paper due to appear in the *Economic History Review*.

limited expansion which the modest and confined capitalist manufacture of the period could not yet achieve itself, and thus make it possible for this modest capitalist sector to break through its pre-capitalist limits. In other words, there was probably at this period not room in the European economy (including its colonies) for the initial industrialization of more than one country. Or, to put it another way round: a widespread simultaneous economic expansion everywhere in the advanced areas of Europe would probably have slowed down the preparation of industrial revolution.[16]

Now the seventeenth century crisis certainly made such a concentration of world resources easier, if only because it eliminated from the economic race some areas which had been formerly dynamic and advanced—*e.g.,* Italy and a large part of Central Europe—leaving, in effect, only the Dutch, the English and possibly the French in the race. (And of these, as we shall see, the feudal-absolutist French were unable to compete effectively, the Dutch unwilling to use their extraordinary monopoly position for the purpose of advancing industrial revolution). But the crisis did more. Wherever we look, we observe it concentrating economic forces: wealth and economic power in large landlords, best able to accumulate and to secure (in plantations and serf-estates) the maximum agricultural export-surplus from colonial countries; markets in large capital cities; and so on.[17] For instance, in the course of that century, while the population of England increased much less than in the sixteenth or eighteenth centuries, London doubled its size, and therefore greatly increased its proportion of the total British population and home market. In this tendency to concentrate, the seventeenth century crisis seems to differ markedly from the fourteenth century cri-

[16] The problem is more fully discussed in E. J. Hobsbawn *op. cit.*, but the argument may be summarized in Berrill's words: "The crux of the argument . . . is that the most vital circumstance of an industrial revolution was the market condition in the trading area and this was only slowly ripening before 1780. Only slowly did purchasing power expand with population, income per head, transport costs and restraints on trade. But the market was expanding and the vital question was when would a producer of some mass consumption goods capture enough of it to allow fast and continuous expansion of their production."

[17] See E. J. Hobsbawm, *op. cit.*, for a full discussion of this complex process.

sis, which led, on the contrary, to economic dispersion—*e.g.*, the break-up of large demesne farming in the west, and of the great industrial concentrations in Italy and Flanders. Hence, taking the European economy as a whole—and this must include both the east-European and overseas colonies—the seventeenth century crisis did not so much lead to a temporary general regression, as to a very rapid economic shift. As the English "old draperies" declined, the "new draperies" rose; the sixteenth century pattern of Baltic trade was replaced, after a few decades, by a geographically and commercially somewhat different new pattern; the old Spanish pattern of colonialism by a far more effective Franco-British-Dutch pattern. It is true that some of these solutions were only temporary. By the mid-eighteenth century the serf-economy of the new east-European magnates and the plantation economy of West Indian and American planters were patently near the limits of their economic potentialities. Nevertheless, they helped to enable the large, and as we have seen increasingly concentrated "capitalist sector" of the European economy, to maintain its growth, and to move straight from the crisis period into an era of extremely rapid and dynamic expansion, notably in England between 1660 and 1700.

But this was no accident. For if the crisis produced conditions of economic concentration which could be used to advance industrial development, it did not necessarily guarantee such development. This is shown by the Dutch, who were the chief initial beneficiaries of this concentration. As we know, they never became the pioneers of the industrial economy; indeed, paradoxically, the far less flourishing Spanish Netherlands (Belgium) and Liège were to become, after England, the first industrialized economy. This was because, alone of all the old fashioned "medieval" business centers, the Dutch—a sort of Venice or Augsburg swollen to seminational scale—were able to carry on business in the old and unprogressive manner, and in doing so tended increasingly to sacrifice the interests of Dutch manufacture to those of Dutch trade and finance. If the only capitalist economies available in the seventeenth century had been of the Dutch type, it is to be doubted whether the subsequent development of industrialism would have been as rapid or as great. A *different* kind of "modern" capitalist economy was needed, if the economic potentialities of the seventeenth century were to be utilized. But in fact, in the course of the century, one such economy emerged: the English.

Whether it did so as the result of a "bourgeois revolution" is a matter for debate. I am not entering this debate about nomenclature here. But it can hardly be denied that sometime in the course of the seventeenth century—say between 1620 and 1670 —England was transformed from a secondary, though interesting and dynamic economy into an economy which looked like being able to initiate and conduct the economic revolution of the world, which indeed it did. The transformation was so rapid, that by the 1690's England seemed actually on the verge of industrial revolution. At all events scholars have been puzzled why the industrial revolution did not grow out of the development of the 1690's, but was delayed until the 1780's. Moreover, this transformation in the world position of the British economy was not due merely to spontaneous economic developments within it, but plainly also to a major revolution in policy, which henceforth subordinated all other ends to an aggressive mercantilism, to the accumulation of capital and profit. Moreover, whoever actually constituted in the ruling class of postrevolutionary England, it is clear that this policy differed in at least one crucial respect from the Dutch: in cases of conflict the interests of the *manufacturing* sector normally prevailed over that of the trading and financial sector. In spite of Davenant's appeal to imitate the free-trading Dutch "consuming at home what is cheap or comes cheaply and carrying abroad what is rich and will yield most money,"[18] the bitter struggle between the home industrialists and the East India Company was unambiguously won by the manufacturing interests in 1700; a victory as important as that of North over South, high-tariff over low-tariff interests was to be for the industrialization of the United States.

Lastly, it may be safely claimed that the full and unfettered adoption of such a policy was impossible before the Revolution. This was so not because it was not advocated on technical grounds, or even anticipated, or because the wealth it produced would not have been recognized as useful by the ancien régime of

[18] *Works* (ed. 1771) I, 102–03.

James and Charles, but because that ancien régime was incapable of applying it effectively; as indeed were all the ancien régimes of the seventeenth century, whether they tried to or not, except bourgeois ones like the Dutch.[19] The striking thing about the reformed absolutist monarchies with which Trevor-Roper makes such play is not that they produced devoted, intelligent, and often remarkably able and perspicacious economic strategists, but that these strategists did not prevail. The impressive thing about late-seventeenth century France is not Colbertism, but its relative failure; not the reform of the monarchy, but its failure, in spite of much greater resources, to compete economically—and therefore, in the end, militarily—with its maritime rivals, and its consequent defeat by those rivals.[20]

For the purposes of this discussion it is not important to settle the name of this new policy, or to discuss in detail how, in terms of politics and ideology it came about, beyond establishing what is in any case obvious, that it came about during the period of crisis, and pretty obviously in some sort of connection with the English Revolutions. What is important is, that such an economy, and such a "bourgeois" state policy emerged nowhere else except in England, and that its emergence made a crucial difference to the subsequent economic development of the world, because it ensured that the resources concentrated by the crisis were increasingly to be absorbed by and subordinated to, a single economy of adequate size, which was likely to make progressive use of them.[21]

It has not been my purpose to argue that, but for the seventeenth century crisis, industrial capitalism would not have developed. If we take a general view of the period from, say 1000 A.D.

[19] H. R. Trevor-Roper, *op. cit.*, attempts to show that the seventeenth century revolutions were unnecessary for the adoption of the desirable economic policies. But much of his article is devoted to demonstrating the incapacity of the pre-revolutionary ancien régimes to adopt them.

[20] *Cf.* R. Mousnier, "Evolution des Finances Publiques en France et Angleterre (*Revue Historique,* 1951).

[21] Admittedly in and through a sort of hostile symbiosis with the Dutch; but from the point of view of subsequent development the important thing is, that the English soon became the dominant power in this partnership, and Dutch resources were thus mobilized for economic growth largely by and through England.

to 1800 A.D., it is reasonable to suppose that the forces making for the disintegration of the feudal economy and the growth of a capitalist economy were powerful enough to secure a break-through sooner or later, somewhere; and it is equally reasonable to suppose, with Marx, that industrialization was the logical product of such a break-through. It has rather been my purpose to show that this replacement of feudalism by capitalism was not, and could not be, a simple linear evolution—that, even in purely economic terms it had to be discontinuous and catastrophic— and to sketch some of the mechanisms of this historic change, and to draw attention to the seventeenth century crisis as a crucial (as it turned out *the* crucial) episode in the decline of the feudal and the victory of the capitalist economy. The question why the industrial revolution was delayed until the late eighteenth century cannot be discussed here.

10   *Lewis Cecil Gray*

Genesis of the Plantation System as an Agency for Colonial Expansion of Capitalism

SIGNIFICANCE OF THE PLANTATION SYSTEM IN ECONOMIC EVOLUTION

The economic life of the ante bellum South frequently has been approached primarily as a study in social pathology, with attention centered on its unprogressiveness and the evil consequences of slavery and the plantation system. We should be incredulous, however, concerning a point of view that reveals only the pathological side of a social and economic régime. That the peculiar institutions of the South came into existence, survived, even increased in importance during more than two centuries is

SOURCE. Lewis Cecil Gray, *History of Argiculture in the Southern United States to 1860* (2 vols.; Washington: Carnegie Institution, 1932), Volume I, Chapter XIV.

ground for the suspicion that they possessed a special fitness, that they comprised an adaptation to the conditions of time and place that was both natural and economic, even though the institutions ultimately became anachronistic.

The typical institutions—servitude, slavery, the plantation system, and the credit system—were not peculiar to the South nor established only by the English race. They appeared also in Central America, the West Indies, and South America, established in the process of colonization by English, French, Spanish, Dutch, and Portuguese. They constitute essential characteristics of a prevalent stage of economic evolution long recognized by writers on the philosophy of colonization in classifying colonies. Many years ago Professor Heeren distinguished four classes of colonies: agricultural, plantation, mining, and trading.[1] Other writers, though employing somewhat different classifications, nevertheless retain the significant distinction between agricultural colonies and plantation colonies.[2]

Professor Albert Galloway Keller has summarized suggestively the contrasts between plantation colonies and agricultural colonies.[3] Agricultural colonies, he holds, tend to develop in temperate, and plantation colonies in tropical, regions. Tropical products are likely to be in demand as luxuries in the mother country, and economic conditions place a premium on the production of a few products in especial demand; therefore in plantation colonies industry is specialized. Since the climate is unfavorable to the labor of European races, compulsory labor of tropical races develops. Agriculture is extensive, and cultivation exploitative. Because of the unhealthful climate and large financial resources of the masters, there is much absentee ownership; and as a result, much cruelty toward the laboring classes. The necessity of marketing goods in the mother country and buying supplies therefrom creates a vital interdependence. The plantation colony is characterized by great estates, more or less specu-

[1] *Political System of Europe and Its Colonies,* 23.

[2] Roscher & Jannasch, *Kolonien, Kolonialpolitik und Auswanderung,* 2 et seq.; Leroy-Beaulieu, *Colonisation chez les Peuples Modernes,* 748 et seq.; Egerton, *Origin and Growth of the English Colonies,* 3.

[3] *Colonization, a Study of the Founding of New Societies,* 3–19: cf. Leroy-Beaulieu, *Colonisation chez les Peuples Modernes,* 742 et seq.

lative in character. Social organization is aristocratic, with definite castes based on racial differences. A great preponderance of males and the small economic importance of women of the colonizing race leads to formal celibacy, but also extreme laxity in relations with the lower race. In the case of agricultural colonies, since their products compete with those of the mother country, commercial interdependence is slight. Local self-sufficiency is apt to prevail in the earlier years, and but little specialization in production. The size of economic units, especially in agriculture, is small. The colonists furnish their own labor. Agriculture soon becomes intensive, and regard is had to soil conservation. Absenteeism is almost unknown. Industry is diversified, and the people resourceful and inventive. The homogeneous population and small economic dependence on the mother country result in a strong tendency to self-government and democratic institutions. Woman is economically important, and the family extremely cohesive.

The contrasts of the plantation Colonies of the South with the agricultural type of colony were not so marked as is suggested in the above characterization. In climate and in social organization the Southern Colonies belong midway between the two extremes described above—extremes best typified by the British West Indies and New England.

The most characteristic institution of the plantation colony was the plantation system, which may be formally defined as follows: *The plantation was a capitalistic type of agricultural organization in which a considerable number of unfree laborers were employed under unified direction and control in the production of a staple crop.* The definition applies to the South, however, only in the ante bellum period, for plantation organization has prevailed since the Civil War on the basis of labor that is at least nominally free. The definition implies also that (1) the functions of laborer and employer were sharply distinct; (2) the system was based on commercial agriculture, except in periods of depression; (3) the system represented a capitalistic stage of agricultural development, since the value of slaves, land, and equipment necessitated the investment of money capital, often of large amount and frequently borrowed, and there was a strong tendency for the planter to assume the attitude of the business man in testing success by ratio of net money income to capital invested; and (4) there was a strong tendency toward specialization—the production of a single crop for market.

It is significant that three of the characteristics developed in manufacturing by the Industrial Revolution—commercialism, capitalism, and specialization—were attained in Southern agriculture as early as the first half of the seventeenth century through the establishment of the plantation system.

The development of plantation organization has frequently been interpreted as an incident of the introduction of Negro slavery. Its early development, however, was mainly on the basis of white servitude,[4] and, although slavery has passed away, it still prevails in the South and in various tropical regions on the basis of indentured (coolie) labor.[5] Slavery itself flourished only under certain favorable conditions: it rested upon ethical standards peculiar to the age; its character was influenced by distinctive commercial policies; and it prevailed only in certain regions, while in others it languished and died. In short, it was not the mere accidental visit of a slave-trading vessel that explains the introduction of slavery in the South. Once established, however, slavery became in turn a *raison d' etre* of the plantation system. Primarily, then, the genesis of the plantation system is to be regarded as a phase of the colonial expansion of capitalism, necessitated by the industrial environment peculiar to certain parts of the New World, the character of the races and populations that entered into the fabric of colonial empire, the commercial and colonial ideals of the several nations participating in the task of colonization, and the technical character of industry in that period. These conclusions will be indicated by reviewing briefly the development of the plantation system in the Spanish, French, and British Colonies in the New World.

BEGINNINGS OF THE PLANTATION SYSTEM IN SPANISH COLONIAL POLICY

The record of the experience of European nations that established colonies in the New World confirms the observation of

---

[4] See [Gray, *History of Agriculture in the Southern United States to 1860*, Vol. I], pp. 308, 348.

[5] *Cf.* Ireland, *Tropical Colonization,* Chaps. IV–VI.

Paul Leroy-Beaulieu, that the policies of colonization must conform to the conditions encountered.[6] Sharp contrasts in colonial policy and accomplishment were due partly to economic and political differences in the colonizing nations but even more to wide differences in the natural environment and native populations of the countries colonized.

Spain and Portugal did not establish what French writers term *colonies de peuplement;* no widespread development of immigration was requisite, for Portuguese colonies in Brazil and Spanish colonies in the West Indies, Mexico, and Peru were built up initially on the basis of native populations. On the other hand, France and England faced the necessity of organizing an extensive stream of immigration from the mother countries and from Africa. The Spaniard found in the larger West Indian islands a numerous population, which had reached the agricultural stage and a settled village life.[7] The original population of Hispaniola was estimated at over 3,000,000 by Las Casas and at over 1,000,000 by Oviedo and Peter Martyr, although both estimates were undoubtedly exaggerated. Peschel estimated the native population of Hispaniola at between 200,000 and 300,000.[8] They were greatly superior in culture and docility to the Caribs in the Windward and Leeward Islands, whose stubborn resistance and cannibalism soon furnished the Spaniards a justification for enslaving them.[9]

On the other hand, when Jamaica, San Domingo, and other islands were wrested from Spain by England or France, the aboriginal inhabitants of the superior culture had been largely extinguished. Most of the earliest original island settlements of the English and French were in the Leeward and Windward Islands, occupied mainly by the Caribs. The most terrible tortures were insufficient to reduce them to submission; when taken into captivity they preferred to commit suicide rather than to work for their captors. The only recourse was to wage wars of extermina-

[6] *Colonisation chez les Peuples Modernes,* 751 *et seq.*

[7] In some parts of the Continent the Spaniards encountered Indians in lower stages of culture. Peschel, *Races of Man and Their Geographical Distribution,* 420.

[8] Bourne, *Spain in America,* 213; Edwards, *British West Indies,* I, 58.

[9] Lucas, C. P., *Historical Geography of the British Colonies,* II, 42.

tion and import the needful labor supply.[10] The Bermudas, Barbados, Antigua, and some of the smaller islands were uninhabited by native tribes.[11] Most of the tribes encountered by the English and French on the Continent, as already noted, were still in the hunting and fishing stage, more or less supplemented by a rude garden cultivation. Therefore, their numbers were few relative to the land area.[12]

The policy inaugurated by the Spaniards for controlling the native races involved in theory the development of a sort of manorial system. The natives, regarded as conquered vassals, were required to pay tribute, and failing that, to render personal services. In 1497 letters patent were issued to Columbus authorizing him to grant repartimientos of lands to Spaniards. The repartimiento, or to use the more common term, the encomienda, was a system of sub-in-feudation, for, according to the constitutional law of the Indies, the land was the domain of the King.[13] It was only a step to the further grant of rights over the inhabitants. In 1498 certain Indian caciques were assigned the task of providing the Spaniards with so many thousand shoots of cassava, with the expectation that they in turn would compel the inhabitants of their villages to produce the required amounts. The system was soon officially recognized. In 1503, under orders from Spain, the natives were divided into groups, giving 50 to 100 Indians to each Spaniard as an encomienda, or commandery. The natives were to spend a portion of their time in working for fixed wages.[14]

As the system was gradually extended, the detailed relation-

[10] Peytraud, *L'Esclavage aux Antilles Françaises*, 5, 12–19, 26 *et seq.*; Edwards, *British West Indies*, I, 358–360, 402, 424.

[11] *Ibid.*, 327, 437; Clark, C., *Summary of Colonial Law*, 175; Jourdain, *Discovery of the Bermudas* (Hakluyt, Early Voyages, V), 185.

[12] See Brinton, *The American Race*, 75–92; Farrand, *Basis of American History*, especially Chaps. XI, XIV.

[13] Helps, *Spanish Conquest*, I, 145 *et seq.*, 152; Roscher, *Spanish Colonial System*, 4; Bourne, *Spain in America*, 256. The Spaniards had employed a somewhat similar policy after the subjugation of the Moriscoes.

[14] Merriman, *Rise of the Spanish Empire*, II, 232; Helps, *Spanish Conquest*, I, 163; Brown, J., *History of St. Domingo*, I, 26, 29. The system was legalized by cedulas issued by Ferdinand, Aug. 14 and Nov. 12, 1509. Lea, "Indian Policy of Spain," in *Yale Review*, VIII, 126.

ship of the encomiendero to his subjects became more precisely defined. The natives occupied substantially the status of villeins regardant, though in legal theory they were minors for life. They were bound to their respective villages, but assigned a definite amount of ground to cultivate for their own benefit. The amounts of tribute in gold, produce, or labor were carefully defined. The natives could not be employed outside of the village except under special circumstances and in compliance with safeguards to prevent excessive demands on their time and strength. There were numerous provisions to protect the native's person from violence and his possessions from confiscation. The encomiendero was under obligation to furnish the villagers protection and religious instruction.[15]

In the course of the gradual development of the policy administrative agencies were provided to enforce the provisions for the protection of the native tribes against exploitation, but in the early decades of colonization circumstances were overwhelmingly against the realization of these ideals. Many of the Spanish adventurers were vicious and lawless, while the barbarity and numerical preponderance of the natives excited the intolerance of their fanatical conquerors and appeared to justify a policy of terrorism.[16] In the early period the natives under the encomienda system were treated as slaves and quickly exterminated by the barbarities that Las Casas eloquently described. In 1533 the native population of Porto Rico was practically extinct, and in 1548 Oviedo doubted whether 500 natives of pure stock remained in Hispaniola.[17]

[15] Martyr, *History of the West Indies* (Hakluyt, Selection of Curious Rare . . . Voyages, Supplement), 626–627; Helps, *Spanish Conquest,* I, 260–263; III, 117; IV, 360–369; Lea, "Indian Policy of Spain," in *Yale Review,* VIII, 140, 144–146, 153–155; Roscher, *Spanish Colonial System,* 6; Pons, *Travels in South America* (Phillips, Collection of Voyages, IV, No. 2), p. 59; Bourne, *Spain in America,* 256–264. In some parts of their dominions, especially in Mexico and Peru, the Spaniards found a sort of native serfdom. Garcilaso de la Vega, *Royal Commentaries of the Incas,* II, 17–50; Cieza de Leon, *Travels,* 149.

[16] Benzoni, *History of the New World,* 8; *cf.* also p. 72; Brown, J., *History of St. Domingo,* I, 35; Merriman, *Rise of the Spanish Empire,* II, 232–235.

[17] Casas, *Oeuvres,* I, 19–21; Lea, "Indian Policy of Spain," in *Yale Review,* VIII, 121–127; Brown, J., *History of St. Domingo,* I, 29–34; Bourne, *Spain in*

From time to time recognition of the inconsistency of existing practices in relation to the legal theory of the system led to half-hearted attempts at reform, soon nullified by the influence of vested interests at the Spanish capital.[18] After more settled conditions were established, however, the encomienda system was gradually modified to a more humane approximation of its legal and theoretical foundation, until finally abolished in the latter part of the eighteenth century.[19]

Although the system was actually an extreme form of slavery in the early decades of Spanish colonization,[20] evidence is not lacking that even in this period of greatest abuse the law was sometimes rigidly enforced. In Peru a Spanish gentleman was punished by 200 lashes for compelling Indians to carry his baggage.[21] In the third decade of the sixteenth century Benzoni wrote of the Province of Fondura, "The Indians scarcely give their masters anything but what belongs to them; and if by chance any Spaniard constrained his people to give him something more; or ill treated them, he would be immediately deprived of them by the governors." Some of the Indians in Mexico were wealthy.[22] William Walton, who visited the Spanish Colonies in the closing years of the eighteenth century, believed that the Indians were treated too leniently to effect their training

---

America, 211–214; Benzoni, *History of the New World*, 108; Gage, *New Survey of the West Indies*, 175; Enriquez de Guzman, *Life and Acts*, 84.

[18] For a detailed account, see Helps, *Spanish Conquest*, I, 506–511; II, 24–34; III, 165; IV, Bk. XVIII, Chaps. I–III; Bk. XIX, Chap. VIII; Lea, "Indian Policy of Spain," in *Yale Review*, VIII, 140.

[19] *Ibid.*, 140, 145, 153–155; Roscher, *Spanish Colonial System*, 6; Helps, *Spanish Conquest*, IV, 360–369; Pons, *Travels in South America* (Phillips, Collection of Voyages, IV, No. 2), p. 59; Bourne, *Spain in America*, 256–264; Humboldt, *Kingdom of New Spain*, I, 183.

[20] *Cf.* quotations by Lea, "Indian Policy of Spain," in *Yale Review*, VIII, 146. For evidence of the milder characteristics of the system in Mexico as compared with its rigorous characteristics in Guatemala and Peru, see Bourne, *Spain in America*, 263; Gage, *New Survey of the West Indies*, 312–315; Casas, *Oeuvres*, I, 227–268, 273; Cieza de Leon, *Travels*, 106.

[21] Simon, *Expedition of Pedro de Ursua and Lope de Aguirre*, 233 n.

[22] *History of the New World*, 145; Gage, *New Survey of the West Indies*, 298.

in the arts of civilization.[23] Humboldt declared they were as well off economically as the lower classes of the Spanish peninsula.[24]

In short, during the sixteenth century the plantation system based on Indian labor gradually ceased to exist in the Spanish West Indies, and on the Continent was gradually transformed into an approximation of the manorial system.

DEVELOPMENT OF THE INSTITUTION OF SLAVERY IN SPANISH COLONIES

In 1492 Columbus sent some of the captured Caribs to Spain, where slavery already existed, with the suggestion that this savage race be converted by wholesale enslavement.[25] In 1498 the Spanish Government authorized the enslavement of those taken in war. It was easy for the scholastic sophistry of that day to justify the capture of natives forced into a warlike attitude by the cruelty of invaders whose savage reputation preceded them.[26]

The Spanish authorities early began importing Negro slaves into their Colonies, ostensibly to alleviate the lot of the Indians. Special privileges of importation were granted powerful private interests, with restrictions on the number introduced. Probably in no year before 1713 was the maximum higher than 4,250. The assiento of that year provided for a maximum of 4,800. A considerable illicit trade had been developed by the English, French, Dutch, and Genoese.[27]

These sources of supply were inadequate to satisfy the demand resulting from extinction of the natives in the islands and the opening up of the mainland. As early as 1523 the Spaniards

[23] *Spanish Colonies*, II, Chap. XVII.

[24] *Kingdom of New Spain*, I, 198.

[25] Helps, *Spanish Conquest*, I, 134, 142. For an account of the beginnings of the slave trade to Europe, see Phillips, U. B., *American Negro Slavery*, 11–13.

[26] Helps, *Spanish Conquest*, I, 165; III, 119–124; Lea, "Indian Policy of Spain," in *Yale Review*, VIII, 121.

[27] Helps, *Spanish Conquest*, II, 19–21; Bourne, *Spain in America*, 269–272; Phillips, U. B., *American Negro Slavery*, 18–19; Moses, *Spanish Rule in America*, 270–273; Campbell, J., *History of the Spanish Americas*, 308–314; Aimes, *Slavery in Cuba*, 8, 16–17, 25.

in Hispaniola protested that the monopolistic policy made slaves
scarce.[28] The freeing of the Indians by the "New Laws" of 1542
nearly paralyzed industry in Cuba.[29] Professor Aimes has
shown that for two centuries Cuba remained undeveloped for
lack of slaves.[30]

The result of the several policies of exclusion, not only of
slaves, but also of white settlers, was that the Spanish possessions
in America remained under-populated. At the close of the eighteenth century, with an area one fifth larger than Europe, they
contained a smaller slave population than Virginia, and most of
the slaves were in the single Province of Caracas.[31] In 1789, for
instance, the French Colony of San Domingo contained 30,826
whites, 27,548 free colored, and 465,429 slaves. In 1785 the
Spanish part of the same island contained 122,640 free persons
and only 30,000 slaves.[32] In the latter part of the eighteenth
century the population of Porto Rico was only 1,500 Spaniards
and mixed breeds and about 3,000 Negroes.[33] The much smaller English island, Barbados, with only about 100,000 acres, was
estimated to contain 50,000 whites and 100,000 Negroes within
fifty years after its first settlement, an estimate probably con-
siderably exaggerated.[34]

Thus, the restrictive policy of Spain resulted, whether for better or worse, in the diversion of the vast stream of Negro slaves
to the possessions of her rivals, England, France, Portugal, and
Holland. "Had the commerce of the islands been reasonably
free, plantation slavery on a large scale would have rapidly de-

[28] Helps, *Spanish Conquest*, III, 211.

[29] Benzoni, *History of the New World*, 57; Aimes, *Slavery in Cuba*, 10–13.

[30] *Ibid.*, Chaps, I–II, *passim*.

[31] Humboldt, *Personal Narrative of Travels*, III, 123; *cf.* Moses, *Spanish
Rule in America*, 55–61; Pons, *Travels in South America* (Phillips, Collection
of Voyages, IV, No. 2), p. 45.

[32] Mackenzie, *Notes on Haiti*, II, 109.

[33] Raynal, *Europeans in the East and West Indies*, IV, 99.

[34] Burke, Edm., *European Settlements in America*, II, 86–88; Edwards,
British West Indies, I, 350; Pitman, *Development of the British West Indies*,
45 n. For population statistics of other possessions of the respective countries,
see Edwards, *British West Indies*, I, 186, 230, 383, 405, 418, 432, 435, 447,
470–471; Bourne, *Spain in America*, 196–200.

veloped, and the history of Haiti and the English islands would have been anticipated a century by the Spaniards."[35]

Humane consideration aside, Spanish colonization policy in the West Indies was far less successful in economic results than the policies adopted by England and France. The sparse slave population and the unprosperous agriculture of the Spanish islands presented a severe contrast to the populous, prosperous Colonies established by Spain's northern rivals. In the former, systematic agriculture was not highly developed, and herding comprised the principal economic activity.[36] Some tobacco, indigo, pimento, ginger, and cacao were produced, and there were a few sugar plantations. It was not until the last quarter of the eighteenth century, when the restrictions on the slave trade were partially removed and the stream of slaves again diverted to the Spanish West Indies, that the sugar industry and plantation system rapidly developed.[37]

EMPLOYMENT OF THE PLANTATION SYSTEM BY THE FRENCH AND BRITISH COLONIZATION COMPANIES

It is not probable that the Spanish plantation system, such as it was, exerted an important direct influence on the beginnings of the system in the British and French Colonies. Certainly the development of the plantation system in Virginia, the first plantation Colony successfully established by England, was not influenced by the Spanish West Indian system; for the prevailing relations of England and Spain were not favorable to extensive friendly intercourse between their Colonies, and Spain was especially hostile toward the Virginia enterprise.[38]

[35] *Ibid.*, 272; *cf.* Roscher, Spanish Colonial System, 10 n.

[36] Campbell, J., *History of the Spanish Americas*, 156; Gage, *New Survey of the West Indies*, 175, 179, 278; Edwards, *French Colony in St. Domingo*, 178, 184; Long, *History of Jamaica*, I, 238.

[37] Aimes, *Slavery in Cuba*, Chap. I, *passim*; Edwards, *British West Indies*, I, 186, 242–247; *idem*, *French Colony in St. Domingo*, 178, 184; Bridges, *Annals of Jamaica*, I, 182; Humboldt, *Cuba*, 213–216, 251–253; Leroy-Beaulieu, *Colonisation chez les Peuples Modernes*, 31–34.

[38] Brown, A., *Genesis*, I, 89, 91, 100, 102–105, 108, 116–124, & *passim*; Beer, G. L., *Origins of the British Colonial System*, 7–10.

It is also unlikely that other British and French plantation Colonies helped to mould the early development of the institutions in Virginia. Barbados, settled in 1624, and St. Christopher, jointly settled by the English and French between 1623 and 1626, were influential original centers from which the plantation system spread to other islands; but plantation organization had been established in Virginia before it had developed materially in either of these Colonies. In a later period, however, there was a well established and frequent communication between the British West Indies and the American plantation Colonies, as well as considerable migration. Barbadians, as we have noted, were influential in the settlement of South Carolina, and there was some migration from Barbados to Virginia.[39] The attack of the French on St. Christopher in 1666 impelled numbers of Englishmen to migrate to Virginia and New England.[40] After the revolution in San Domingo large numbers of French refugees fled to South Carolina and other parts of the South. The joint British and French occupation of St. Christopher, the British occupation of Jamaica after 1655, the temporary British occupation of Cuba and Florida in 1763, the British occupation of the French Colony of St. Lucia, where the French system of law was allowed to remain in force, were a few of the many opportunities for the cross-fertilization of culture, while commercial intercourse must have worked powerfully in the same direction.[41]

In undertaking to establish *colonies de peuplement,* France was handicapped by the general aversion of the French population toward emigration. Political ambition and the desire for extending commerce were dominant motives back of colonial expansion. The impulse for emigration came from above, rather than from below. The seigneurs, having obtained seignorial commissions, sought to induce families of cultivators to follow them in order to people their fiefs with feudal retainers and tenants.[42]

[39] Washington, *Journal on a Tour to Barbadoes,* Pref., p. 12; McKinnon, *Tour through the British West Indies,* 23.

[40] Letter of Michael Smith to Richard Chandler, June 11, 1666, in Great Britain, *Calendar of State Papers, America and West Indies,* 1661–1668, p. 387.

[41] Clark, C., *Summary of Colonial Law,* 23.

[42] Benoit du Rey, *Recherches sur la Politique Coloniale de Colbert,* 30; *cf.* Pauliat, *Politique Coloniale,* 105–108; Chailley-Bert, *Compagnies de Colonisation,* 32–35.

Agents of the colonizing companies travelled the length and breadth of France gathering laborers for the French Colonies. *Engagés* (indentured servants) were transported free on condition of serving three years, and were sold to the colonists at low prices. To persons of the better class the companies advanced expenses of transport and settlement on condition that the debt be paid out of the earliest harvests. Frequently the urgent need for colonists led to the sending out of criminals and paupers.[43]

It was no accident, therefore, that caused the French to make a great success of their plantation Colonies while failing to secure a strong foothold in Canada. The provincial nobility and the wealthy, energetic bourgeoisie were extremely capable in conducting plantation colonization, based on the labor of others, but they were less inclined to the rigorous labors of an agricultural colony.[44]

In the earliest attempts at colonization neither the English nor the French proposed to rely upon Negro slaves. More than a decade elapsed after the settlement of Virginia before the first slaves were introduced; and during the first three quarters of a century the plantation system was based mainly on indentured servitude.[45] In the island of Barbados white servants were a large element in the population for several decades. According to an official report in 1643, there were 18,600 Englishmen in the island, and not more than 6,400 Negroes. Early conditions in Jamaica after British occupation were similar.[46] Slaves were not systematically introduced in French St. Christopher during the earlier years, for the attention of the Compagnie des Iles de l'Amérique was centered upon the introduction of white settlers, 7,000 of whom had been sent out by 1642.[47]

[43] Pauliat, *Politique Coloniale*, 114–117; Brown, J., *History of St. Domingo*, I, 59, 90–91; Long, *History of Jamaica*, II, 267 n.

[44] Cordier, *Compagnies à Charte et la Politique Coloniale*, 44.

[45] See [Gray, *History of Agriculture in the Southern United States*, Vol. I,] Chap. XVI.

[46] Davis, N. D., *Pages from the Early History of Barbadoes* [Newspaper clippings, Library of Congress]; Lucas, C. P., *Historical Geography of the British Colonies*, II, 179; see especially Pitman, *Development of the British West Indies*, 45–48; Nisbit, *Slavery not Forbidden by Scripture, etc.*, 11.

[47] Peytraud, *L'Esclavage aux Antilles Françaises*, 12.

Before the slave trade became important, a stable white society had been established in the French West Indies. Gradually, as in the English islands, the development of a staple crop and the introduction of Negro slaves resulted in the disappearance of the small proprietorships.[48]

If the planting of *colonies de peuplement* involved the problem of labor, it involved much more that of providing the capital needed for two classes of expenses: first, the public and semi-public expenses connected with the preliminary preparation of colonization, such as exploration, surveys, road-building, and military protection; and second, the expenses connected with the transport and settlement of the colonist. Since the white immigrant of the lower class rarely possessed so large a sum, it was necessary that some form of organization be devised which would unite the requisite labor and capital in the work of colonization. The primitive commercial organization of Spain did not provide a sufficient number of private adventurers willing to embark capital in distant projects. Consequently the government was compelled to assume the chief rôle in the early furtherance of colonization.[49] Though successful conquistadors organized expeditions on their own account out of the gains from former exploits, such expeditions were forays rather than colonizing enterprises. By the seventeenth century, however, England and France had attained a more advanced stage of economic development. In each country there were large bodies of free capital seeking investment in foreign enterprises, and the commercial classes had developed in economic strength and initiative. The colonial activity of both England and France, therefore, was largely the result of the effort of the private capitalist to find a profitable investment in the unlimited opportunities opened up by discovery and exploration, and accordingly, the colonizing companies usually excited popular enthusiasm for investment.[50]

The necessities of colonization in the period of foundation, as

[48] Leroy-Beaulieu, *Colonisation chez les Peuples Modernes*, 161; Morris, H. C., *History of Colonization*, I, 396.

[49] Cheyney, *European Background of American History*, I, 132–137. Concerning the financing of Menéndez' Florida settlements, see above, p. 10.

[50] Chailley-Bert, *Compagnies de Colonisation*, 71–76; Bonnassieux, *Les Grandes Compagnies de Commerce*, 369.

well as the economic ideas of the time, led to the employment of
the privileged company as an instrument for foreign investment.
Between the years 1599 and 1789 about seventy-five colonizing
companies were chartered in France. Thirty-four trading companies were created in England in the latter part of the sixteenth
century and in the seventeenth century.[51] The magnitude of the
task of initial colonization and the political and international relations involved precluded the effective activity of the individual
enterpriser and necessitated unity of control. The colonizing
agency must wage war against colonial rivals, maintain armed
fleets, build forts, and sometimes even send ambassadors and
consuls. Colonial governments must be set up, a commercial
code established, a land policy created, and roads constructed. In
dealing with native people, unity and continuity in aim and policy were essential.[52] Where so much of the task was not immediately connected with profit-making, competing individuals or
companies would have neglected the public phases of the enterprise. Moreover, a single merchant arriving with his cargo of
goods was likely to find that a competitor had already glutted his
market.

The earliest companies were of the "regulated" type. They
were granted a monopoly of trade and extensive powers for establishing and regulating trading relations and for defending
their monopoly, but did not employ a permanent capital nor seek
to earn profits. Expenses were defrayed from membership fees
and various fees and charges levied on members and others in
payment for trading facilities provided by the organization. Individual members, however, traded on their own account. Such
companies resembled partnerships rather than corporations, particularly in equality of individual contributions, lack of free
transfer of individual interests, and unlimited liability of

[51] Chailley-Bert, *Compagnies de Colonisation*, 21–25; Kingsbury, "Comparison of the Virginia Company with the Other English Trading Companies," in
Amer. Hist. Assn., *Annual Report*, 1906, I, 162.

[52] Epstein, *Levant Company*, 25; Cordier, *Compagnies à Charte et la Politique Coloniale*, 81; Chailley;Bert, *Compagnies de Colonisation*, 16; Cheyney,
European Background of American History, 161.

members.[53] Gradually it was found desirable to modify the character of the regulated companies. Right of participation was finally made available to anyone possessing the requisite funds. It ceased to be feasible to separate quasi public functions of development from purely commercial functions. More continuity of activity was provided, for annual expeditions of individual merchants were not adequate to perform the functions of colonization.[54]

The earliest English and French companies organized for operation abroad concerned themselves primarily in commercial transactions, in fishing, or in the fur trade, without attempting, except for a few feeble efforts, to establish populous colonies.[55] When, however, serious attention began to be given to investment in the New World, a new type of enterprise was required. Mining and agriculture promised enormous profits, but only by means of settled colonies. The problem that confronted the companies was to accomplish the foundation of these colonies in such a way as to result in profits to the capitalist.

Some of the companies undertook to attain this object by requiring quitrents from all landholders, but many went a step further. Instead of merely levying toll on the laborer's land, leaving him free to conduct his own operations, they sought to employ the laborer himself in the business of production. These enterprises became the prototypes of the plantation system. The earliest policy of the Virginia Company was of this character.[56] The same plan was followed in establishing the Plymouth Colony, the capitalists and colonists having formed an association in the interest of which the entire productive activity of the Colony was carried on.[57] A similar project was proposed by the Company

---

[53] Cawston & Keane, *Early Chartered Companies*, 10–13, 20–31, 68; Epstein, *Levant Company*, 23–40, & *passim;* Scott, W. R., *Joint-Stock Companies*, II, 1–36, 84, 242–245.

[54] Concerning various stages in the transition, see *ibid.*, 36, 92–111.

[55] Cawston & Keane, *Early Chartered Companies*, 10, 68, 89 *et seq.;* Scott, W. R., *Joint-Stock Companies*, II, 1–17, 36, 69, 83–88.

[56] See [Gray, *History of Agriculture in the Southern United States*, Vol. I,] Chap. XV.

[57] See Scott, W. R., *Joint-Stock Companies*, II, 306–311.

for New England, but proved abortive.[58] The proposed Huguenot settlement in South Carolina, promoted by William Boswell, Samuel Vassal, Hugh l'Amy, and Peter de Licques, was to be organized in several plantations, each ten miles square and worked during the first ten years by fifty men in the joint interest of the investors.[59] In the earliest colonial establishment of the Providence Company, the communal type of organization which characterized the early years of the Colony of Virginia was employed.[60] The Swedes organized a joint-stock company in effecting their first steps in colonization on the Delaware. For several years the great majority of the colonists were the industrial servants of the company, working on several tobacco plantations.[61]

When the nucleus of colonization was once established the essential rôle of the monopolistic companies was terminated. The performance of the quasi public functions entrusted to them proved a grievous burden to companies whose primary object was profit. They were no longer necessary to investment in New World industry; and like their predecessors, the trading companies, they excited the jealousy of private individuals who desired to encroach upon their monopoly, and encountered the opposition of the colonists, who found themselves hampered by restrictive policies.

The private plantation system was the natural successor of the colonizing company. With the quasi public functions of colonial foundation accomplished and the functions of government taken over by public agencies, the remaining task was to finance immigration and settlement. The plantation system afforded a convenient method of uniting capital and labor in the business of production. It would have been impracticable for the European capitalist to advance to each laborer the necessary expenses of

[58] Great Britain, *Calendar of State Papers, America and West Indies, 1574–1660*, pp. 30, 45, 47, 137, 204.

[59] *Ibid.*, 115.

[60] Kingsbury, "Comparison of the Virginia Company with the Other English Trading Companies," in Amer. Hist. Assn., *Annual Report*, 1906, I, 167.

[61] Johnson, A., *Swedish Settlements on the Delaware*, I, Chaps. XIII, XXI, XXXII; II, App. B.

emigration and settlement, leaving him to work out his own success and to repay the debt at will. The planter was the effective agent through whom European capital might be so employed, and the plantation was the agency of colonial expansion which brought together and combined three separate factors in utilizing the natural resources of the New World; the labor of the industrial servant or the slave, the capital furnished by the European merchant, and the directive activity of the planters. In some instances, of course, planters themselves furnished a part or all of the capital.

11 FROM   *Stuart Bruchey*

The Planters: Sources of Operating Capital

I have referred to the larger planters as men who could more easily "afford" large estates, servants or slaves, tools and implements for clearing land, and other necessary means of devoting their resources more fully to commercial production. What were the sources of the operating capital with which they made and then worked the fixed capital of land? Where did they obtain the purchasing power they were able to convert into these two forms of "real" capital? Their main sources appear to have been threefold: British loans and investments; equipment, supplies, and claims to American land brought by emigrants from England; and earnings from planting "ploughed back" into the land. While it is impossible to quantify these sources so as to display their relative significance, it appears that the two British channels deserve most emphasis.

Great quasi-public trading companies, privileged, chartered, and joint-stock, and served as the initial funnels through which

SOURCE. "The Planters: Sources of Operating Capital" in *The Roots of American Economic Growth 1607–1861*, by Stuart Bruchey Copyright © 1965 by Stuart Bruchey. Reprinted by permission of Harper & Row, Publishers, Inc.

English capital funds and labor sought to exploit the new-world opportunities opened by voyages of discovery and exploration. Overwhelmed by heavy costs of settlement and blinded by fools-gold schemes for easy wealth, they had failed to return profits to their investors. So too had failed the subsidiary colonizing associations which in some instances grew out of them. The private plantation, a method of uniting English capital, the labor of indentured servant or slave, and the resident management of the planter, emerged from these early failures. "Venture" and "capital," previously united in the person of an English absentee investor, split off from each other: the venturer now came in person to America to manage his enterprises and drew upon English capital in the form of mercantile credit. Some of these early enterprisers, Gray believes, "undoubtedly brought with them all or a part of the requisite capital." Certainly the "ambitious younger sons of middleclass families" who came to Virginia in the wave of the second generation of emigrants between 1640 and approximately 1670 brought "material advantages" with them. The recent researches of Bernard Bailyn have shown that they brought with them family claims to land in the colony, inherited shares of the original Company stock, or "a variety of forms of capital that might provide the basis for secure family fortunes."

Probably upon most planters, however, as upon colonial enterprise generally, pressed the scarcity of capital funds and labor that characterizes a newly-opened country. Even as late as 1680, in reply to the question "What obstruction do you find to the improvement of the trade and navigation of your Corporation?" the Governor of Connecticut specified the "want of men of estates to venture abroad, and of money at home for the management of trade, and labor being so deare with us." Scattered evidence suggests that interest rates were high. Gray reports they ranged from 8 to 10 per cent on well-secured loans in South Carolina during the greater part of the colonial period. Just before the Revolution the legal rate was lowered to 8 per cent in both that colony and Georgia. Massachusetts in 1641 restricted the rate to 8 per cent so that there would not be "usury amongst us contrary to the laws of God," but it lowered the rate to 6 per cent in 1693. However, in the judgment of Victor S. Clark, the costs of capital funds in relation to profit margins were not "excessive." That the productivity of funds was higher in America than in Britain in 1765 is suggested by James Habersham's remark to an English correspondent that 8 per cent could be "as well if not better paid by a Carefull Person either in the commercial or planting way here, than £ 5 per Ct. [5 per cent] with you."

It is this greater marginal efficiency of capital funds that attracted British loans and investments to America, in shipbuilding, iron works, the seventeenth-century fisheries, trade, manufacturing, and southern agriculture. Immediately after the Revolution John Lord Sheffield remarked that the "greater part of the colony commerce was carried on by means of British capitals," with "at least four-fifths" of the importations from Europe being "at all times made upon credit." "The greater part both of the exportations and coasting trade of America," Adam Smith asserts in *The Wealth of Nations* (1776), "is carried on by the capitals of merchants who reside in Great Britain. Even the stores and warehouses from which goods are retailed in some provinces, particularly in Virginia and Maryland, belong many of them to merchants who reside in the mother country." Victor S. Clark says further: "Until the very end of the colonial period, speculative enterprises in America, including the most important manufacturing undertakings, were financed very largely with English or German money, though occasionally wealthy colonists cooperated in these projects." That the achievement of political independence did not automatically bring to an end American dependence upon British capital, particularly in the case of the southern planter, is clearly seen in the following evaluation made in June 1792 by William Heth of Bermuda Hundred, Virginia, for the benefit of Alexander Hamilton: "The trade of this state is carried on chiefly with foreign capital. Those engaged in it, hardly deserve the name of merchants, being the factors, agents and Shop-keepers of the Merchants and Manufacturers of Gt. Britain —and their business to dispose of the goods of that, for the produce of this country, and remit it to the order of their principals with whom the profits of the trade of *course* centre.—"

Because of the cheapness of land and the ability to obtain headright claims to it by importing servants or slaves, the amount of funds required by the southern planters was not as large as it was to be in the later pre-Civil War period. Gray reports that about the year 1775 the establishment of a tobacco plantation of two thousand acres involved an expenditure of approximately £ 1,000 for slaves, £ 300 for buildings and furniture, £ 60 for implements and arms, £ 50 for a small sloop, £ 265 for livestock, £ 40 for land fees, and £ 100 for orchard and small miscellaneous items. The total came to £ 1,915 sterling. At about the same period the cost of a rice or indigo plantation of "moderate" size amounted to approximately £ 1,000 more. Leila Sellers presents an estimate of about £ 2,500 for a South Carolina rice plantation of two hundred acres (£ 100), forty "working hands" (£ 1,800), annual wages of an overseer (£ 50), and various tools and supplies.

English merchants customarily provided these supplies on one-year credit, with thes planter's crop serving as security for the advance. In the early years of settlement, credit purchases of servants and slaves were of less importance to Virginia and Maryland than to South Carolina and Georgia. The two tobacco colonies very largely used indentured servants for the first three-quarters of the seventeenth century, and the initial costs of servants usually amounted only to about one-fifth those of slaves. But the indebtedness of the tobacco planters mounted in the late seventeenth and eighteenth centuries with the increasingly rapid introduction of slaves.

Were figures for British capital exports to America available, they would undoubtedly show the mainstream flowing into the plantation agriculture of the southern mainland and British West Indies. The southern planter, according to Gray, borrowed "much" of his capital funds, and in the British West Indies "Most of the estates" were burdened with heavy encumbrances to persons residing in Great Britain. British law flowed in the wake of British capital in an effort to protect profit margins on these investments. While this body of law will be examined more closely later, it should be noted here that the profits to be won by transshipping tobacco from Great Britain to the Continent led to the "enumeration" of that article in the Navigation Acts. And if tobacco was thus forbidden by law to be shipped by colonial merchants to any point outside the British empire, so too was rice (to which, however, limited concessions were made after 1750) and indigo. However it was not colonial merchants but English merchants, not colonial shipping but English shipping (and after the Act of Union of 1707, that of the Scots as well) that dominated the greatest trade route of the colonial period, the route which ran back and forth across the Atlantic between Great Britian and her southern and West Indian colonies. As late as 1769–1771 four-fifths of the traffic crossing the Atlantic was carried in British bottoms. In a word, British mercantile houses provided the credit required for production and marketing, and with the aid of laws enacted to promote the interests of the merchants and the navy of Great Britain, the same houses provided almost the entire machinery of marketing itself.

Geography facilitated this dominance in the case of the tobacco colonies. The numerous navigable rivers of Maryland and Virginia diffused trade throughout the two provinces, long preventing its concentration in port cities under the control of native merchants. There was no need for the intermediation of natives: English ships simply penetrated the country to the wharves of the larger planters, unloaded their supplies, and put on tobacco for the homeward voyage. The cargo was consigned to the same merchant who had shipped the supplied, and it represented payment on account of obligations thus incurred as well as previous ones. Many smaller planters and farmers less favorably situated with respect to navigable waters purchased supplies from the larger planters and sold or consigned their tobacco to them. With the movement of tobacco away from the Tidewater into the Piedmont after the early eighteenth century, the consignment system gradually gave way to a method of direct purchase. Finding English merchants in control of Tidewater business, Scottish mercantile houses dispatched factors to supervise the general operations of chains of stores opened in the backcountry of both provinces. The stores seem to have offered merchandise on credit to any grower "from whom a purchase of at least 300 hogsheads of tobacco could be made annually," the typical scarcity of currency in the backcountry making it natural to resort to a system of bookkeeping barter. One of the most recent students of their practices, James H. Soltow, makes clear that the planters' accounts were supposed to be settled at the close of the crop year. But it was sometimes a difficult policy to enforce, and some balances remained unpaid as long as four or five years.

South of Virginia the shoal channels of the inland streams did not obstruct navigation by small craft but prevented oceangoing vessels from penetrating inland. It was a situation inviting both urbanization and the rise of a numerous group of small native middlemen, known at the time as "country" factors. Charleston emerged after 1670 as the commercial funnel for an agricultural district embracing South Carolina, parts of North Carolina, Georgia, and, after 1763, East and West Florida as well. At Charleston, and also at smaller ports in the district, country factors served as retail middlemen between planters and larger wholesale merchants, buying from the former and selling to the latter. Sometimes, however, they imported goods from colonies to the north, from the West Indies, and even from England. Despite the differences between the Carolina country and the region of the Chesapeake, "the masters of business," the men in "command of the shipping and wholesale trade," to use the language of Leila Sellers, were, in both areas, the factors of British merchants. It was they who provided indentured servants, slaves, and other supplies to planters on credit and directed the exportation of the planters' staples.

British credit thus came to southern agriculture through a number of channels, sometimes directly, sometimes circuitously, in the latter case being extended first to a resident factor, storekeeper, or colonial merchant and then by one of them to the planter. Larger planters, who had themselves obtained credit directly from an English mercantile house—on a "wholesale" basis, as it were—often proceeded to "retail" it to the smaller planters and farmers in their neighborhoods. To what extent was the shortage of capital funds in the hands of the southern planters owing to their intimate dependency upon the British?

12   *Eric Williams*
British Industry and the Triangular Trade

Britain was accumulating great wealth from the triangular trade. The increase of consumption goods called forth by that trade inevitably drew in its train the development of the productive power of the country. This industrial expansion required finance. What man in the first three-quarters of the eighteenth century was better able to afford the ready capital than a West Indian sugar planter or a Liverpool slave trader? We have already noticed the readiness with which absentee planters purchased land in England, where they were able to use their wealth to finance the great developments associated with the Agricultural Revolution. We must now trace the investment of profits from the triangular trade in British industry, where they supplied part of the huge outlay for the construction of the vast plants to meet the needs of the new productive process and the new markets.

THE INVESTMENT OF PROFITS FROM THE TRIANGULAR TRADE

Banking

Many of the eighteenth century banks established in Liverpool and Manchester, the slaving metropolis and the cotton capital respectively, were directly associated with the triangular trade. Here large sums were needed for the cotton factories and for the canals which improved the means of communication between the two towns.

Typical of the eighteenth century banker is the transition from tradesman to merchant and than the further progression from

SOURCE. From *Capitalism and Slavery* by Eric Williams. Copyright 1944 by the University of North Carolina Press. Chapter V.

merchant to banker. The term "merchant," in the eighteenth century context, not infrequently involved the gradations of slaver captain, privateer captain, privateer owner, before settling down on shore to the respectable business of commerce. The varied activities of a Liverpool businessman include: brewer, liquor merchant, grocer, spirit dealer, bill-broker, banker, etc. Writes the historian: "One wonders what was covered by that 'etc.' "[1] Like the song the sirens sang, that "etc." is not beyond all conjecture. It included, at some time or other, some one or more aspects of the triangular trade.

The Heywood Bank was founded in Liverpool in 1773 and endured as a private bank until 1883, when it was purchased by the Bank of Liverpool. Its founders were successful merchants later elected to the Chamber of Commerce. "They had their experience," the historian writes, "of the African trade," besides privateering. Both appear in the list of merchants trading to Africa in 1752 and their African interests survived up to 1807. The senior partner of one of the branches of the firm was Thomas Parke, of the banking firm of William Gregson, Sons, Parke and Morland, whose grandfather was a successful captain in the West Indian trade. Typical of the commercial interrelationships of the period, the daughter of one of the partners of the Heywoods later married Robertson, son of John Gladstone, and their son, Robertson Gladstone, obtained a partnership in the bank. In 1788 the firm set up a branch in Manchester, at the suggestion of some of the town's leading merchants. The Manchester branch, called the "Manchester Bank," was well known for many years. Eleven of fourteen Heywood descendants up to 1815 became merchants or bankers.[2]

The emergence of Thomas Leyland on the banking scene was

[1] J. Hughes, *Liverpool Banks and Bankers, 1760–1817* (Liverpool, 1906), 56–57, 217.

[2] *Ibid.*, 91–97; L. H. Grindon, *Manchester Banks and Bankers* (Manchester, 1878), 42, 54, 79–82, 185–189; J. B. Botsford, *English Society in the Eighteenth Century as Influenced from Oversea* (New York, 1924) , 122; H. R. F. Bourne, *English Merchants, Memoirs in Illustration of the Progress of English Commerce* (London, 1866), II, 78–79; E. Donnan, *Documents Illustrative of the History of the Slave Trade to America* (4 Vols.; Washington, D.C., 1930–1935), II, 493, 656.

delayed until the early years of the nineteenth century, but his
investments in the African slave trade dated back to the last
quarter of the eighteenth, Leyland, with his partners, was one of
the most active slave traders in Liverpool and his profits were
immense. In 1802 he became senior partner in the banking firm
of Clarkes and Roscoe. Leyland and Roscoe: curious combination! Strange union of the successful slaver and the consistent
opponent of slavery! Leyland struck off on his own in 1807, in
a more consistent partnership with his slave partner Bullins, and
the title of Leyland and Bullins was borne proudly and un-
smirched for ninety-four years until the amalgamation of the
bank, in 1901, with the North and South Wales Bank Limited.[3]

The Heywoods and Leylands are only the outstanding examples of the general rule in the banking history of eighteenth century Liverpool. William Gregson, banker, was also slave trader,
shipowner, privateer, underwriter, and owner of a ropewalk.
Francis Ingram was a slave trader, member of the African Company in 1777, while he also had a share in a ropery business,
and embarked on a privateering enterprise in partnership with
Thomas Leyland and the Earles. The latter themselves had
amassed a huge fortune in the slave trade, and remained slave
traders right up to 1807. The founder of Hanly's bank was Captain Richard Hanly, slave trader, whose sister was herself married to a slave trader. Hanly was a prominent member of the
"Liverpool Fireside," a society composed almost entirely of captains of vessles, slavers, and privateers, with a sprinkling of superior tradesmen. Robert Fairweather, like Hanly, was slave trader, member of the Liverpool Fireside, merchant and banker.

Jonas Bold combined both slave and West Indian trades. One
of the Company of Merchants trading to Africa from 1777 up to
1807, Bold was a sugar refiner, and became a partner in Ingram's bank. Thomas Fletcher began his career as apprentice to
a merchant banker who carried on an extensive trade with Jamaica. Raised to a partnership, Fletcher later became successive-
ly Vice-Chairman and Chairman of the Liverpool West India
Association, and at his death his assets included interests in

---

[3] Hughes, *op. cit.*, 170–174. In 1799 Leyland had four ships in the slave
trade, which carried 1,614 slaves. Donnan, *op cit.*, II, 646–649.

mortgages on a coffee and sugar plantation, with the slaves there-
on, in Jamaica. Charles Caldwell, of the banking firm of
Charles Caldwell and Co., was a partner in Oldham, Caldwell,
and Co., whose transactions were principally in sugar. Isaac
Hartman, another banker, owned West Indian plantations; while
James Moss, banker and prominent citizen in the eighteenth century, had some very large sugar planations in British Guiana.[4]

What has been said of Liverpool is equally true of Bristol,
London and Glasgow. Presiding over the meeting of the influential committee set up in Bristol in 1789 to oppose abolition was
William Miles. Among the members of the committee were Al-
derman Daubeny, Richard Bright, Richard Vaughan, John Cave
and Philip Protheroe. All six were bankers in Bristol. Cave,
Bright and Daubeny were partners in the "New Bank" established in 1786. Protheroe was partner in the Bristol City Bank.
William Miles bought a leading partnership in the old banking
house of Vaughan, Barker and Company; two of his sons were
mentioned in 1794, and "Miles's Bank," as it was popularly
called, had a lengthy and prosperous career.[5]

For London only one name need be mentioned, when that
name is Barclay. Two members of this Quaker family, David
and Alexander, were engaged in the slave trade in 1756. David
began his career in American and West Indian commerce and
became one of the most influential merchants of his day. His
father's house in Cheapside was one of the finest in the city of
London, and was often visited by royalty. He was not merely a
slave trader but actually owned a great plantation in Jamaica
where, we are told, he freed his slaves, and lived to find that "the
black skin enclosed hearts full of gratitude and minds as capable
of improvement as the proudest white." The Barclays married
into the banking families of Gurney and Freame, like so many
other intermarriages in other branches of industry which kept

[4] Hughes, *op. cit.*, 74–79, 84–85, 107–108, 111, 133, 138–141, 162, 165–166,
196–198, 220–221. For the Earles see Botsford, *op. cit.*, 123; Bourne, *op. cit.*, II,
64. In 1799 the Earles had three ships in the slave trade, which carried 969
slaves; Ingram, in 1798, three ships, with 1,005 slaves; Bold, in 1799, two
ships, with 539 slaves. Donnan, *op cit.*, II, 642–649.

[5] J. Latimer, *Annals of Bristol in the Eighteenth Century* (Bristol, 1873),
297–298, 392, 468, 507; *Annals of Bristol in the Nineteenth Century*, 113, 494;
Bourne, *op. cit.*, II, 18.

Quaker wealth in Quaker hands. From the combination sprang Barclay's Bank whose expansion and progress are beyond the scope of this study.[6]

The rise of banking in Glasgow was intimately connected with the triangular trade. The first regular bank began business in 1750. Known as the Ship Bank, one of the original partners was Andrew Buchanan, a tobacco lord of the city. Another was the same William Macdowall whose meeting with the sugar heiresses of St. Kitts had established both the fortunes of his house and those of the city. A third was Alexander Houston, one of the greatest West Indian merchants of the city, whose firm, Alexander Houston and Company, was one of the leading West Indian houses in the kingdom. This firm itself only grew out of the return of the two Scotch officers and their island brides to the city. For three-quarters of the century the firm carried on an immense trade, owning many ships and vast sugar plantations. Anticipating the abolition of the slave trade, it speculated on a grand scale in the purchase of slaves. The bill, however, failed to pass. The slaves had to be fed and clothed, their price fell heavily, disease carried them off by the hundreds. The firm consequently crashed in 1795, and this was the greatest financial disaster Glasgow had ever seen.

The success of the Ship Bank stimulated the formation of other banks. The Arms Bank was founded in the same year, with one of the leading partners Andrew Cochrane, another tobacco lord. The Thistle Bank followed in 1761, an aristocratic bank, whose business lay largely among the rich West Indian merchants. One of the chief partners was John Glassford, who carried on business on a large scale. At one time he owned twenty-five ships and their cargoes on the sea, and his annual turnover was more than half a million sterling.[7]

[6] W. C. Barclay, *A History of the Barclay Family* (London, 1924–1934), III, 235, 242–243, 246–247, 249; A. T. Gary, *The Political and Economic Relations of English and American Quakers, 1750–1785* (Oxford University D. Phil. Thesis, 1935), 194, 221, 455, 506; Bourne, *op. cit.*, II, 134–135; Botsford, *op. cit.*, 120–121, 295. Another prominent banking name in London associated with the slave trade was Baring. Gary, *op. cit.*, 506.

[7] G. Eyre-Todd, *History of Glasgow* (Glasgow, 1934), III, 151, 218–220, 245, 372; J. Buchanan, *Banking in Glasgow During the Olden Time* (Glasgow, 1862), 5–6, 17, 23–26, 30–34.

Heavy Industry

Heavy industry played an important role in the progress of the Industrial Revolution and the development of the triangular trade. Some of the capital which financed the growth of the metallurgical industries was supplied directly by the triangular trade.

It was the capital accumulated from the West Indian trade that financed James Watt and the steam engine. Boulton and Watt received advances from Lowe, Vere, Williams and Jennings —later the Williams Deacons Bank. Watt had some anxious moments in 1778 during the American Revolution when the West Indian fleet was threatened with capture by the French. "Even in this emergency," wrote Boulton to him hopefully, "Lowe, Vere and Company may yet be saved, if ye West Indian fleet arrives safe from ye French fleet . . . as many of their securities depend on it."[8]

The bank pulled through and the precious invention was safe. The sugar planters were among the first to realize its importance. Boulton wrote to Watt in 1783: ". . . Mr. Pennant, who is a very amiable man, with ten or twelve thousand pounds a year, has the largest estate in Jamaica; there was also Mr. Gale and Mr. Beeston Long, who have some very large sugar plantations there, who wish to see steam answer in lieu of horses."[9]

One of the leading ironmongers of the eighteenth century, Antony Bacon, was intimately connected with the triangular trade. His partner was Gilbert Francklyn, a West Indian planter, who later wrote many letters to the Lord President of the Committee of Privy Council emphasizing the importance of taking over the French sugar colony of Saint Domingue in the war with revolutionary France.[10] Bacon, like so many others, ventured into the African trade. He began a lucrative commerce in first victualling troops on the coast and then supplying seasoned and able Ne-

---

[8] J. Lord, *Capital and Steam-Power, 1750–1850* (London, 1923), 113.

[9] *Ibid.*, 192.

[10] Liverpool Papers, Add. *MSS. 38227*, ff. 43, 50, 140, 141. Sept. 7 and 14, Nov. 15 and 17, 1791.

groes for government contracts in the West Indies. During the years 1768–1776 he received almost £67,000 under this latter heading. In 1765 he set up his iron works at Merthyr Tydfill which expanded rapidly owing to government contracts during the American war; in 1776 he set up another furnace at Cyfartha. The iron ore for his furnaces was exported from Whitehaven, and as early as 1740 Bacon took a part in improving its harbor.

Bacon made a fortune out of his artillery contracts with the British government. He retired in 1782 having acquired a veritable mineral kingdom. His ironworks at Cyfartha he leased to Crawshay, reserving for himself a clear annuity of £10,000, and out of Cyfartha Crawshay himself made a fortune. He sold Penydaren to Homfray, the man who perfected the puddling process; Dowlais went to Lewis and the Plymouth works to Hill. The ordinance contract had already been transferred to Caroon, Roebuck's successor. No wonder that it was stated that Bacon considered himself as "moving in a superior orbit."[11]

William Beckford became a master ironmonger in 1753.[12] Part of the capital supplied for the Thorncliffe ironworks, begun in 1792, came from a razor-maker, Henry Longden, who received a bequest of some fifteen thousand pounds from a wealthy uncle, a West Indian merchant of Sheffield.[13]

Insurance

In the eighteenth century, when the slave trade was the most valuable trade and West Indian property among the most valuable property in the British Empire, the triangular trade occupied an important position in the eyes of the rising insurance companies. In the early years, when Lloyd's was a coffee house and

---

[11] L. B. Namier, "Antony Bacon, *Journal of Economic and Business History* (Nov., 1929)," 25–27, 32, 39, 41, 43; T. S. Ashton, *Iron and Steel in The Industrial Revolution* (Manchester, 1924), 52, 136, 241–242; J. H. Clapham, *An Economic History of Modern Britain, The Early Railway Age, 1820–1850* (Cambridge, 1930), 187–188.

[12] A. Beaven, *The Aldermen of The City of London* (London, 1908–1913), II, 131.

[13] Ashton, *op. cit.*, 157.

nothing more, many advertisements in the London Gazette about runaway slaves listed Lloyd's as the place where they should be returned.[14]

The earliest extant advertisement referring to Lloyd's, dated 1692, deals with the sale of three ships by auction. The ships were cleared for Barbados and Virginia. The only project listed at Lloyd's in the bubbles of 1720 concerned trade to Barbary and Africa. Relton, the historian of fire insurance, states that insurance against fires in the West Indies had been done at Lloyd's "from a very early date." Lloyd's, like other insurance companies, insured slaves and slave ships, and was vitally interested in legal decisions as to what constituted "natural death" and "perils of the sea." Among their subscriptions to public heroes and merchant captains is one of 1804 to a Liverpool captain who, on passage from Africa to British Guiana, successfully beat off a French corvette and saved his valuable cargo. The third son of their first secretary, John Bennett, was agent for Lloyd's in Antigua in 1833, and the only known portrait of his father was recently discovered in the West Indies. One of the most distinguished chairmen of Lloyd's in its long history was Joseph Marryat, a West Indian planter, who successfully and brilliantly fought to maintain Lloyd's monopoly of marine insurance against a rival company in the House of Commons in 1810, where he was opposed by another West Indian, father of the famous Cardinal Manning.[15] Marryat was awarded £15,000 compensation in 1837 for 391 slaves in Trinidad and Jamaica.[16]

In 1782 the West Indian sugar interest took the lead in starting another insurance company, the Phoenix, one of the first companies to establish a branch overseas—in the West Indies.[17]

---

[14] F. Martin, *The History of Lloyd's and of Marine Insurance in Great Britain* (London, 1876), 62.

[15] C. Wright and C. E. Fayle, *A History of Lloyds* (London, 1928), 19, 91, 151, 212, 218–219, 243, 293, 327. Other prominent names associated with Lloyd's were Baring, and the abolitionists, Richard Thornton and Zachary Macaulay. *Ibid.*, 196–197.

[16] *H. of C. Sess. Pap.*, 1837–8, Vol. 48. The exact figure was £15,095.4.4 (pp. 12, 165, 169).

[17] Clapham, *op. cit.*, 286.

The Liverpool Underwriters' Association was formed in 1802. Chairman of the meeting was the prominent West Indian merchant, John Gladstone.[18]

THE DEVELOPMENT OF BRITISH INDUSTRY
TO 1783

Thus it was that the Abbé Raynal, one of the most progressive spirits of his day, a man of wide learning in close touch with the French bourgeoisie, was able to see that the labors of the people in the West Indies "may be considered as the principal cause of the rapid motion which now agitates the universe."[19] The triangular trade made an enormous contribution to Britain's industrial development. The profits from this trade fertilized the entire productive system of the country. Three instances must suffice. The slate industry in Wales, which provided material for roofing, was revolutionized by the new methods adopted on his Carnarvonshire estate by Lord Penrhyn,[20] who, as we have seen, owned sugar plantations in Jamaica and was chairman of the West India Committee at the end of the eighteenth century. The leading figure in the first great railway project in England, which linked Liverpool and Manchester, was Joseph Sandars, of whom little is known. But his withdrawal in 1824 from the Liverpool Anti-Slavery Society is of great importance, as at least showing a reluctance to press the sugar planters.[21] Three other men prominently identified with the undertaking had close connections with the triangular trade—General Gascoyne of Liverpool, a stalwart

[18] Wright and Fayle, op. cit., 240–241.

[19] G. S. Callender, Selections from the Economic History of the United States (New York, 1909), 78–79.

[20] A. H. Dodd, The Industrial Revolution in North Wales (Cardiff, 1933), 37, 91, 125, 204–208, 219. See also C. R. Fay, Imperial Economy and its place in the formation of Economic Doctrine (Oxford, 1934), 32.

[21] Huskisson Papers, Add. MSS. 38745, ff. 182–183. Huskisson to Sandars, Jan. 22, 1824, agreeing with his withdrawal. See also J. Francis, A History of the English Railway; its Social Relations and Revelations, 1820–1845 (London, 1851), I, 93.

champion of the West India interest, John Gladstone and John Moss.[22] The Bristol West India interest also played a prominent part in the construction of the Great Western Railway.[23]

But it must not be inferred that the triangular trade was solely and entirely responsible for the economic development. The growth of the internal market in England, the ploughing-in of the profits from industry to generate still further capital and achieve still greater expansion, played a large part. But this industrial development, stimulated by mercantilism, later outgrew mercantilism and destroyed it.

In 1783 the shape of things to come was clearly visible. The steam engine's potentialities were not an academic question. Sixty-six engines were in operation, two-thirds of these in mines and foundries.[24] Improved methods of coal mining, combined with the influence of stream, resulted in a great expansion of the iron industry. Production increased four times between 1740 and 1788, the number of furnaces rose by one-half.[25] The iron bridge and the iron railroad had appeared; the Carron Works had been founded; and Wilkinson was already famous as "the father of the iron trade." Cotton, the queen of the Industrial Revolution, responded readily to the new inventions, unhampered as it was by the traditions and guild restrictions which impeded its older rival, wool. Laissez faire became a practice in the new industry long before it penetrated the text books as orthodox economic theory. The spinning jenny, the water frame, the mule, revolutionized the industry, which, as a result, showed

[22] See *Hansard*, VI, 919, where Gascoyne opposed the prohibition of the British slave trade to new colonies conquered during the Napoleonic wars as a violation of faith. April 25, 1806. For Gladstone, see Francis, *op. cit.*, I, 123; F. S. Williams, *Our Iron Roads; their history, construction, and social influences* (London, 1852), 323–324, 337. For Moss, see Francis, *op. cit.*, I, 123; Hughes, *op. cit.*, 197–198.

[23] V. Sommerfield, *English Railways, their beginnings, development and personalities* (London, 1937), 34–38; Latimer, *Annals of Bristol in the Nineteenth Century*, 111, 189–190. Three of the directors were connected with the West Indies, and subscribed £51,800 out of £217,500.

[24] Lord, *op. cit.*, 166.

[25] H. Scrivenor, *A Comprehensive History of The Iron Trade* (London, 1841), 86–87. In 1740: 17,350 tons in 89 furnaces; in 1788: 68,300 tons in 85 furnaces.

a continuous upward trend. Between 1700 and 1780 imports of. raw cotton increased more than three times, exports of cotton goods fifteen times.[26] The population of Manchester increased by nearly one-half between 1757 and 1773,[27] the numbers engaged in the cotton industry quadrupled between 1750 and 1785.[28] Not only heavy industry, cotton, too—the two industries that were to dominate the period 1783–1850—was gathering strength for the assault on the system of monopoly which had for so long been deemed essential to the existence and prosperity of both.

The entire economy of England was stimulated by this beneficent breath of increased production. The output of the Staffordshire potteries increased fivefold in value between 1725 and 1777.[29] The tonnage of shipping leaving English ports more than doubled between 1700 and 1781. English imports increased fourfold between 1715 and 1775, exports trebled between 1700 and 1771.[30] English industry in 1783 was like Gulliver, tied down by the Lilliputian restrictions of mercantilism.

Two outstanding figures of the eighteenth century saw and, what was more, appreciated the irrepressible conflict: Adam Smith from his professorial chair, Thomas Jefferson on his plantation.

Adam Smith denounced the folly and injustice which had first directed the project of establishing colonies in the New World. He opposed the whole system of monopoly, the keystone of the colonial arch, on the ground that it restricted the productive power of England as well as the colonies. If British industry had advanced, it had done so not because of the monopoly but in spite of it, and the monopoly represented nothing but the sacri-

[26] J. Wheeler, *Manchester, Its Political, Social and Commercial History, Ancient and Modern* (Manchester, 1842), 148, 170. Imports: from 1,985,868 to 6,700,000 pounds; exports: from £23,253 to £355,060.

[27] W. T. Jackman, *The Development of Transportation in Modern England* (Cambridge, 1916), II, 514 n. From 19,837 to 27,246.

[28] Butterworth, *op. cit.*, 57; Wheeler, *op. cit.*, 171. From 20,000 to 80,000.

[29] Lord, *op. cit.*, 143.

[30] P. Mantoux, *The Industrial Revolution in the Eighteenth Century* (London, 1928), 102–103.

fice of the general good to the interests of a few, the sacrifice of the interest of the home consumer to that of the colonial producer. In the colonies themselves the ban on colonial manufactures seemed to him "a manifest violation of the most sacred rights of mankind . . . impertinent badges of slavery imposed upon them, without any sufficient reason, by the groundless jealousy of the merchants and manufacturers of the mother country." British capital had been forced from trade with neighboring countries to trade with more distant countries; money that could have been used to improve the lands, increase the manufactures, and extend the commerce of Great Britain had been expended in fostering a trade with distant areas from which Britain derived nothing but loss (!) and frequent wars. It was a fit system for a nation whose government was influenced by shopkeepers.[31]

The *Wealth of Nations* was the philosophical antecedent of the American Revolution. Both were twin products of the same cause, the brake applied by the mercantile system on the development of the productive power of England and her colonies. Adam Smith's role was to berate intellectually "the mean and malignant expedients"[32] of a system which the armies of George Washington dealt a mortal wound on the battlefields of America.

[31] Adam Smith, *The Wealth of Nations* (Cannan ed.; N.Y., 1937), 549, 555, 558–559, 567, 573, 576, 579, 581, 595, 625–626.

[32] *Ibid.*, 577.

13 FROM   *C. L. R. James*
The West Indies in the History of European Capitalism

Prosperity is not a moral question and the justification of San Domingo was its prosperity. Never for centuries had the western world known such economic progress. By 1754, two years before the beginning of the Seven Years' War, there were 599 plantations of sugar and 3,379 of indigo. During the Seven Years' War (1756–1763) the French marine, swept off the sea by the British Navy, could not bring the supplies on which the colony depended, the extensive smuggling trade could not supply the deficiency, thousands of slaves died from starvation and the upward rise of production, though not halted, was diminished. But after the Treaty of Paris in 1763 the colony made a great stride forward. In 1767 it exported 72 million pounds' weight of raw sugar and 51 million pounds of white, a million pounds of indigo and two million pounds of cotton, and quantities of hides, molasses, cocoa and rum. Smuggling, which was winked at by the authorities, raised the official figures by at least 25 per cent. Nor was it only in quantity that San Domingo excelled but in quality. Each coffee tree produced on an average a pound weight, equal sometimes to that of Mocha. Cotton grew naturally, even without care, in stony ground and in the crevices of the rocks. Indigo also grew spontaneously. Tobacco had a larger leaf there than in any other part of the Americas and sometimes equalled in quality the produce of Havana. The kernel of San Domingo cocoa was more acidulated than that of Venezuela and was not inferior in other respects, experience proving that the chocolate made of the two cocoas in combination had a more delicate flavour than that made from the cocoa of Venezuela alone.

If on no earthly spot was so much misery concentrated as on a

SOURCE. From *The Black Jacobins: Toussaint L'Ouverture and the San Domingo Revolution,* Second Edition, by C. L. R. James, 1963, pp. 45–67. By permission of the author.

slave-ship, then on no portion of the globe did its surface in proportion to its dimensions yield so much wealth as the colony of San Domingo.

And yet it was this very prosperity which would lead to the revolution.

From the beginning the colonists were at variance with the French Government and the interests it represented. The French, like every other Government in those days, looked upon colonies as existing exclusively for the profit of the metropolis. Known as the Mercantile system in England, the French called this economic tyranny by a more honest name, the Exclusive. Whatever manufactured goods the colonists needed they were compelled to buy from France. They could sell their produce only to France. The goods were to be transported only in French ships. Even the raw sugar produced in the colonies was to be refined in the mother-country, and the French imposed heavy duties on refined sugar of colonial origin. "The colonies," said Colbert, "are founded by and for the metropolis." This was not true. The colonists had founded San Domingo themselves, and the falsehood of the claim made the exploitation all the harder to bear.

In 1664 the French Government, in accordance with the custom of those days, handed over the rights of trade with San Domingo to a private company. But the monopolists either could not or would not send out all the goods that the colonists wanted, and charged them nearly twice as much as they were accustomed to pay. The colonists revolted and the Governor was compelled to ease the restrictions. In 1722 the same thing happened. Agents received from the company the exclusive grant of the African trade, in return for supplying San Domingo with 2,000 Negroes every year. But by 1720 the colonists were needing 8,000 slaves a year, and they knew that in addition to supplying them with only one-quarter of their needs, the company would raise the price. There was another insurrection. The colonists arrested the Governor and put him in prison, and the Government had to modify the privileges of the company. The colonists saw themselves held in check by the Exclusive for the benefit of the metropolis, and as their prosperity grew they found the restrictions more and more intolerable. Political dependence on the mother-country was now retarding the economic growth of San Domingo. The colonists wished to shake off these shackles as Britain's American colonies were to shake off theirs. Thus if big whites and small whites were in permanent conflict with each other, they were united against the Mulattoes on the one hand and against the French bourgeoisie on the other. They could persecute the Mulattoes, but against the French bourgeoisie they could do nothing but rage. Long before 1789 the French bourgeoisie was the most powerful economic force in France, and the slave-trade and the colonies were the basis of its wealth and power.

The slave-trade and slavery were the economic basis of the French Revolution. "Sad irony of human history," comments Jaurès. "The fortunes created at Bordeaux, at Nantes, by the slave-trade, gave to the bourgeoisie that pride which needed liberty and contributed to human emancipation." Nantes was the centre of the slave-trade. As early as 1666, 108 ships went to the coast of Guinea and took on board 37,430 slaves,[1] to a total value of more than 37 millions, giving the Nantes bourgeoisie 15 to 20 per cent on their money. In 1700 Nantes was sending 50 ships a year to the West Indies with Irish salt beef, linen for the household and for clothing the slaves, and machinery for sugar-mills. Nearly all the industries which developed in France during the eighteenth century had their origin in goods or commodities destined either for the coast of Guinea or for America. The capital from the slave-trade fertilized them; though the bourgeoisie traded in other things than slaves, upon the success or failure of the traffic everything else depended.[2]

Some ships took on the way wine from Madeira for the colonists and dried turtle from Cape Verde for the slaves. In return they brought back colonial produce to Nantes whence Dutch vessels took it to Northern Europe. Some made the return journey by way of Spain and Portugal, exchanging their colonial cargo for the products of those countries. Sixty ships from Rochelle and Oberon brought their salted cod to Nantes, to go to the inland market or out to the colonies to feed the slaves. The year

[1] This section is based on the work of Jaurès, *Histoire Socialiste de la Révolution Française*, Paris, 1922, pp. 62–84.

[2] Gaston-Martin, *L'Ere des Négriers (1714–1774)*, Paris, 1931, p. 424.

1758 saw the first manufactory of Indian cloth, to weave the raw cotton of India and the West Indian islands.

The planters and small manufacturers of San Domingo were able to establish themselves only by means of the capital advanced by the maritime bourgeoisie. By 1789 the Nantes merchants alone had 50 millions invested in the West Indies.

Bordeaux had begun with the wine industry which gave its ship-builders and navigators an opportunity to trade all over the world; then came brandy, also to all ports, but above all to the colonies. By the middle of the eighteenth century, 16 factories refined 10,000 tons of raw sugar from San Domingo every year, using nearly 4,000 tons of charcoal. Local factories supplied the town with jars, dishes and bottles. The trade was cosmopolitan —Flemings, Germans, Dutchmen, Irishmen and Englishmen came to live in Bordeaux, contributing to the general expansion and amassing riches for themselves. Bordeaux traded with Holland, Germany, Portugal, Venice, and Ireland, but slavery and the colonial trade were the fount and origin and sustenance of this thriving industry and far-flung commerce.

Marseilles was the great centre for the Mediterranean and Eastern trade, and a royal decree at the beginning of the century had attempted to exclude it from the trade with the colonies. The attempt failed. San Domingo was the special centre of the Marseilles trade. Marseilles sent there not only the wines of Provence: in 1789 there were in Marseilles 12 sugar refineries, nearly as many as in Bordeaux.

In the early years most of this trade had been carried in foreign-built or foreign-owned ships. But by 1730 the maritime bourgeois began to build themselves. In 1778 Bordeaux ship-owners constructed seven vessels, in 1784 they constructed 32, with a total of 115 for the six years. A Marseilles ship-owner, Georges Roux, could fit out a fleet on his own account in order to take vengeance on the English fleet for the prizes it had taken.

Nantes, Bordeaux and Marseilles were the chief centres of the maritime bourgeoisie, but Orleans, Dieppe, Bercy-Paris, a dozen great towns, refined raw sugar and shared in the subsidiary industries.[3] A large part of the hides worked in France came

[3] Deschamps, *Les Colonies pendant la Révolution*, Paris, 1898, pp. 3–8.

from San Domingo. The flourishing cotton industry of Normandy drew its raw cotton in part from the West Indies, and in all its ramifications the cotton trade occupied the population of more than a hundred French towns. In 1789 exchanges with the American colonies were 296 millions. France exported to the islands 78 millions of flour, salted meats, wines and stuffs. The colonies sent to France 218 millions of sugar, coffee, cocoa, wood, indigo and hides. Of the 218 millions imported only 71 millions were consumed in France. The rest was exported after preparation. The total value of the colonies represented 3,000 millions, and on them depended the livelihood of a number of Frenchmen variously estimated at between two and six millions. By 1789 San Domingo was the market of the new world. It received in its ports 1,587 ships, a greater number than Marseilles, and France used for the San Domingo trade alone 750 great vessels employing 24,000 sailors. In 1789 Britain's export trade would be 27 million pounds, that of France 17 million pounds, of which the trade of San Domingo would account for nearly 11 million pounds. The whole of Britain's colonial trade in that year amounted to only five million pounds.[4]

The maritime bourgeoisie would not hear of any change in the Exclusive. They had the ear of the Minister and the Government, and not only were the colonists refused permission to trade with foreign countries, but the circulation of all French currency, except the very lowest, was forbidden in the islands, lest the colonists use it to purchase foreign goods. In such a method of trade they were at the mercy of the bourgeoisie. In 1774 their indebtedness was 200 millions, and by 1789 it was estimated at between 300 and 500 millions.[5] If the colonist complained of the Exclusive, the bourgeoisie complained that the colonists would not pay their debts, and agitated for stricter measures against the contraband.

Rich as was the French bourgeoisie, the colonial trade was too big for it. The British bourgeois, most successful of slave-traders, sold thousands of smuggled slaves every year to the French colo-

[4]Brougham, *The Colonial Policy of the European Powers*, Edinburgh, 1803, vol. II, pp. 538–540.

[5] Deschamps, *Les Colonies pendant . . .*, p. 25.

nist and particularly to San Domingo. But even while they sold
the slaves to San Domingo, the British were watching the progress of this colony with alarm and with envy. After the independence of America in 1783, this amazing French colony suddenly
made such a leap as almost to double its production between
1783 and 1789. In those years Bordeaux alone invested 100 millions in San Domingo. The British bouregois were the great rivals of the French. All through the eighteenth century they
fought in every part of the world. The French had jumped glee-
fully in to help drive them out of America. San Domingo was
now incomparably the finest colony in the world and its possibilities seemed limitless. The British bourgeoisie investigated the
new situation in the West Indies, and on the basis of what it saw,
prepared a bombshell for its rivals. Without slaves San Domingo
was doomed. The British colonies had enough slaves for all the
trade there were ever likely to do. With the tears rolling down
their cheeks for the poor suffering blacks, those British bourgeois who had no West Indian interests set up a great howl for
the abolition of the slave-trade.

A venal race of scholars, profiteering panders to national vani-
ty, have conspired to obscure the truth about abolition. Up to
1783 the British bourgeoisie had taken the slave-trade for granted. In 1773 and again in 1774, the Jamaica Assembly, afraid of
insurrection and seeking to raise revenue, taxed the importation
of slaves. In great wrath the British Board of Trade disallowed
the measures and told the Governor that he would be sacked if
he gave his sanction to any similar Bill.[6] Well-meaning persons
talked of the iniquity of slavery and the slave-trade, as well-
meaning persons in 1938 talked about the native question in Africa or the misery of the Indian peasant. Dr. Johnson toasted the
next slave insurrection in the West Indies. Stray members of parliament introduced Bills for the abolition of the slave-trade
which the House rejected without much bother. In 1783 Lord
North turned down a petition against the trade:[7] the petition did
credit to the Christian feelings, and to the humane breast, etc.,
etc., but the trade was necessary. With the loss of America, however, a new situation arose.

[6] *House of Commons: Accounts and Papers*, 1795–1796, vol. 100.
[7] *Parliamentary History*, XXIII, pp. 1026–1027.

The British found that by the abolition of the mercantile system with America, they gained instead of losing. It was the first great lesson in the advantages of free trade. But if Britain gained the British West Indies suffered. The rising industrial bourgeoisie, feeling its way to free trade and a greater exploitation of India, began to abuse the West Indies, called them "sterile rocks,"[8] and asked if the interest and independence of the nation should be sacrificed to 72,000 masters and 400,000 slaves.[9]

The industrial bourgeois were beginning their victorious attack upon the agricultural monopoly which was to culminate in the Repeal of the Corn Laws in 1846. The West Indian sugar-producers were monopolists whose methods of production afforded an easy target, and Adam Smith[10] and Arthur Young,[11] the forerunners of the new era, condemned the whole principle of slave-labour as the most expensive in the world. Besides, why not get sugar from India? India, after the loss of America, assumed a new importance. The British experimented with sugar in Bengal, received glowing reports and in 1791 the first shipments arrived.[12] In 1793 Mr. Randle Jackson would preach to the company's shareholders, a little sermon on the new orientation. "It seemed as if Providence, when it took from us America, would not leave its favourite people without an ample substitute; or who should say that Providence had not taken from us one member, more seriously to impress us with the value of another."[13] It might not be good theology, but it was very good economics. Pitt and Dundas saw a chance of capturing the continental market from France by East India sugar. There was cot-

[8] *The Right in the West Indian Merchants to a Double Monopoly of the Sugar Market of Great Britain, and the expedience of all monopolies examined.* (n.d.)

[9] Chalmers, *Opinions on Interesting Subjects of Law and Commercial Policy arising from American Independence,* London, 1784, p. 60.

[10] Smith, *Wealth of Nations,* vol. I, p. 123. "It appears from the experience of all ages and nations . . . that the work done by freemen comes cheaper in the end than that performed by slaves."

[11] Young, *Annals of Agriculture,* 1788. Vol. IX, pp. 88–96. "The culture of sugar by slaves is the dearest species of labour in the world."

[12] *East India Sugar,* 1822, appendix I, p. 3.

[13] *Debate on the Expediency of cultivating sugar in the territories of the East India Company,* East India House, 1793.

ton and indigo. The production of cotton in India doubled in a few years. Indian free labour cost a penny a day.

But the West Indian vested interests were strong, statesmen do not act merely on speculation, and these possibilities by themselves would not have accounted for any sudden change in British policy. It was the miraculous growth of San Domingo that was decisive. Pitt found that some 50 per cent of the slaves imported into the British islands were sold to the French colonies.[14] It was the British slave-trade, therefore, which was increasing French colonial produce and putting the European market into French hands. Britain was cutting its own throat. And even the profits from this export were not likely to last. Already a few years before the slave merchants had failed for £700,000 in a year.[15] The French, seeking to provide their own slaves, were encroaching in Africa and increasing their share of the trade every year. Why should they continue to buy from Britain? Holland and Spain were doing the same. By 1786 Pitt, a disciple of Adam Smith, had seen the light clearly. He asked Wilberforce to undertake the campaign.[16] Wilberforce represented the important division of Yorkshire, he had a great reputation, all the humanity, justice, stain on national character, etc., etc., would sound well coming from him. Pitt was in a hurry —it was important to bring the trade to a complete stop quickly and suddenly. The French had neither the capital nor the organisation to make good the deficiency at once and he would ruin San Domingo at a stroke. In 1787 he warned Wilberforce that if he did not bring the motion in, somebody else would,[17] and in 1788 he informed the Cabinet that he would not stay in it with those who opposed.[18] Pitt was fairly certain of success in England. With truly British nerve he tried to persuade the European

[14] *Report of the Committee of Privy Council for Trade and Plantations,* 1789, Part IV, Tables for Dominica and Jamaica. See also Dundas' statistics, April 18, 1792.

[15] Clarkson, *Essay on the Impolicy of the African Slave Trade,* London, 1784, p. 29.

[16] Coupland, *The British Anti-Slavery Movement,* London, 1933, p. 74.

[17] Coupland, *Wilberforce,* Oxford, 1923, p. 93.

[18] Fortescue MSS. (Historical Manuscripts Commission, British Museum), Pitt to Grenville, June 29, 1788. Vol. I, p. 342.

Governments to abolish the trade on the score of inhumanity. The French Government discussed the proposal amicably, but by May, 1789, the British Ambassador wrote sadly that it seemed as if all the French Government's negotiations had been to "compliment us and to keep us quiet and in good humour."[19] The Dutch, less polite, gave a more abrupt negative. But here a great stroke of luck befell Pitt. France was then stirring with pre-revolutionary attacks on all obvious abuses, and one year after the Abolitionist Society had been formed in Britain, a group of Liberals in France, Brissot, Mirabeau, Pétion, Condorcet, Abbé Grégoire, all the great names of the first years of the revolution, followed the British example and formed a society, the Friends of the Negro. The leading spirit was Brissot, a journalist who had seen slavery in the United States. The society aimed at the abolition of slavery, published a journal, agitated. This suited the British down to the ground. Clarkson went to Paris, to stimulate "the slumbering energies"[20] of the society, gave it money, supplied France with British anti-slavery propaganda.[21] Despite the names that were to become so famous and a large membership, we must beware of thinking that the Friends of the Negro represented a force. The colonists took them seriously, the maritime bouregeoisie did not. It was the French Revolution which, with unexpected swiftness, would drag these eloquent Frenchmen out of the stimulating excitement of philanthropic propaganda and put them face to face with economic reality.

These then were the forces which in the decade preceding the French Revolution linked San Domingo to the economic destiny of three continents and the social and political conflicts of that pregnant age. A trade and method of production so cruel and so immoral that it would wilt before the publicity which a great revolution throws upon the sources of wealth; the powerful British Government determined to wreck French commerce in the Antilles, agitating at home and intriguing in France among men who, unbeknown to themselves, would soon have power in their

[19] *Liverpool Papers* (Additional Manuscripts, British Museum). Lord Dorset to Lord Hawkesbury. Vol. 38224, p. 118.

[20] R. I. and S. Wilberforce, *Life of Wilberforce*, London, 1838, vol. I, p. 228.

[21] *Cahiers de la Révolution Française*, Paris, 1935, No. III, p. 25.

hands; the colonial world (itself divided) and the French bourgeoisie, each intent on its own purposes and, unaware of the approaching danger, drawing apart instead of closer together. Not one courageous leader, many courageous leaders were needed, but the science of history was not what it is to-day and no man living then could foresee, as we can foresee to-day, the coming upheavals.[22] Mirabeau indeed said that the colonists slept on the edge of Vesuvius, but for centuries the same thing had been said and the slaves had never done anything.

How could anyone seriously fear for such a wonderful colony? Slavery seemed eternal and the profits mounted. Never before, and perhaps never since, has the world seen anything proportionately so dazzling as the last years of pre-revolutionary San Domingo. Between 1783 and 1789 production nearly doubled. Between 1764 and 1771 the average importation of slaves varied between ten and fifteen thousand. In 1786 it was 27,000, and from 1787 onwards the colony was taking more than 40,000 slaves a year. But economic prosperity is no guarantee of social stability. That rests on the constantly shifting equilibrium between the classes. It was the prosperity of the bourgeoisie that started the English revolution of the seventeenth century. With every stride in production the colony was marching to its doom.

The enormous increase of slaves was filling the colony with native Africans, more resentful, more intractable, more ready for rebellion than the creole Negro. Of the half-million slaves in the colony in 1789, more than two-thirds had been born in Africa.

These slaves were being used for the opening up of new lands. There was no time to allow for the period of acclimatisation, known as the seasoning, and they died like flies. From the earliest days of the colony towards the middle of the eighteenth century, there had been some improvement in the treatment of the slaves, but this enormous number of newcomers who had to be broken and terrorised into labour and submission caused an increase in fear and severity. In 1784 the administrators, who visited one of the slave shops which sometimes served as a market-place instead of the deck of the slaver, reported a revolting pic-

[22] Written in 1938.

ture of dead and dying thrown pell-mell into the filth. The Le Jeune case took place in 1788. In 1790 de Wimpffen states that not one article of the Negro Code was obeyed. He himself had sat at table with a woman, beautiful, rich and very much admired, who had had a careless cook thrown into the oven.

The problem of feeding this enormous increase in the slave population was making the struggle between the planters and the maritime bourgeoisie over the Exclusive more bitter than ever, and the planters after 1783 had forced a slight breach in the strait jacket which clasped them. Having tasted blood, they wanted more.

Mulattoes educated in Paris during the Seven Years' War had come home, and their education and accomplishments filled the colonists with hatred and envy and fear. It was these last years that saw the fiercest legislation against them. Forbidden to go to France, where they learnt things that were not good for them, they stayed at home to increase the strength of the dissatisfied.

With the growth of trade and of profits, the number of planters who could afford to leave their estates in charge of managers grew, and by 1789, in addition to the maritime bourgeois, there was a large group of absentee proprietors in France linked to the aristocracy by marriage, for whom San Domingo was nothing else but a source of revenue to be spent in the luxurious living of aristocratic Paris. So far had these parasites penetrated into the French aristocracy that a memoir from San Domingo to the King could say: "Sire, your court is creole," without too much stretching of the truth.

The prosperity affected even the slaves. More of them could save money, buy their freedom, and enter the promised land.

This was the San Domingo of 1789, the most profitable colony the world had ever known; to the casual eye the most flourishing and prosperous possession on the face of the globe; to the analyst a society torn by inner and outer contradictions which in four years would split that structure into so many pieces that they could never be put together again.

It was the French bourgeoisie which pressed the button. This strange San Domingo society was but a garish exaggeration, a crazy caricature, of the *ancien régime* in France. The royalist bureaucracy, incompetent and wasteful, could not manage the finances of France; the aristocracy and the clergy bled the peasantry dry, impeded the economic development of the country, gobbled up all the best places, and considered themselves almost as superior to the able and vigorous bourgeois as the white planters considered themselves superior to the Mulattoes.

But the French bourgeoisie too was proud and no members of it were prouder than the maritime bourgeois. We have seen their wealth. They knew that they were the foundation of the country's prosperity. They were buying up the land of the aristocracy. They built great schools and universities, they read Voltaire and Rousseau, they sent their linen to the colonies to be washed and to get the right colour and scent, they sent their wine for two or three voyages to the colonies and back to give it the right flavour. They, along with the other bourgeois, chafed at their social disadvantages; the chaotic state of French administration and finance handicapped them in their business. A hard winter in 1788 brought matters to a head. The monarchy was already bankrupt, the aristocracy made a bid to recover its former power, the peasants began to revolt, and the bourgeoisie saw that the time had come for it to govern the country on the English model in collaboration with its allies, the radical aristocracy. In the agitation which began the French Revolution, the maritime bourgeoisie took the lead. The bourgeoisie of Dauphiné and Britanny, with their ports of Marseilles and Nantes, attacked the monarchy even before the official opening of the States-General, and Mirabeau, the first leader of the revolution, was the deputy for Marseilles.

From all over the country the cahiers, or lists of grievances, poured in. But the French people, like the vast majority of Europeans to-day, had too many grievances of their own to be concerned about the sufferings of Africans, and only a few cahiers, chiefly from clergymen, demanded the abolition of slavery. The States-General met. Mirabeau, Pétion, Mayor of Paris, Abbé Grégoire, Condorcet, all members of the Friends of the Negro, were deputies, all pledged to abolition. But abolition for the maritime bourgeois was ruin. For the moment, however, the States-General grappled with the King.

While the French bourgeoisie led the assault on the absolute monarchy at home, the planters followed suit in the colonies.

And, as in France, the geographical divisions of San Domingo and their historical development shaped the revolutionary movement and the coming insurrection of the slaves.

The pride of the colony was the great North Plain of which Le Cap was the chief port. Bounded on the north by the ocean, and on the south by a ridge of mountains running almost the length of the island, it was about 50 miles in length and between 10 and 20 miles in breadth. Cultivated since 1670, it was covered with plantations within easy reach of each other. Le Cap was the centre of the island's economic, social and political life. In any revolutionary upheaval, the planters of the North Plain and the merchants and lawyers of Le Cap would take the lead. (But the slave-gangs of the North Plain, in close proximity to each other and the sooner aware of the various changes in the political situation, would be correspondingly ready for political action.)

Very different was the West Province, with its isolated plantations scattered over wide areas. In districts like the Artibonite, Verrettes, Mirabelais, and St Marc, there were many Mulatto proprietors, some of great wealth.

The South Province was a sort of pariah, somewhat sparsely populated, with a majority of Mulattoes. The eastern end, Cape Tiburon, was only some 50 miles from Jamaica and here the contraband trade was particularly strong.

Early in 1788 the North Province took the lead. It formed a secret committee to secure representation in the States-General. In Paris the group of wealthy absentee noblemen formed a committee for the same purpose, the two groups collaborated and the Paris noblemen refused to accept the veto of the King. At the end of 1788 the colonists summoned electoral assemblies and elected a delegation, some of whom consisted of their allies in Paris. In their cahier they claimed abolition of military justice and the institution of a civil judiciary; all legislation and taxes to be voted by provincial assemblies subject only to the approval of the King and a Colonial Committee sitting at Paris but elected by themselves. By restricting political rights to owners of land the planters effectively excluded the small whites who took little interest in all this agitation. Of the slaves and Mulattoes, they said not a word. Slaves did not count, and the Mulattoes secured permission from the frightened bureaucracy to send a deputation to

Paris on their own account. But a number of the planters at
home, and quite a few in Paris, the Club Massiac, viewed this
desire to be represented in the States-General with distrust. The
agitation for abolition of the slave-trade in England, the propaganda of the Friends of the Negro, the revolutionary temper of
France, filled them with foreboding. Representation in the
States-General by a few deputies could effect nothing, and it
would bring the full glare of publicity and awakening political interest on the state of society in San Domingo, which was exactly
what they did not want. But while the pro-representation group
were in a minority, having a positive aim they were bold and
confident. Their opponents, with bad consciences and aiming
only at avoiding trouble, could oppose no effective resistance.
Colonial representation in a metropolitian assembly was an innovation unheard of at that time, but the San Domingo representatives, profiting by the revolutionary ferment in Paris, circumvent-
ed the objections of the King and Minister. They petitioned the
nobility who cold-shouldered them. But when Louis tried to in-
timidate the Third Estate, and the deputies went to the tennis-
court and swore that being the representatives of the people they
would never adjourn, Gouy d'Arsy, leader of the colonists, boldly led his group of colonial noblemen into this historic meeting.
Out of gratitude for this unexpected support, the bourgeoisie
welcomed them, and thus France admitted the principle of colonial representation. Full of confidence these slave owners
claimed 18 seats, but Mirabeau turned fiercely on them: "You
claim representation proportionate to the number of the inhabitants. The free blacks are proprietors and tax-payers, and yet
they have not been allowed to vote. And as for the slaves, either
they are men or they are not; if the colonists consider them to be
men, let them free them and make them electors and eligible for
seats; if the contrary is the case, have we, in apportioning deputies according to the population of France, taken into consideration the number of our horses and our mules?"

San Domingo was allowed only six deputies. In less than five
minutes the great Liberal orator had placed the case of the
Friends of the Negro squarely before the whole of France in un-
forgettable words. The San Domingo representatives realised at
last what they had done; they had tied the fortunes of San Do-

mingo to the assembly of a people in revolution and thenceforth the history of liberty in France and of slave emancipation in San Domingo is one and indivisible.

Unaware of these portentous developments the colonists in San Domingo were going from victory to victory. As in France, the last months of 1788 in San Domingo had been hard. France had had to prohibit the export of grain, and under these circumstances the Exclusive was a tyrannical imposition threatening the island with famine. The Governor opened certain ports to foreign ships; the Intendant, Barbé de Marbois, agreed to the first small breaches but refused to sanction their extension. The matter went to the King's Council who repudiated the Governor, recalled him, and appointed a new Governor, with the colonists calling for the blood of the Intendant. This was the situation when on a day in September a boat sailed into the harbour, and the captain, hurrying ashore, ran down the streets of Le Cap, shouting the news of July 14th. The King had been preparing to disperse the Constituent Assembly by force, and the Paris masses, arming themselves, had stormed the Bastille as the symbol of feudal reaction. The great French Revolution had begun.

PARLIAMENT AND PROPERTY

Nearly all the creoles in San Domingo donned the red cockade, foremost among the agitators being those planters most heavily indebted to the maritime bourgeoisie. The militia was transformed into a National Guard in imitation of the National Guards of revolutionary France. The colonists gave themselves striking uniforms and military decorations, christened themselves captains, brigadiers and generals. They lynched the few who openly opposed them, and having no enemy to fight against they invented some. A detachment of the National Guard marched out of Le Cap against some rebel Negroes and after hours of weary tramping returned to the town with one of their number mortally wounded, not by the revolting Negroes (there were none) but by the bullets of his own companions. When, two years later, the insurrection broke out, the first chiefs were the blacks who had served as guides in this idiotic expedition.

To escape lynching, Barbé de Marbois and some of the most unpopular bureaucrats fled to France and, in defiance of the Governor, the Provincial Committee claimed the direction of affairs and began to make preparations for an election in the North Province. In January, 1790, came authority from the Minister to form a Colonial Assembly, and three Provincial bodies summoned this Assembly to meet in the town of St Marc.

De Peynier, the Governor, was an old man and weak, but even a strong man would have been in difficulties. For the absolute monarchy, paralysed by the revolution in Paris, could no longer give support to its representatives in the colonies. The small whites, as soon as they heard of the fall of the Bastille, had deserted their friends the bureaucracy and joined the revolution. There was only one hope for the bureaucrats—the Mulattoes, and the Governor instructed the commandants of the districts to adopt a new attitude towards them. "It has become more necessary than ever not to give them any cause for offence, to encourage them and to treat them as friends and whites."[23] The retreat of race prejudice had begun. Sad though it may be, that is the way that humanity progresses. The anniversary orators and the historians supply the prose-poetry and the flowers.

The plan succeeded admirably and the Mulattoes, in sheer self-defence against the murderous violence of the small whites and the revolutionaries, everywhere supported the royalist bureaucracy and military. Greed fortified prejudice. At the beginning of the agitation when the rich whites controlled the movement, they had made overtures to the rich Mulattoes. But the entry of the small whites changed this completely. The fiery (and heavily indebted) politicians who were now leading the revolution in San Domingo and the propertyless small whites wanted to exterminate the Mulattoes and confiscate their property. The whites were only 30,000. The Mulattoes and free blacks were about the same, and increasing at a far greater rate than the whites. Embittered by their persecution they called the whites intruders and themselves nationals. The revolutionaries spread it

[23] Michel, *La Mission du Général Hédouville à Saint-Domingue*, Port-au-Prince,.Haiti, 1929, Vol. 1, pp. 11–12.

that unless the Mulattoes were held down they would soon out-number the whites and drive them out of the colony. And now the Mulattoes had joined the counter-revolution.

Near the end of the year came the news of Mulatto success in Paris. On October 22nd, the National Assembly had received them, and the president in reply to their petition had said that no part of the nation would appeal for its rights in vain to the assembled representatives of the French people. On December 4th, one of the leading lights of the revolution at that time, the Count Charles de Lameth, in revolutionary enthusiasm uttered the famous words, "I am one of the greatest proprietors in San Domingo, but I declare to you that I would prefer to lose all I possess there rather than violate the principles that justice and humanity have consecrated. I declare myself both for the admission of the half-castes into the administrative assemblies and for the liberty of the blacks!" Not only political rights for Mulattoes but the abolition of slavery. The news of this drove white San Domingo to fury. How could they know that these words were merely spoken in a Pickwickian sense, that Lameth, a right-wing Liberal, would be one of the most tenacious enemies of both political rights for the Mulattoes and abolition. They began to terrorize the Mulattoes.

Lacombe, a Mulatto, claimed for his people social and political rights. The whites of Le Cap hanged him on the spot: giving the reason that in heading his petition "In the name of the Father, of the Son and of the Holy Ghost," he had departed from the established formula. M. de Baudière, a white-haired seneschal, drafted a moderate petition for some Mulattoes seeking to improve their status. The whites from the surrounding district lynched him, paraded his head on a pike and shamefully mutilated his dead body. Leaders in this terror were the small whites: the managers and stewards of the plantations and the mass of the townsmen. In some parishes of the North, white planters had summoned the Mulattoes to the primary assemblies. The small whites refused to have them, and their example gradually spread to the country where these small whites enjoyed sitting in assemblies from which the wealthy coloured proprietors were excluded. One primary assembly of the West Province even declared that the men of colour would not be allowed to take the civic oath without adding to the general formula the promise of respect for the whites.

The Mulattoes of Artibonite and Verrettes, rich and numerous, refused to take any such oath and issued the call for an insurrection to their brothers all over the island. The whites summoned all their forces and the rising petered out. But at this the richer planters were thoroughly frightened. The Mulatto chiefs fled and there were only a few arrests. Despite the shrill clamour of the small whites, the rich planters attempted no reprisals. The planters all over the country, and especially in the West Province, were becoming nervous of the behaviour of the small whites. Formerly respectful, they had been for a moment flattered by being treated as equals. But they were pushing forward, eager to use the revolution for the purpose of becoming officials and masters. In the elections for the new Assembly they used intimidation and violence against the richer whites in order to ensure majorities. The rich planters began to look more to the hitherto hated royal authority, and towards a compromise with the other caste of slave-owners, the rich Mulattoes. San Domingo had received the news of the fall of the Bastille in September. Now, barely six months after, in face of the revolutionary small whites, and the extreme revolutionaries in the Colonial Assembly, wealthy San Domingo was following the bureaucrats and drawing nearer to the rich Mulattoes. God had undoubtedly made the black blood inferior to the white, the Exclusive was a monstrous imposition, the bureaucracy was a burden. But these owners of hundreds of slaves were already prepared to turn a blind eye to these century old tenets of their caste in face of the dangers they saw ahead.

The Colonial Assembly, says Deschamps, sincerely believed itself to be a miniature Constituent Assembly. But the coarse San Domingo whites had no spark of that exalted sentiment which drove the revolutionary bourgeoisie elsewhere to dignify its seizure of power with the Declaration of Independence or the Rights of Man. They wasted no time but struck blow after blow at the Exclusive, repudiated the control of the National Assembly, and acknowledged allegiance only to the King. But here their troubles began.

The Assembly of the North Province was composed chiefly of lawyers and Le Cap merchants who represented the great financial and commercial interests of the maritime bourgeois. For them any break with France would have been ruin. Under this new constitution the men of St Marc would have had the last word on the millions of francs they owed to France. And when the Assembly of St Marc passed a decree condemning the usury of the merchants and lawyers of Le Cap the Provincial Assembly of the North (of course on the highest grounds of patriotism) broke with St Marc instantly, withdrawing its members. But although they were opposed to the Assembly of St Marc, the men of the North Plain were themselves bourgeois, linked to the maritime bourgeois of France and, therefore, supporters of the revolution and enemies of the royalist bureaucracy. San Domingo, therefore, had three white parties: the royalist bureaucracy, in other words the counter-revolution, growing stronger every day as the rich planters continued to withdraw from the Assembly of St Marc; the Assembly of St Marc itself, the Patriots, as they called themselves; and the Provincial Assembly of the North, watching both sides but for the time being supporting the Government as the link with France. All three despised the bastard Mulattoes, but all three needed them. The Provincial Assembly of the North had begun by making overtures to them. The royalist bureaucracy was openly cultivating good relations. The Assembly of St Marc now made advances in return for support in the struggle for independence.[24] The Mulattoes would not listen to them, whereupon the Patriots returned to the belief that free men of colour were contrary to the laws of God and man and should be exterminated. To them in this ferocious mood came the decree of March 8th, passed by the Constituent Assembly in France.

[24] Commissioner Roume to the Committee of Public Safety, *Les Archives du Ministère des Affaires Etrangères. Fonds Divers, Section Amérique*, No. 14, folio 258. See also in this connection, Garran-Coulon, *Rapport sur les Troubles de Saint-Domingue, fait au nom de la Commission des Colonies, des Comités de Salut Public, de Législation, et de la Marine, Réunis*, 4 volumes, Paris, 1798, Vol. II, pp. 7–8.

14   *Jay R. Mandle*

The Plantation Economy: An Essay in Definition

The recent work of A. G. Frank and the comments which it has stimulated, especially those of Ernesto Laclau, extend to the Western hemisphere a debate which originally was concerned with Western Europe.[1] Twenty years ago in the pages of *Science & Society*, Paul M. Sweezy and Maurice Dobb, among others, engaged in a discussion which centered on the need to specify the essential elements of feudalism and capitalism, and to understand the nature and timing of the transition from one system to the other.[2] In the more recent case of Frank and Laclau, the debate centers on the question of whether Latin American societies from the sixteenth century onward should properly be considered feudal or capitalist. In this case the question is posed so as to cast light on the failure of Latin and other New World societies to achieve high levels of economic development.

In the present paper we attempt to do two things. In the first place we examine and analyze the methodological differences which separate the participants in these discussions. In the second, on the basis of this analysis, we apply the tools and definitions which seem most useful to several different societies in the New World. In the course of doing so we consider whether plantation-dominated societies might have a set of social relations which distinguish them from both feudal and capitalist societies,

SOURCE. Jay R. Mandle, "The Plantation Economy: An Essay in Definition," *Science & Society*, XXXVI (Spring, 1972), pp. 49–62. Copyright © 1972 by Science & Society.

[1] Andre Gunder Frank, *Capitalism and Underdevelopment in Latin America* (New York, 1967) and *Latin America: Underdevelopment or Revolution* (New York, 1969); Ernesto Laclau, "Imperialism in Latin America," *New Left Review*, May/June, 1971, 67.

[2] This debate which includes seven articles by five authors has been reprinted as a symposium by *Science & Society* under the title *The Transition from Feudalism to Capitalism* (New York, 1963). Hereafter, this will be referred to as *The Transition*.

the categories which are employed by all of the authors cited. As a result we attempt to develop the conception of a "plantation society."

Despite the different regions with which they are concerned, I think it is fair to argue that Sweezy and Frank on one side and Dobb and Laclau in opposition to them share a fundamental methodological core and a common analytic starting point. The Sweezy-Frank argument places great stress on the role market relations play in defining the character and the nature of change in a given society. In the original discussion with Dobb, for example, Sweezy argues that "the crucial feature of feudalism . . . is that it is a system of production for use. The needs of the community are known and production is planned and organized with a view to satisfying these needs."[3] Further, he argues that ". . . the growth of trade was the decisive factor in bringing about the decline of western European feudalism."[4] In contrast, Dobb emphasizes productive relations. He declares that feudalism was "virtually identical with what we usually mean by serfdom: an obligation laid on the producer by force and independently of his own volition to fulfill certain economic demands of an overlord, whether these demands take the form of services to be performed or of dues to be paid in money or in kind."[5] While conceding that ". . . the growth of market towns and of trade played an important role in accelerating the disintegration of the old mode of production," Dobb argues that ". . . trade exercised its influence to the extent that it accentuated the internal conflicts within the old mode of production."[6] These pressures resulted from ". . . the inefficiency of Feudalism as a system of production, coupled with the growing needs of the ruling class for revenue . . . since this need for additional revenue promoted an increase in the pressure on the producer to a point where this pressure became literally unendurable."[7]

[3] *The Transition*, p. 2.
[4] *Ibid.*, p. 8, fnte, 10.
[5] Maurice Dobb, *Studies in the Development of Capitalism* (New York, 1947), p. 35.
[6] *The Transition*, p. 23.
[7] Dobb, *Studies in the Development of Capitalism*, p. 42.

A similar definitional disagreement separates Laclau and Frank. Though Frank nowhere clearly defines what he means by capitalism, he acknowledges that his work ". . . centers on and emerges from the metropolis-satellite structure of the capitalist system."[8] That is, his work concentrates on the unequal market relationships which emerge within the international capitalist economy and within domestic economics. For Frank, as with Sweezy, an economic system which produces for long-distance markets, as the New World colonies necessarily had to do, given the circumstances of their origin, is a capitalist system, and this is the case even though the mother country was at best in a transitional stage between feudalism and capitalism.

Disagreeing with Frank, and himself paralleling the arguments of Dobb, Laclau cites the cases of Mexico, Peru, Bolivia, and Guatamala where, he argues, during the period under consideration labor coercion continued to prevail and the alienation of property still had not proceeded very far in these societies.[9] Accordingly, the argument states that it is inappropriate to describe these economies as capitalist. Similarly in the West Indies the economies were characterized by slave labor while in mining areas a form of disguised slavery emerged, again requiring at the least that these regions be considered noncapitalist.[10] Thus while Frank and Sweezy argue that developed market relations, especially in international trade, are the key to both the definition and the evolution of capitalism, Dobb and Laclau argue that the circumstances surrounding the domestic labor force and their conditions of employment are central to both of these issues. Though each side in this debate appeals by quotation to the authority of Marx to legitimize its position, the Dobb-Laclau position is much closer to orthodox Marxism than the Sweezy-Frank view.[11] By emphasizing the conditions of employment of the la-

[8] Frank, *Capitalism and Underdevelopment in Latin America*, p. vii.

[9] Laclau, "Imperialism in Latin America," pp. 25, 28, 30.

[10] *Ibid.*, p. 30.

[11] This seems to be the case with respect to method despite the fact that E. J. Hobsbawm considers Sweezy's position on the transition from feudalism to capitalism closer to Marx's actual historical description than Dobb's. Karl Marx, *Pre-capitalist Economic Formations*, "Introduction" by Eric J. Hobsbawm (New York, 1964), p. 46.

bor force, Dobb and Laclau at least attempt to define the "relations of production" in the historical context in which they are
dealing, something which Sweezy and Frank fail to do. Similarly,
in seeing the dynamics of historical change as residing primarily
in the conflict between the inefficiency of the organization of production and the increasing needs of the current ruling class,
Dobb and Laclau hypothesize a conflict between the forces of
production (improving and increasingly efficient technology)
and the relations of production (the social organization of production) in a way similar to that suggested by Marx, while
Frank and Sweezy generally ignore this possible source of historical change. In method of analysis then, the Sweezy-Frank position, while broadly working within the Marxist framework by
employing the Marxist stages of history schema, represents a significant departure from orthodoxy by placing greatest emphasis
on external market relations as a source of change in contrast to
seeing dynamism emerging from the internal conflict between developing technology and the social structure.

To say this, of course, is not by any means to say that because
they depart from classical Marxism Sweezy and Frank are necessarily wrong. On the contrary, such an attempt at revising and
up-dating conventional Marxism has been only too conspicuous
by its absence in the history of radical scholarship. The importance of this kind of reinterpretation is doubly emphasized since
on one hand Dobb himself agrees that evidence supporting his
view ". . . is neither very plentiful nor conclusive," while at the
same time he asserts that he by no means denies ". . . that the
growth of market towns and of trade played an important role in
accelerating the disintegration of the old mode of production."[12]
In the case of Latin America, as Frank emphasizes, we are dealing with a region whose economic origins were the result of the
expansion of international trade. This alone meant that the degree to which this area engaged in long distance trade was much
greater than in classically feudal areas. As a result, it is entirely
plausible to argue that traditional Marxist method might have
placed too little emphasis on the international context in which a

---

[12] Dobb, *Studies in the Development of Capitalism*, p. 47; *The Transition*,
p. 23.

society functioned as a defining characteristic of that society—a view which seems close to the starting point of the analysis by Sweezy and Frank. In any event, the position adopted by the latter ought properly be considered as a new set of hypotheses offered in the framework of Marxism. As a result, it should be investigated both with respect to its internal logic and its ability to help explain the dynamics of the real world.

With that said, however, it is readily apparent that there are grave weaknesses in the Sweezy-Frank approach. One problem is that while Sweezy sees international market participation as an engine of growth and as a mechanism of transforming a backward society into a progressive one, Frank sees that same participation as being responsible for the long-term stagnation of the Latin American economies. For Sweezy the growth of long-distance trade resulted in "the superior efficiency of more highly specialized production, . . . greater gains to be made by producing for the market rather than for immediate use and the greater attractiveness of town life to the worker." These were the factors which ". . . made it only a matter of time before the new system . . . would win out."[13] For Frank, on the other hand, participation in such trade has "generated underdevelopment in the peripheral satellites whose economic surplus was expropriated, while generating economic development in the metropolitan centers which appropriated that surplus. . . ."[14]

The important point to note is that each of these contradictory interpretations of the impact of participation in international markets has had empirical confirmation in the real world; and since this is the case, it obviously is not trade *per se* which accounts for whether a country or area stagnates or expands. Frank's position with respect to the negative effects of trade is in many ways similar to that advanced by Gunnar Myrdal[15] and others. The argument that resources are expropriated from one market participant to another involves at least the implicit assumption that one of these entrants exercises considerable market power over the other. If, for example, the metropolitan coun-

[13] *The Transition*, p. 10.
[14] A. G. Frank, *Capitalism and Underdevelopment*, p. 3.
[15] Gunnar Myrdal, *Economic Theory and Underdeveloped Regions* (New York, 1957).

try acts as a monopsonist, it is quite likely that the prices received for the satellite's output will be abnormally low. Similarly, assuming that the metropole is a monopolist with respect to the supply of goods and services to the hinterland, the prices charged will be relatively high. While the examples of a monopsonist and monopolist are extreme, it seems fair enough to argue that in the context of New World Colonialism, some such degree of market power may well have prevailed. As a result it would not be surprising, at least in Latin America, to discover that with the establishment of artificially high prices for European goods and artificially low prices for domestically produced products, resources were drained from the satellite to the metropolitan country in much the way Frank describes.

If, however, one does not make the assumption of inequality in market power, the Sweezy argument for the stimulative effects of expanding trade has a high degree of plausibility, and, of course, bears a marked resemblance to the beliefs of the classical economists. Long-distance trade presumably widens market opportunities and increases the number of potentially profitable investment opportunities. This, in turn, provides incentives for more firms and businessmen to initiate production, and as a result pressure is generated to remove social obstacles which prevent the expansion of production and the achievement of improved technological efficiency. If, then, profits are achieved, and are reinvested domestically, in contrast to the Frank case where they are lost overseas, both increased output and improving efficiency can be the associated consequences of participating in long-distance trade.

Two issues then are central in identifying whether the Frank retardative effect or the Sweezy expansionary effect is the result of increasing market participation. The first is the parity of market power which exists between trading partners; the second is the extent to which there are supply responses to widening market opportunities. But clearly in both cases the implications of international trade—either positively or negatively—have much more to do with the internal conditions of the country than with the trade itself. Whether or not resources are drained from one country to another depends upon the relative market power of the traders, which, in turn, reflects the development of the pro-

ductive forces of each. Whether a metropolitan country is able to
act as a monopolist, and hence drain resources, depends upon
the extent to which the hinterland country is successful in searching for alternate market outlets and widening its structure of production. The degree to which a metropole can act as a monopolist depends upon the ability of the satellite to find new sources
of supply and engage in a form of import-substitution.

Alternatively, whether trade is to act as a stimulant depends
upon the ability of the society to respond to changing opportunities. Three responses are possible to a widening of market opportunities, only one of which is development-promoting. In the first
case an international market may expand, but the country may
be unable to take advantage of the situation and production remains as before. In the second case the response to the growing
market may take the form of expanding output, but within the
constraints imposed by traditional technology and social structure. As we shall see, this response, characteristic of large parts
of the New World, failed to achieve either the efficiency improvement or institutional change required by economic development. Finally, of course, there may be a dynamic response to
market growth with all that this implies for methods of production and social organization.

The crucial point is that the effects of international trade are
largely determined by what goes on inside the society. The extent
to which market power either is achieved by or is denied to others depends on the internal capacity of the economy; the extent
to which modernization of technology and institutions is the consequence of widening markets similarly depends upon internal
social structure. It is this—the determinant role of internal struc-
to which modernization of technology and institutions is the concerned with the importance of international trade come to opposite conclusions with respect to its stimulative or retardative
effects. For in the case which concerns Sweezy, Europe in the late
middle ages, there was generally a rough equality between trade
participants at least to the extent that no area possessed an obvious technological superiority sufficient to exercise market
power. At the same time wide areas of European society were
opening up sufficiently to allow the dynamic effects of trade to
be the dominant influence. In the Latin American case, however,

this was obviously not the situation, especially since the New World societies were established to service specific European needs. As a result, expanding trade merely reinforced the original rigid social structure. In short, trade provides alternative avenues of change. Which avenue is realized, however, depends not on the trade itself, as Sweezy and Frank would have it, but on the nature of the response to the widening market.

To argue that internal structure is the key to social dynamism leaves open, of course, the question of which elements of the society are most important in defining different social structures. As we have seen, Dobb argues that the crucial distinction between feudalism and capitalism centers on the social relations of the labor force. A labor force free to sell its labor power is considered characteristic of a capitalist economy, and where restrictions are placed on such freedom and/or a tie to the land is maintained which inhibits labor market participation, feudalism prevails. Yet, as Eric Hobsbawm has pointed out, the effect of so defining these two different kinds of societies is to make feudalism something of a residual category. Clearly, an important degree of asymmetry is involved in carefully defining capitalism and leaving feudalism as a term to be applied to the non-capitalist societies. Its result has been ". . . to bring into currency a vast category of feudalism which spans the continents and the millennia, and ranges from say, the emirates of Northern Nigeria to France in 1788, from the tendencies visible in Aztec society on the eve of the Spanish conquest to czarist Russia in the nineteenth century."[16]

For analytic purposes, the definitional imprecision involved in utilizing the same category to describe such a diffuse collection of societies is highly unsatisfactory. Indeed, it is significant that even Laclau, in the course of his critique of Frank, shies away from the use of the word feudal in describing Latin societies, moving to the hardly more satisfactory term "semi-feudal." Interestingly, Bettelheim uses that same phrase to describe modern Indian rural conditions,[17] suggesting that the avoidance of the

[16] Eric J. Hobsbawm (ed.), *Pre-Capitalist Economic Formations* by Karl Marx (New York, 1964), p. 63.

[17] Charles Bettelheim, *India Independent* (New York and London, 1968), p. 22–23.

phrase hardly lessens the confusion involved in failing to specify the components of noncapitalist, but yet not really feudal societies. This is especially so if by feudalism we mean something close to what existed in Europe in the middle ages. In the argument that follows the effort will be to develop a general framework which will be useful in analyzing the pattern of development achieved in the New World.

Since the late 17th century the plantation has been the dominant unit of production in many parts of the New World. Charles Wagley has described "plantation America" as extending ". . . from about midway up the coast of Brazil into the Guianas, along the Caribbean coast, throughout the Caribbean itself and into the United States."[18] In this extended region the technological and organizational characteristics of the dominant productive units have decisively influenced the pattern of change and development which has been experienced. Organization of these units has on one hand produced very low incomes for the bulk of the population, while at the same time yielding profits high enough to attract major international investors and corporations: low levels of labor productivity, but a continual and generally successful search for improved technology and reduced costs of production; a vigorous participation in international commodity markets, but virtually moribund domestic markets either for produce or for labor; and finally, a system of labor force control which has extended from slavery, abolished in Brazil as late as 1888, to other mechanisms such as indentured immigration, share-cropping, or the contrived absence of alternatives to which the labor force could turn. Quite clearly in their market responsiveness, their profit orientation and their heavy participation in international trade, the economies of "plantation America" exhibited markedly non-feudal propensities. At the same time, however, the nature of labor force control either through slavery or some other non-market mechanism makes it impossible by Dobb's definition to classify them as capitalist. For analytic reasons, therefore, we will refer to the economies of the New World where plantations were dominant as "plantation economies" by

[18] Charles Wagley, "Plantation America: A Culture Sphere," in Vera Rubin (ed.), *Caribbean Studies: A Symposium* (Seattle, 1960), p. 3.

which we mean regimes which can be considered neither capitalist nor feudal and which have their own dynamic pattern based upon the technology and social relations which inhere in the plantation as the dominant unit of output.

New World scholars have contributed an extensive literature to the discussion of plantations. Typically, in defining what they mean by a plantation, writers emphasize its commercial characteristics, its relatively large scale of production and its labor-intensive, low-skill methods of production. Thus, for example, in the *International Encyclopedia of the Social Sciences,* William O. Jones defines a plantation as ". . . an economic unit producing agricultural commodities . . . for sale and employing a relatively large number of unskilled laborers whose . . . are closely supervised."[19] However, this kind of definition, which receives wide currency in the literature, is misleading since it confines the meaning of the phrase to the productive unit itself and ignores the distinctive kinds of social relations which emerge from the plantation structure.

A starting point in the search for a more satisfactory definition is provided by anthropologist E. R. Wolfe. Wolfe points out that "wherever the plantation has arisen, or wherever it was imported from the outside, it always destroyed antecedent cultural norms and imposed its own dictates, sometimes by persuasion, sometimes by compulsion, yet always in conflict with the cultural definitions of the affected population. The plantation, therefore, is also an instrument of force, wielded to create and to maintain a class-structure of workers and owners, connected hierarchically by a staff-line of overseers and managers."[20] What Wolfe does not point out is that the plantation's use of force stemmed directly from its labor-intensive patterns of production. In order for the plantation to be productive, masses of low-wage undifferentiated workers were needed, and it is this need which accounted for the planter regime's harsh and brutal methods of congregat-

[19] David Sills (ed.), *The International Encyclopedia of the Social Sciences,* XII, p. 154.

[20] Eric R. Wolfe, "Specific Aspects of Plantation Systems in the New World: Community Sub-Cultures and Social Classes," in *Plantation Systems of the New World* (Washington, 1959), p. 136.

ing and disciplining labor, either by disrupting indigenous societies or importing whole new populations. Especially in the circumstances of the New World colonial period, when labor was
relatively scarce but the need for workers enormous, labor markets could not be depended upon to provide the requisite number
of workers at profitable wage rates. As a result, the plantation
owners resorted to non-market mechanisms of labor force mobilization—in the first instance slavery—to achieve their desired
levels of output. But it is precisely this—the use of the extra-
market means of congregating and utilizing labor—which distin-
guishes these plantation-dominated economies from capitalist
ones, where the market is relied upon to allocate labor.

A plantation economy then not only is defined by the nature
of its production function and typical participation in international markets, but also by the distinctive mechanisms of labor
force control which emerge from it. Where plantations are dominant, their manpower requirements are such that these needs,
not only come to set the pattern of social relations on the estate,
but have important implications for the wider society. A plantation economy is one in which, because of the plantation's economic dominance and the characteristic chronic relative shortage
of labor associated with this kind of production, some form of
coercion is required to satisfy its manpower requirements. As a
result of this coercion, work as unskilled labor on the estates is
the only employment option available to the population, and ultimately such labor is made compulsory by the state through
officially sanctioned legislation and violence. In no real sense is a
domestic labor market operative in plantation-dominated societies. At the same time, the plantations themselves are intensely
profit-oriented commercial enterprises, which respond readily to
changing international market signals, at least with respect to the
volume of output which can be profitably marketed. As a result,
a plantation society is marked by profound inequalities, in which
the "modern" profit and market-oriented ruling class, institution-
ally based in the owner's plantations, dominates the rest of the
population, which is organized and employed strictly as "brawn
power."

Historically, several mechanisms of social control have successfully supported plantation economies. Though slavery was

the foundation upon which New World plantation societies were originally constructed, the history of these societies subsequent to emancipation suggests that slavery alone did not define the social system. Emancipation did severely shake the hegemony of the plantocracy, but its survival under formally changed circumstances of labor control, in several different countries, indicates that juridical ownership of people could be eliminated and yet the essential attributes of the plantation society be retained. Thus in some parts of the West Indies, emancipation meant practically nothing to the social organization because of the absence of unutilized land. With legal freedom the ex-slaves had no alternative employment opportunities available to them and thus *de facto* were compelled to continue to work on the estates as before. In other parts of the West Indies, where land was available and where the ex-slaves did vacate the plantations, indentured immigration became the mechanism by which the plantation-dominated societies remained intact. Thus in Trinidad, Guyana, and to some extent in Jamaica, a state-supported program of immigration resulted in an annual supply of new labor above and beyond the supply which came from the resident population. In this way the plantations were provided with a sufficiently large and cheap supply of labor independently of the operation of a labor market. These immigrants were legally required to work for a specified number of years on sugar plantations and it was this process, combined with official discouragement to the creation of alternative industries, which allowed the plantation to continue to earn profits on the old labor-intensive, low-income and low labor-productivity basis for more than a century after emancipation.[21] Finally in other parts of Plantation America, such as the Southern United States, share-cropping emerged as a new form of labor force control. In this case while the unit of ownership, the plantation, was retained, it ceased to be administered as one single productive enterprise. Rather, individual "croppers" cultivated their own acreage, under the close supervision of the owner to whom a percentage of the output was delivered as rental. Typically, the share-cropper furnished only his labor and that of his

[21] For a discussion of this process, see my *Population and Economic Change in Guyana* (unpublished).

family to production, while receiving equipment, supplies and even food from the owner. In return, by means of his control of credit, sales, and bookkeeping, the landlord was able to maintain overall control of production as well as the labor force itself. As a 1935 summary of field studies put it, "the plantation system developed during slavery and it continues on the old master and slave pattern" under share cropping.[22]

In each of these cases the essential social relations of production of plantation agriculture were retained; monopolization of the productive assets by a small planter class, production of a staple for external markets, absence of a vital domestic labor market, use of low-productivity, low-wage labor, and a highly uneven distribution of income. What therefore seems to be essential to a plantation society is not the form of the non-market mechanism by which labor is mobilized in large numbers for low productivity agricultural work, but simply that some such non-market mechanism exists. Slavery, indentured immigration, share-cropping, or the artificial maintenance of monocultural plantation production, can all serve to guarantee the labor force requirements of the plantation system and all can do so in the absence of a viable labor market mechanism, an essential aspect of a functioning capitalist economy. As a result, the adaptability of the plantation system is greater than is sometimes assumed, for wherever and under whatever circumstances such a mobilization occurs, the plantation, with its attendant symbiotic relations between the "modern" plantation entrepreneur and the "traditional" unskilled labor force, can prove viable.

It is easy to show that a plantation organization of society is inconsistent with the process of modern economic development.[23] For while development is typically characterized by the emergence of new economic sectors, based on increasing levels of labor productivity, a plantation economy militates in the direction of stability in the structure of output and continuity in

[22] Charles S. Johnson, Edwin R. Embree, W. W. Alexander, *The Collapse of Cotton Tenancy*, Summary of Field Studies and Statistical Surveys, 1933–35 (Chapel Hill, 1935), p. 10.

[23] For a more detailed discussion of this see George Beckford, "Toward An Appropriate Framework for Agricultural Development Planning and Policy." *Social and Economic Studies*, Vol. 17, no. 3, Sept., 1968.

methods of production. And it is precisely through the mechanisms of social control which are essential to the plantation society that such tendencies are put into operation. For as long as labor remains a cheap and abundant factor of production, profit-maximizing entrepreneurs such as plantation owners will have no incentive to substitute machinery for labor and thus raise levels of output per man. Similarly, as long as domestic levels of income remain low, these same businessmen will feel no strong incentive to turn from the international market where they sell their staple to local markets. Indeed, the history of all plantation societies in the New World provides eloquent testimony to the proposition that "rational" economic behavior by profit-seeking firms, depending on the circumstances, actually serves to prevent social economic development even as the individual businessmen prosper.

Moreover, it is clear that neither expanding nor contracting international markets can be relied upon to break down the plantation structure. International market expansion may well serve merely to reinforce the plantation structure. This is especially so when the supply of labor to the estates remains at least equal to the requirements generated by the expanding market. Similarly, market contraction alone may serve to reinforce the system by virtue of the redundancy of labor created by declining output. Such a redundancy would serve to reinforce the pattern of production characteristic of estates.

The key to the plantation society rests in the mechanism of labor force control which enables the estates to carry on production in their characteristic pattern. And as we have seen there is no one such mechanism. In each case, however, the essential problem of the plantation society involves the mobilization of a sufficiently large number of low-wage workers to enable profitable production to be carried out. Once this is done the peculiar mix of capitalist enterprise and archaic labor relations which typifies the plantation economy is made viable. Thus, in the course of history, international firms made profits even though the process by which they achieved those profits resulted in the stagnation of the societies within which they carried out production.

In conclusion, the argument presented here is that the Dobb-Laclau method of searching for the key to social organization is sound. When this is done, however, and particularly when the search centers on the mechanism by which labor is mobilized and allocated, many New World societies seem not to fall easily within the category of either feudalism or capitalism. For as to the latter, plantation economies are characterized by the absence of viable labor markets; and as to the former, differences in labor organization, as well as profound differences between New World plantation owners and European feudal lords with respect to profit motivation and market responsiveness, make it more confusing than enlightening to apply the phrase feudalism to both 15th century Europe and 19th or 20th century Caribbean colonies. As a result, we suggest the usefulness of the concept "plantation economy" in making clear the pattern of economic change experienced in Western Hemisphere countries.